MAJOR EUROPEAN AUTHORS

A study of Nietzsche

BOOKS IN THIS SERIES

PREVIOUS BOOKS BY THE AUTHOR

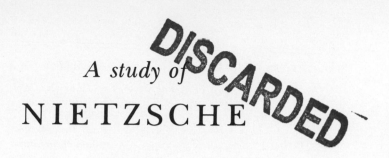

A study of NIETZSCHE

J. P. STERN

Professor of German, University College London

CAMBRIDGE UNIVERSITY PRESS

Cambridge

London · New York · Melbourne

Published by the Syndics of the Cambridge University Press
The Pitt Building, Trumpington Street, Cambridge CB2 1RP
Bentley House, 200 Euston Road, London NW1 2DB
32 East 57th Street, New York, NY 10022, USA
296 Beaconsfield Parade, Middle Park, Melbourne 3206, Australia

First published 1979

Printed in Great Britain
at the University Press, Cambridge

Library of Congress Cataloguing in Publication Data
Stern, Joseph Peter.
A study of Nietzsche.
(Major European authors)
Bibliography: p.
Includes index.
1. Nietzsche, Friedrich Wilhelm, 1844–1900.
I. Title.
B3317.S69   193   78–54328
ISBN 0 521 22126 9

To my friends at University College London

Contents

Preface

'Mad genius...evil Teuton...satanic mind' were words applied
by a respectable critic to Nietzsche when I first wrote about him
more than twenty-five years ago. The atmosphere which
provoked those irate remarks no longer prevails, but now his
writings are threatened by an opposite danger – that of being
read as though he were a cool, systematic philosopher or a poet
needing his symbols counted and his images classified; his
relationship to twentieth-century totalitarian politics is almost
entirely ignored. These oscillations are not surprising. His work
is a seismograph, as well as one of the volcanoes, of modern
Europe. Any attempt at a coherent interpretation of writings
so hybrid and at times so contradictory in content, and so
remarkably versatile in form, is bound to be problematic. The
desire to do justice to this versatility and neither to hide nor to
exaggerate the contradictoriness must be my excuse for urging
the reader to abandon a number of traditional distinctions:
between literature and philosophy, between formal, published
statements and informal notes, between life and work.

A study of Nietzsche's work raises a number of questions: first,
who was he, what was the setting in which his life and writings
should be placed, and what was the philosophical tradition with
which he took issue? Secondly, what did he write? Thirdly, how
are we to read him? And finally, what critical reception and what
influence has his work had during the last ninety years?

The reader may like to know at the outset that I have not given
full answers to all these questions. I have presented Nietzsche's
biography mainly in a series of brief extracts from his and other
people's letters, and have restricted the historical setting to the
barest minimum. Nietzsche's involvement with the traditions of
German Protestantism and of philosophical idealism deserves
fuller examination than it has received here, and so does his
life-long *agon* with Schopenhauer. Apart from looking into

Nietzsche's philosophical antecedents I have tried to show some
of his affinities with the linguistic philosophy that came after him.
My main aim has been a *critical* reconstruction of what Nietzsche
wrote and (in the last chapter) a characterization of his mode of
writing; such a characterization is intended to suggest with what
expectations we should read him. I have said little about the
critical reception of Nietzsche's work, and about his influence
(which is second to none) on writers as diverse as Rilke, Yeats,
Valéry, H. G. Wells, D. H. Lawrence, Thomas Mann and George
Bernard Shaw; as far as German literature is concerned,
Gottfried Benn hardly exaggerates when he writes to a friend:
'...really, you know, *he* has anticipated and formulated everything, absolutely everything we poke around in – what else have
we done these last fifty years but trot out and vulgarize *his*
gigantic thoughts and suffering.'[1] On the subject of Nietzsche's
influence on twentieth-century politics (ignored or minimized by
all recent critics of his work) it seemed appropriate to take up
and extend arguments begun in a previous book.[2]

Having consulted and learned from the available translations
(see pp. 212–13), I decided to offer my own versions of
quotations from Nietzsche's works. As on previous occasions I
am deeply grateful to Sheila Stern for help in revising them.
Nietzsche's writings, especially those published posthumously,
abound in typographical emphases; I have reproduced these only
where not to do so would have altered his meaning.

I am grateful to the Rockefeller Foundation and to my own
College for making it easy for me to write this study: the former
by inviting me to the Villa Serbelloni, their study centre at
Bellagio above Nietzsche's beloved Lake Como, where I enjoyed
such magnificent hospitality as Nietzsche on his restless wan-
derings never knew; the latter by granting me a term's sabbatical
leave to complete the work.

For permission to reprint, thanks are offered to the editors
of *The Journal of European Studies*, *Encounter*, and *Nietzsche:
Imagery and Thought* (ed. J. M. S. Pasley and published by
Methuen), in whose pages different versions of parts of the last
chapter are to be found. A shortened version of this *Study* has
appeared in the Fontana Modern Masters series.

Finally, I am happy to acknowledge my gratitude to four

[1] To F. W. Oelze, 28 November 1949.
[2] J. P. Stern, *Hitler: the Führer and the People* (London 1975).

friends: Nicholas Boyle read and criticized an earlier version of the last chapter and the conclusion; Bernard Williams read the entire typescript and asked a number of challenging questions, some of which I may have succeeded in answering; with Michael Silk I have discussed many of the issues raised here; and Chris Waller offered many suggestions for the improvement of my text and helped generously by tracing references and quotations, especially in the new and as yet uncompleted critical edition of Nietzsche's work.

J.P.S.

University College London
July 1977

Abbreviations

A	*Der Antichrist*
EH	*Ecce Homo*
FaW	*Der Fall Wagner* (The Wagner Case)
FW	*Die Fröhliche Wissenschaft* (The Joyous Science)
GD	*Die Götzen-Dämmerung* (The Twilight of the Idols)
GM	*Zur Genealogie der Moral* (The Genealogy of Morals)
GT	*Die Geburt der Tragödie* (The Birth of Tragedy)
J	*Jenseits von Gut und Böse* (Beyond Good and Evil)
M	*Morgenröte* (Aurora)
MA	*Menschliches, Allzumenschliches* (Human, All-Too-Human). I, II
Mus	*Gesammelte Werke*, Musarionausgabe
NS	*Nietzsche Studien*
Schlechta	*Werke in drei Bänden*
U	*Unzeitgemässe Betrachtungen* (Thoughts Out of Season), I–IV
WKG	*Werke: Kritische Gesamtausgabe*, referred to by numbers indicating section, volume and page, e.g. VII/2 p. 104
WzM	*Der Wille zur Macht* (The Will to Power)
Z	*Also sprach Zarathustra* (Thus Spoke Zarathustra)

1

A chronology of Nietzsche's life

O, what a noble mind is here o'erthrown!

(*Hamlet* III: 1)

1844

15 October: Nietzsche born[1] in Röcken near Lützen, in the Prussian province of Saxony. Christened by his father, Carl Ludwig Nietzsche (1813–49), a Lutheran pastor who had received preferment from King Friedrich Wilhelm IV of Prussia ('My son, Friedrich Wilhelm shall be your name, in remembrance of my royal benefactor, on whose birthday you were born'). Nietzsche's mother (Franziska, née Oehler, 1826–97), married at the age of 17, was the daughter of a Saxon country vicar. On both sides of his family Nietzsche came from a long line of Lutheran clergymen.

1846

10 July: Elisabeth, his only sister, is born.

1849

30 July: Father dies, supposedly as the result of a brain injury sustained in a fall eleven months earlier; another report (see under 1858 below) speaks of a congenital disease of the brain. Nietzsche remembers him for his musical compositions and his extemporizing on the piano.

---

[1] This chronology is derived mainly from Nietzsche's correspondence; I have also used the biographical sections of W. Kaufmann's and Karl Jaspers's studies (*Nietzsche: Philosopher, Psychologist, Antichrist*, Princeton [4]1974; *Nietzsche: Einführung in das Verständnis seines Philosophierens*, Berlin 1947); the chronology in *Schlechta*, vol. III, pp. 1359–82; E. F. Podach, *Gestalten um Nietzsche* (Weimar 1932), and *Nietzsches Zusammenbruch* (Heidelberg 1930); C. A. Bernoulli, *Franz Overbeck und Friedrich Nietzsche: eine Freundschaft* (2 vols. Jena 1908); P. Deussen, *Erinnerungen an Friedrich Nietzsche* (Leipzig 1901); and Ivo Frenzel, *Friedrich Nietzsche* (rororo, Reinbek 1966).

1850

The family move to Naumburg. The boy's main companion is his sister, his upbringing is entirely in the hands of women: his mother, his ambitious grandmother, and two aunts.

1852

After a false start at the local elementary school, Nietzsche enters a private preparatory school and then, aged 8, the Naumburg 'Domgymnasium'. The atmosphere at home is precious and devout; many years later Nietzsche remembers that at the age of 12 he had 'a vision of God in his full glory'. According to a fictitious tradition to which Nietzsche clings throughout his life, the family claims Polish aristocratic ancestry.

The boy mixes very little with others, but has two close friends; their conversations are precocious and highly literary. One of them (Wilhelm Pinder) writes: 'From earliest childhood he loved solitude and the freedom to pursue his own ideas, avoiding the company of men, and seeking out those regions which Nature alone had furnished with sublime beauty.'

His sister Elisabeth reports an occasion (Easter 1857) when both came home with excellent school reports: 'When Fritz and I were alone, he asked me "whether it was not strange that we both learned so well and knew so many things that other children didn't know".' In the summer of 1856 the boy is absent from school because of severe headaches and pain in the eyes.

1858

In a diary begun at this time Nietzsche recalls his own musical beginnings (he wrote his first motet aged 10), and reviews his literary productions: some fifty poems on 'natural scenery, disasters at sea, and thunderstorms with fires', but also on 'Fortune's changes, illustrated by a wanderer slumbering in the ruins of Carthage'. In the house of one of his friends his musical education is broadened (Geheimrat Krug was a friend of Mendelssohn's), in the house of another he is introduced to the German classics. The boy's critical comments on his own and other people's writings, though self-consciously and convention-ally worded, are unusually perceptive; he confesses (in 1864) to 'a true passion for universal knowledge', and is conscious of lacking a sense of order. His dominant urge is to appropriate, articulate, re-create in his own terms – *to write*.

October 1858 to September 1864. Leaves Naumburg with a school record good enough to gain a scholarship at Schulpforta, Germany's best and most famous Protestant boarding school (the poet Klopstock, the philosopher Fichte and the historian Ranke had been among its pupils). Receives a brilliant classical education, discovers Hölderlin, 'whom the majority of his nation knows hardly by name'. For Nietzsche, Hölderlin is not only the supreme lyrical poet, but also (as the author of *Hyperion*, 1797–9) the incisive critic of 'our barbarism...what he hated in the German was the mere expert, the Philistine'.

At Easter 1861 Nietzsche is confirmed, together with his closest schoolfriend, Paul Deussen, in a spirit of great religious enthusiasm; but at this time, too, he reads D. F. Strauss's 'demythologizing' *The Life of Jesus* (1836, George Eliot's English translation 1846). His subsequent loss of faith seems to have been gradual and undramatic, not caused by any traumatic event.

His health continues indifferent; an entry in the school's hospital record (1862) reads: '...a full-blooded, thick-set man with noticeably staring eyes, shortsighted, often plagued by headaches. His father was conceived in old age and died young of softening of the brain, the son was conceived during the father's illness. No grave symptoms are visible yet, but clearly his medical antecedents have to be borne in mind.' During his vacations in Naumburg he founds (with two friends) *Germania*, an artistic society. They subscribe to a musical periodical and write original works which are subjected to mutual criticism. The society's last funds are spent on extracts from *Tristan und Isolde*, arranged for the piano.

1864

Summer and early autumn: Leaves school with good marks in all subjects except mathematics, and outstanding marks in classics. A Latin school essay on the poet Theognis of Megara is extended into a full-scale study after Nietzsche leaves Schulpforta.

October: Matriculates in the University of Bonn, attends a variety of lectures, including theology, but his classical studies are affected by the violent quarrels of his two teachers, Otto Jahn and Friedrich Wilhelm Ritschl. Nietzsche makes some effort to take part in the social life of the place (he joins a student corporation, 'Franconia', sings in a musical festival in Cologne, Whitsun 1865), but he is conscious of remaining an outsider and cutting an awkward figure. Writes a number of musical compositions, influenced by Schumann.

The academic year at Bonn is a failure, yet he can write at the end of it: 'I hope that it will be possible one day to record this year too, from the vantage point of memory, as a necessary link in my development' (30 August 1865). His friend Paul Deussen recalls the following episode: 'One day in February 1865 Nietzsche had gone to Cologne by himself and there was shown the sights by a porter whom finally he asked to take him to a restaurant. But the porter took him to a house of ill-repute. "I found myself," Nietzsche told me the next day, "suddenly surrounded by a half dozen apparitions in sequins and gauze, who were looking at me expectantly. Then, as if in this company it were the only creature with a soul, I instinctively made for the piano and struck a few chords, which freed me from my numbed state. Then I fled." After he told me this, and in view of everything I know about Nietzsche, I'm inclined to believe that the words of a Latin biography of Plato apply to him: mulierem numquam attigit.'

1865

October: Moves with Ritschl to Leipzig, for four semesters. In November, at a time of deep depression and search for 'a way of building a suitable life of my own', he discovers Schopenhauer. On Ritschl's suggestion he founds a philological society and lectures there. Beginning of his longest friendship, with fellow-classicist Erwin Rohde (author of *Psyche*, 1893). Inconclusive evidence that Nietzsche may at this time have consulted two doctors for a syphilitic infection. (Thomas Mann conjectures that it may have been contracted during the visit to a Cologne brothel; he places the whole story at the centre of his *Doktor Faustus*, 1946.)

1866

Spring: Ritschl encourages him to rewrite and publish (1867) his study of Theognis and other papers. Summer: reads F. A. Lange's

History of Materialism (1866, English 1923), on which he was to draw extensively, not least for his views on Kant. Summer in Naumburg: 'My Schopenhauer, the music of Schumann, my solitary walks – these are the three things that provide my few moments of recreation.' He admires various actresses from a distance. His sympathies in the Austro-Prussian war are firmly on Prussia's and Bismarck's side.

1867

9 October: begins military service in the cavalry company of an artillery regiment stationed in Naumburg ('the best horseman among thirty recruits'), and lives at home. Wins a university prize on a theme set by Ritschl, *The Sources of Diogenes Laertius*, a writer Nietzsche later uses for his gossip about Socrates.

1868

March: A chest injury while mounting a horse takes a long time to heal; during extensive sick-leave from the army Nietzsche resumes his studies.

October: returns to Leipzig for his last Winter Semester, full of doubts about 'the philological brood . . . its molish activities, full cheek-pouches and blind eyes, their delight when they catch a worm, their indifference to the true and urgent problems of life' (to Rohde, 20 November). Nietzsche now conceives vague plans to study chemistry. November: first meeting with Richard Wagner at the house of Wagner's sister Ottilie Brockhaus (wife of the publisher), who is a friend of Frau Ritschl. Enthusiastic discussion of Schopenhauer's philosophy of music.

1869

21 January: overwhelming impression made by *Meistersinger* première in Dresden. 13 February: nominated Extraordinary Professor of Classical Philology at Basle, on Ritschl's enthusiastic recommendation and before Nietzsche has completed either his doctorate or his 'Habilitationsarbeit'. Duties: six lectures a week (at 7 a.m.), one seminar, six classes of Greek at the 'Paedagogium' (local grammar school). 17 April: he becomes a Swiss citizen. 17 May (Whitsun): first visit to Wagner and Cosima von Bülow at

Tribschen near Lucerne. 18 May: inaugural lecture on 'Homer and Classical Philology'.

First meetings with the historian Jakob Burckhardt. Letter to Wagner: '...the best and most sublime moments of my life are connected with your name and with that of your great spiritual brother, Arthur Schopenhauer, of whom I think with equal veneration, indeed *religione quadam*' (22 May).

1870

9 April: nominated full Ordinary Professor; 11–13 June with Rohde at Tribschen ('What evokes this religious mood is the presence of the gods in the house of the genius...', to Cosima von Bülow, 19 June).

11 August: leave from Basle to serve as volunteer medical orderly in the Franco-Prussian War; accompanying a transport of wounded (Alsace, Lunéville, Nancy) he falls ill, 7 September, with dysentery and diphtheria. Convalescing in Naumburg, by the end of October he is back in Basle. His attitude toward the war is romantically pro-German, even chauvinistic, yet he also speaks of Prussian power as 'the greatest danger to culture' (7 November).

Friendship with Franz Overbeck (1837–1905), the new Professor of Church History, with whom Nietzsche will share lodgings for the next five years. He expresses strong feelings of revulsion for the ethos of the profession ('the most burdensome thing of all is that I have forever to *represent* – a teacher, a philologist, a human being...' to Rohde, early February; 'No entirely radical truth [Wahrheitswesen] is possible [in the universities]. More specifically, nothing truly revolutionary can ever originate here' (to Rohde, 15 December), yet he feels that classical studies can be justified. For the first time Nietzsche is conscious of a great personal pedagogic task, a 'scientific and ethical education of our nation' (to Carl von Gersdorff, 12 December), in which Greece and music, Wagner and Schopenhauer, would all play their part.

1871

January: in a letter to the University's chief administrator Nietzsche complains of states of exhaustion, which he sees as symptoms of his reluctance to continue as a classical philologist.

Proposing Erwin Rohde as his successor, he offers himself as a candidate for the (then vacant) chair of philosophy; nothing comes of his plan.

From 15 February to the end of the semester on sick-leave, travelling with his sister and Gersdorff in the Swiss Alps. Meetings, with Wagner at Tribschen (April) and at a concert in Mannheim (23 December). Nietzsche has resumed composing, the autumn is taken up with writing his first book.

1872

1 January: *The Birth of Tragedy from the Spirit of Music* (Leipzig: E. W. Fritsch; for last edn see 1886). Wagner writes: 'I have never read anything more beautiful than your book!' And Cosima Wagner: 'In this book you have conjured spirits which I believed owed obedience only to our maëstro' (18 January).

January–March: before the Basle 'Academic Society' Nietzsche delivers five public lectures, *On the Future of our Educational Institutions* (published posthumously); its tenor is still romantic–nationalistic; the attacks on contemporary 'Bildung' and 'Kultur' are well received – Nietzsche is now at the height of his public success. There follows a swift reversal. At first not a single German review of *The Birth of Tragedy* appears. Ritschl is deeply embarrassed by the book, his private comment is, 'geistreiche Schwiemelei' ('brilliant but unsound'). The silence is broken by a young Berlin classicist, Ulrich von Wilamowitz-Moellendorff (1848–1931), 'What a bumptious-Jewish [sic] sickly laddie!' Nietzsche writes to Gustav Krug (24 July). Wilamowitz's hostile pamphlet, *Philology of the Future! A Reply to Friedrich Nietzsche's Birth of Tragedy!*, evokes Rohde's scurrilous *Afterphilologie: Epistle of a Philologist to Richard Wagner*.

Winter Semester: only two students (a lawyer and a Germanist) attend Nietzsche's lectures: 'what hurts me is the harm I have done to this small university, which so honoured me with its confidence' (to Wagner, November). The public censure by a Bonn colleague ('Anyone who has written a thing like that is finished as a scholar [ist wissenschaftlich tot]', H. Usener) is accepted by 'the profession'. Ten years later Nietzsche himself writes: 'Zarathustra is a scholar no more'.

25 April: the last of Nietzsche's twenty-three visits; the Wagners leave Tribschen. 22 May: with Rohde and Gersdorff

he attends the laying of the foundation-stone of the Bayreuth theatre, followed by a memorable performance of Beethoven's Ninth Symphony. 28–30 June in Munich: with Gersdorff and Malwida von Meysenbug (1816–1903), whom he first met at Bayreuth, Nietzsche attends two performances of *Tristan*, conducted by Hans von Bülow. Nietzsche sends him his *Manfred Meditation*, in which von Bülow finds no musical merit.

October: a journey to Italy is abandoned for no tangible reason at Bergamo, but returning through Switzerland Nietzsche discovers the beauty of the high Alpine valleys. November: meeting with the Wagners at Strasbourg. Christmas with family at Naumburg, in Weimar he hears *Lohengrin* for the first time, visits Ritschl in Leipzig.

This is a year of momentous though entirely undramatic changes: *the first* of sixteen years of Nietzsche's creative life, *the last* in which he was to enjoy tolerable health.

1873

The first of *Thoughts out of Season*, an attack on D. F. Strauss's *Der alte und der neue Glaube* is published and very favourably reviewed. The essay – a polemic against the author of *The Life of Jesus* as a complacent 'Kulturphilister' – argues that Germany's warlike superiority over France and the founding of the 'Empire' are not only no proof of the superiority of German culture but, on the contrary, will lead to its undoing. Gottfried Keller (to Emil Kuh, 18 November) regards Nietzsche's essay as a publicity stunt.

Wagner is offended by Nietzsche's turning down an invitation to spend the New Year at Bayreuth. 'I cannot think how, in all important matters, one could be more faithful to Wagner [than I am]. . . but I must exercise what I would almost call a necessary "hygienic" abstention from *more frequent* personal contacts, to preserve my freedom' (to von Gersdorff, 24 February). A visit to Bayreuth (with Rohde, 6–12 April) restores friendly relations. Financial difficulties and chaos accompany Wagner's ambitious Bayreuth venture. Nietzsche's archly censorious appeal for funds ('Exhortation to the German Nation') is turned down during a disillusioning meeting of the delegates of the nation-wide 'Wagner Societies' (Bayreuth, 30 October – 2 November).

Close contact with Franz Overbeck, first meeting with Paul Rée (1849–1901), author of *Psychological Meditation* (1875), a work overpraised by Nietzsche. Composes a 'Hymn to Friendship'.

June–October: during repeated attacks of migraine accompanied by worsening eyesight, Nietzsche is looked after by his sister in Basle and Graubünden.

1874

Thoughts Out of Season: II: 'On the Use and Disadvantage of History for Life'; *III:* 'Schopenhauer as Educator'. The former is an evaluation of the study of history (Nietzsche misconstrued Burckhardt's criticism of it as praise; see letter to Rohde, 19 March), the latter is his greatest paean to the man and the philosopher, written at the point when the influence of his work on Nietzsche is already waning. 8–9 June; Nietzsche attends two Brahms concerts and plays Brahms's music in Bayreuth to Wagner, whom this infuriates (15 August); in mid-November he takes great pleasure in Berlioz's *Carnaval Romain*.

By now a pattern of cures, extensive journeys in the Swiss Alps, and university terms at Basle under his sister's care, is established as the mode of Nietzsche's life. He chafes under a burden of lectures (Aeschylus's *The Cup Bearers*; Aristotle's *Rhetoric*; history of Greek literature; etc.) which are not well attended. His university vacations are shortened by his teaching duties in the 'Paedagogium'.

1875

Nietzsche receives an original of Dürer's etching 'Knight, Death, and the Devil' (mentioned extensively in *Human, All-too-Human*, 1886). Readings in political economy, Sir Walter Scott, *Don Quixote*. Friendship with a young musician, Heinrich Köselitz (pseud. Peter Gast, 1854–1918), who will write to Nietzsche's dictation and act as his amanuensis.

From a letter to von Meysenbug: 'People like us never suffer *only physically*, with us everything is deeply permeated by spiritual [geistig] crises, so that I cannot conceive how mere pharmacies and dietary cooking could ever restore my health...' (11 August). To Gersdorff: 'I practise unlearning *the haste of wanting-to-know*, from which all scholars suffer...I shall not acquire health sooner than I really *deserve* it...' (13 December).

The 'spiritual crises' are mounting: immense delight in the piano arrangement of *Götterdämmerung* (Easter) undermines his highly critical attitude to Wagner's exhumations of the Germanic past, at the same time as the Schopenhauerian rejection of life begins to look suspiciously like 'the Judaeo-Christian phraseology'.

1876

Thoughts Out of Season IV: 'Richard Wagner in Bayreuth': a highly ambivalent and (in Nietzsche's own view, to Rohde, 7 October 1875) far from uncritical appraisal of the musician and myth-makcr in the modern world. Wager (too busy to read it properly?) regards the essay as 'immense', and a great tribute.

With von Gersdorff (Lake of Geneva, March) Nietzsche reads *I promessi sposi*, and Voltaire, whose house he visits.

Repeated plans to marry 'some wealthy bride': these seem hardly more serious than Nietzsche's sudden proposal of marriage to a young Dutchwoman, Mathilde Trampedach, after an acquaintance of four days and on the strength of a common admiration for Longfellow's *Excelsior*; the letter (11 April) containing this proposal and also announcing his departure, though clearly not a joke, seems in doubtful taste. Several friends marry and increase his feeling of solitude.

The atmosphere during the Bayreuth festival becomes intolerable ('I dread each of those long artistic evenings...I have absolutely had enough' to his sister, 1 August); Nietzsche flees into the Bavarian Forest, where he begins writing *Human, All-too-Human*. Acquaintance with Louise Ott, a married Parisian lady.

From 15 October one year's sick-leave. With Rée in Genoa and by boat to Naples, then, throughout the winter, with Malwida von Meysenbug in Sorrento. The Wagners too are there. A few days before his departure (5 November), in the course of a long walk on the beach, Wagner enthusiastically and with a great show of sincerity expounds the Christian motifs and symbolism of *Parsifal*. Stony silence greets Wagner's effusion. In his letters Nietzsche speaks of Wagner's newly-acquired Christian convictions as 'mere play-acting', a wholly expedient attempt 'to come to an arrangement with Germany's ruling powers, which have now turned pious'; Elisabeth Förster-Nietzsche also reports Wagner as saying, 'Nowadays the Germans don't want to hear anything about heathen gods and heroes, they want to see something Christian [...die wollen "was Christliches sehn"]'. Nietzsche, deeply offended by what he regards as the coarseness and cynicism of Wagner's attitude, curtly and angrily excuses himself and disappears into the growing dusk – or so he claims;

Cosima Wagner's diary for 5 November records Nietzsche's visit, but no quarrel or coldness. The two men will never meet again.

1877

Sorrento until May, then Ragaz; from 1 September Nietzsche keeps house with his sister and Peter Gast. Criticizes Wagner's music for its 'mannerism and trick...of giving an impression of liveliness at all costs'; he writes to a musical critic advising him 'to use expressions which belong to Schopenhauer's metaphysic of music as little as possible; for I believe – forgive me, I think I *know* – that these expressions are spurious, and that all writings which are couched in this terminology will soon become incomprehensible' (to Carl Fuchs, July).

'I cannot bear life without feeling that I am *useful*, and the Basle people are the only ones who let me know that I am. All that my very problematic thinking and writing have ever done for me was to make me very ill; as long as I was really a scholar, I was healthy! But then came all that nerve-racking music and metaphysical philosophy, and my worries about a thousand things which don't really concern me at all' (to von Meysenbug, 1 July); yet a month later, thanking Paul Deussen for his first book, *Elements of Metaphysics*, with its strong Schopenhauerian and Indian mystical elements: 'I personally only regret one thing: that I didn't receive such a book as this several years earlier! How much more grateful I would have been! As it is, and seeing the direction one's thoughts take, your book serves me, strangely enough, as a happy *collection of all that I no longer believe to be true.*'

Meets the editor of *Mind*, G. Croom Robertson of University College London. Reading *Prometheus Unbound*: 'I bow deeply before one who can experience *this* within himself and is capable of bodying it forth' (to Rohde, 28 August).

'"I yearn for *myself*" – that has really been the continuous theme of my last ten years. Now that, thanks to being with myself for a whole year, everything has become quite clear and manageable, I can find no words to express how rich, how creative, *in spite* of all the suffering, I feel as soon as I am left alone – now I may tell you that I shall not be returning to Basle for good' (to Marie Baumgartner, his French translator, 30 August).

In a letter to Nietzsche's physician (23 October) Richard

Wagner volunteers the opinion that Nietzsche's agitated state of mind is caused by excessive masturbation and advises cold showers; there is little doubt that Nietzsche was informed of this diagnosis well before Wagner's death in 1883.

December: Nietzsche breaks with von Gersdorff on the latter's marriage to a Catholic Italian girl.

1878

Human, All-too-Human: a Book for Free Spirits. Philosophy in a new key, the key of 'becoming: there are *no eternal facts,* just as there are no absolute truths. Therefore what is needed from now on is *historical philosophizing,* and the virtue of being content with that'.

4 January (to Seydlitz): 'Yesterday Wagner sent me a copy of *Parsifal.* Impression on a first reading: more Liszt [Cosima's father] than Wagner; spirit of the Counter-Reformation. Being too much accustomed to all that is Greek and belongs to our common humanity, I find it all too Christian, time-bound, limited; the psychology is wholly phantastic; no flesh and much too much blood... moreover, I don't care for hysterical women; many things which are accepted by the inner eye will hardly be tolerable during a performance – just *think* of our actors, praying, trembling, craning their necks ecstatically... The language sounds like a translation from a foreign tongue. Ah, but the situations and their sequence – is that not the highest poetry? Is that not music's last challenge?'

Nietzsche's bitter complaint about 'the estrangement of so many friends and acquaintances' (to Peter Gast, 31 May) goes hand in hand with declarations of the need for solitude.

In June Nietzsche's Basle household is dissolved, perhaps because of (first?) quarrels with his sister, who returns to Naumburg. August: Wagner, on receiving *Human, All-too-Human,* writes an irritated attack in the *Bayreuther Blätter*: 'It hurt, but not in the place where Wagner wanted to hurt' (to Overbeck, 3 September). 'Wagner himself is *old* and has no Spring to look forward to – but truth does not grow old and in these [cultural and musical] matters, truth's Spring is still to come' (to Carl Fuchs, end of summer).

In a letter of 15 July (to Mathilde Maier) Nietzsche for the first time describes himself as '*a philosopher of life*' (to distinguish himself from the philosophers of death? asks Heidegger).

On 18 November he speaks of 'my shattered health. Outwardly my life is that of a very old man'; and to Marie Baumgartner (29 December): 'I am half dead with pain and exhaustion'.

1879

Publishes an aphoristic supplement (the first half of vol. 2) to *Human, All-too-Human*: 'Solitary as I was, deeply suspicious of myself, and not without inward rage, I now took sides *against* myself and *for* everything that would hurt *me* – me especially – and would come hard to me' (from the 1886 preface).

14 June: with his physical state deteriorating, Nietzsche resigns his chair and is granted an annual pension of 3000 S.F. for the next six years by the Basle Senate; Overbeck administers the fund. This is supplemented throughout Nietzsche's life by the income from a small inheritance.

Visits the Engadine for the first time, spends 'the least sunny winter of my life' in Naumburg, but the search for tolerable conditions in which to work continues restlessly, endlessly. 'What I need is some *real work* that costs time and *effort*, without straining the mind. Did my father not say that I would be a gardener one day?' (to his mother, 21 July). Reads Gogol, Lermontov, Mark Twain, E. A. Poe, Luther documents ('it seems no more than a matter of *national* taste, North and South, that *we* should *prefer* Luther as a man to Ignatius Loyola!').

To Peter Gast, 11 September: 'I am at the end of the thirty-fifth year of my life; "the middle of life" it used to be called throughout one-and-a-half millennia. Dante had his vision at that age, and speaks of it in the first words of his poem. Yet in the middle of life I am so "surrounded by death" that it may take me any hour: with my kind of illness I must think of a sudden death through convulsions (although I would a hundred times prefer to die lingeringly and with a clear mind, so as to be able to speak with my friends, even if it were more painful). In this respect I feel like the oldest man alive, but also in the sense that my life's work is done. A goodly drop of oil has been poured out through me, I know, and what I have done won't be forgotten. Fundamentally I have already put my view of life to the test – many others will yet do so. Up to this moment my mind is not yet depressed by my continuous and painful suffering. Sometimes it seems to me as though I felt more cheerful and more benevolent than in my whole previous life: to whom do I owe this strengthening and healing effect? Not to other men because, with the exception of very few, they have all "been annoyed with me" [haben sich alle "an mir geärgert"], and have not scrupled to let me know it. Read these last manuscripts of mine, dear friend, and ask yourself whether any traces of suffering and stress can be found in them: *I do not believe so...*'; yet to the same (5 October): 'The manuscript you received from St Moritz was purchased so dearly and with so much hardship that nobody who had the choice would have written it at that price. In reading it now, especially the longer passages, I often shudder at the ugly memory [of the writing of it].'

1880

Concluding section of *Human: All-too-Human*, vol. 2, 'The Wanderer and his Shadow' is published; the influence of the *moralistes*, especially La Rochefoucauld, is at its height.

Naumburg and Bolzano, three months in Venice, summer in Marienbad, Frankfurt am Main, Heidelberg, Locarno and Stresa, the winter in Genoa, in a freezing garret without a stove.

Reading Stifter's *Der Nachsommer*. To Peter Gast, from Marienbad, 20 August: 'I live *incognito*, like the most modest of visitors taking the waters – in the list of foreign guests I appear as "Herr Lehrer N." There are many Poles here who, oddly enough, take me to be one of them, come up to me and greet me in the Polish manner, and refuse to believe me when I tell them I am Swiss. "It *is* the Polish race" one of them observed, taking his leave of me quite sadly, "but the heart is turned God only knows which way"...Have you read Sainte-Beuve's eighteenth-century essays? They are exquisite human portraits, and Sainte-Beuve is a splendid painter. But above every figure I can see a further overarching reflection which he does not see, and this advantage I owe to my philosophy. *My* philosophy? The devil take me!'

1881

Aurora [or *The Dawn*]: *Thoughts on Moral Prejudices*. If Kant and Robespierre between them have brought the modern age into being, the age in which 'morality has abolished itself', nevertheless we remain 'men of conscience': what, then, is to be the valid, unassailable content of that conscience?

To Overbeck (Church historian and atheist) he writes the following astonishing statement: 'As for my attitude to Christianity, there is one thing you will surely believe: in my heart I have never really vilified it [ich bin in meinem Herzen nie gegen dasselbe gemein gewesen], and from my childhood days I frequently made a great inward effort towards its ideals, though in the last years I always came up against sheer impossibility' (23 June).

Genoa, Recoaro near Vicenza, then – 4 July to 1 October – Nietzsche's first stay in Sils Maria in the valley of the Upper Inn. Reading Spinoza, or at least Kuno Fischer on Spinoza. Here, '6000 feet above man and time', during a walk on the shore of Lake Silvaplana, in early August, he experienced the first of those moments of euphoria and elation which are now thought to have been symptomatic of his final disease. In the course of this experience there came to him what he later (in *Ecce Homo*, written 1888) called 'the conception fundamental to *Zarathustra*, that is, the idea of the *Eternal Recurrence*, the highest formula of assent [to life] that can ever be reached...'

Such moments of elation, however, are followed by periods of depression and feelings of exposure, of being a victim or tool of...what god, what power? To Gast, end of August: 'There is something about [my writings] which continually offends my sense of shame: they are the mirror-images of an incomplete, suffering creature who has hardly any control over his vital organs – I think of myself as the scrawl which an unknown power scribbles across a sheet of paper, to try out *a new pen*'.

27 November in Genoa Nietzsche hears Bizet's *Carmen* for the first time.

1882

The Joyous Science. Is all morality a function of 'the will to life', the instinct that works for the preservation of the species? What is that will and the world it builds, *really*: a tragic affair, or an 'aesthetic spectacle'? This is the last of the 'aphoristic books' of Nietzsche's middle period. In §§ 108 and 125 the words of 'the Madman's message', 'God is dead', are pronounced for the first time. In a note sent with the book to Burckhardt (September, from Naumburg) Nietzsche hopes to anticipate his criticism: '...it is all-too-personal, and everything personal is really *comic*.'

Nietzsche is perfectly capable of seeing his own work with
Burckhardt's eyes, yet he does not cease to believe that all value
is deeply 'personal'.

Bernhard Förster (1843–89), schoolmaster, Wagnerian, mem-
ber of the political anti-Semitic movement and later Elisabeth's
husband, lectures on Nietzsche in Berlin.

In Rome, as the guest of Malwida von Meysenbug, Nietzsche
falls in love with Lou von Salomé (1861–1937), the daughter of
a Russian general, later wife of a Protestant theologian called
Andreas, mistress of Rilke and confidante of Freud. This is
Nietzsche's most momentous and perhaps only love-affair; it lasts
from April to November, its bitter aftermath throughout the next
year. Details are hard to disentangle since most of the relevant
letters have either been destroyed or amended or forged by the
jealous Elisabeth. In May Nietzsche, Rée, Lou and her mother
travel to Orta and Lucerne (where a most peculiar photograph,
of Lou standing with a toy whip over Nietzsche and Rée in
harness, is taken). Nietzsche then 'prepares' and dispatches
Elisabeth and Lou to attend the *Parsifal* première at Bayreuth
(26 July), while he himself stays away. In August Nietzsche sets
Lou's prose poem, 'Prayer to Life', to music and revises her
collection of aphorisms. To Overbeck (September): 'My philosophical discussions with Lou were the most useful thing I did
this summer. Our intelligences and tastes are most deeply
related, yet there are so many contrasts between us that we serve
each other as the most instructive objects of observation. I have
never met anybody capable of extracting from their experiences
so many *objective insights*.' Similarly to Peter Gast (13 July): 'Dear
Friend, you will assuredly do us both the honour of not
associating the notion of a love-affair with our relationship.'
Nevertheless there is no doubt that Nietsche was deeply in love,
although his shyness in contact with women (the obverse of the
bravado of his observations on them) prevailed once more. He
asked Paul Rée, himself in love with Lou, to propose marriage
to her on his behalf (the episode is used in Mann's *Doktor
Faustus*), and both were turned down, though Rée lived with her
for some time. Elisabeth's vilification of Rée and Lou finally leads
to Nietzsche's complete break with his friends. He flees to Rapallo
(23 November), breaks off all contact with his family.

To Lou and Rée (mid-December): 'Don't be too worried about
those outbursts of my "megalomania" or "wounded vanity" –
if it should happen that, under the influence of some strong

feeling, I were to take my life, that should not cause too many tears either. What do my fantasies matter to you? Even my truths have not mattered to you. I should like you both to ponder that I am a headache-plagued half-lunatic, crazed by too much solitude.'

It is the direst betrayal he has ever suffered; he writes about it on Christmas Day to Overbeck, in Baudelaire's imagery: 'If I can't discover the alchemists' trick of turning even this – filth – into gold, then I am lost. This gives me the *finest* opportunity to prove that to me "all experiences are useful, all days holy and all men divine"!!!! All men divine... Pity, my dear friend, is a sort of hell, whatever Schopenhauer's followers may say.'

Here is Lou Andreas-Salomé's characterization (written in 1894): 'Solitude – that was the strong impression that made Nietzsche so striking on first acquaintance. To the casual observer there was nothing remarkable in his appearance: he was of medium height, always very simply but extremely carefully dressed, with calm features and brown hair brushed smoothly back... The fine and very expressive lines of the mouth were almost entirely hidden by a large drooping moustache combed forwards; he had a soft laugh, a quiet way of speaking and a cautious, meditative walk, with the shoulders slightly hunched; it was hard to imagine this figure in a large crowd of people... Nietzsche had such incomparably beautiful and delicately shaped hands that one's eyes were involuntarily drawn to them, and he himself believed they were the outward sign of his intellect... He ascribed similar significance to his unusually small and well-modelled ears, of which he said that they were really "ears for the unheard-of".

His eyes too betrayed his true self. Though they were half blind, they had none of the peering, blinking, unconsciously importunate look of many myopic people; rather they seemed like guardians of their own treasures, of silent secrets not to be bared to a casual glance...

Nietzsche's behaviour made a similar impression of secrecy and reserve. In daily life he was very polite and as gentle, almost, as a woman, with an unvaryingly benign, even temper – he delighted in the courteous forms of sociability and set great store by them. But there was always an element of the love of disguise as well – his manners were a cloak and mask for an inner life that was hardly ever revealed.'

1883

Thus Spoke Zarathustra: a Book for All and None, parts I and II.
Nietzsche's own estimates swing from one extreme to the other.
To von Gersdorff (28 June): 'The time of silence is over...let
my *Zarathustra* show you how high my will has flown. Don't allow
the legendary style of the book to deceive you: behind all those
simple and strange words lies my deepest seriousness and my
whole philosophy.' Similarly to Peter Gast (end of August) while
waiting for the page-proofs: 'I haven't yet got an objective
impression of the whole; but it seems to me to amount to a
considerable victory over the Spirit of Heaviness [Geist der
Schwere], seeing how difficult [schwer] it is to represent the
problems with which the book is concerned.' But then again, to
Overbeck (before 24 March): 'The worst is that I no longer
understand the point of my living on for another six months,
everything is boring, painful, *dégoûtant*. I suffer too much, too
many deprivations, and I have a boundless sense of the
imperfection, the mistakes and real disasters of my entire
intellectual past...Nothing can be made good any more, I shall
make nothing good any more. Why make anything? Which
reminds me of my latest foolishness – I mean my *Zarathustra*.
(Can you read this? I write like a pig.) Every so often I actually
forget about it. I am curious to know whether it has *any* value
at all – I myself am incapable of a judgement this winter, and
could be grossly mistaken about its value or worthlessness...
Only my general tiredness day after day prevented my cancelling
the order to the printer...' Yet whatever evaluation he may make
of the book, Nietzsche knows that with it he has reached a new
stage on his philosophical journey. To Malwida von Meysenbug
(end of March): 'Are you looking for a new name for me? The
language of the Church has one: I am — *the Antichrist.*'

From now on till 1888 Nietzsche spends his summers in Sils
Maria and his winters in Nice, moving from place to place in the
spring and autumn. 'I wish I had enough money to build myself
a sort of ideal kennel here,' he writes to von Gersdorff from Sils
Maria (28 June) – 'by which I mean a frame house with two
rooms, on a peninsula which goes out into the lake of Sils, where
there was once a Roman castellum. I find it impossible to live for
any length of time in these peasant-houses (as I have done
hitherto): the rooms have low ceilings which press down on one,
and there is always some disturbance going on...'

13 February: Richard Wagner dies in Venice; to Overbeck from Rapallo (22 February): 'Wagner was by far the *fullest* man I have ever known, and in this sense I have experienced a great deprivation these last six years [i.e. since the break in Sorrento in November 1876]. But something like a deadly insult lay between us...'; and to Gast (19 February); '...I even believe that Wagner's death was the most important relief that could come my way just now. It was hard to be for six years the enemy of the man one most reveres, and I am not made grossly enough for that.'

Extensive reading of Democritus; in a letter to Overbeck: '...I am absolutely astounded how little Plato I know' (22 October). Pressure from mother and sister to seek a university post; temporary reconciliation when Elisabeth gets engaged to Förster, but 27 October Nietzsche writes to Overbeck of his decision 'not to live in Germany, and not to live with my relations'.

The agony of last year's betrayal has not abated. To von Meysenbug (August): '...the Schopenhauerian notion of "pity" has hitherto always been the main source of havoc in my life – which is why I have reason to think well of all those moral schemes which include a few other motives in their idea of morality, and which do not attempt to reduce all human effectiveness to "sym-pathies"...In order to enforce one's ideal of man one must impose it on one's fellow-men and overwhelm them with it – that is, one must act creatively! But for that it is necessary to economize one's feelings of pity, and to treat as enemies all those who act against one's ideals, e.g. such riff-raff as L[ou] and R[ée]'; but to Overbeck (summer): 'Every contemptuous word written against Rée and Miss Salomé makes my heart bleed.'

1884

Thus Spoke Zarathustra part III (containing the doctrine of the Eternal Recurrence).

At work on the fourth and last part of the book, Nietzsche is beginning to emphasize the systematic nature of his philosophizing. He now looks back on *Aurora* and *The Joyous Science* as 'preparations and commentaries on *Zarathustra*. It is a fact that I wrote the commentary *before* the text' (to Overbeck, 7 April); and he also looks forward to the next five or six years in which he will study 'a whole range of new disciplines', including biology, for the purpose of 'elaborating a scheme in which I have traced out my "philosophy"'. These projects for a system seem always to be connected with moments of great euphoria: 'Since Voltaire there has been no such attack on Christianity – and, truth to tell, not even Voltaire had any inkling that Christianity could be attacked *in this way*' (to Overbeck, before 28 August 1883); 'I am now in all probability *the most independent man in Europe*. My goals and tasks reach wider than those of anyone else' (to the same, before 2 May 1884).

Such moments of elation are also reflected in Nietzsche's evaluations of *Zarathustra*. At present 'its meaning is entirely personal, it is my own "book of devotion and encouragement", whereas to everyone else it appears dark and hidden and ridiculous', but (he believes) its eventual standing as philosophy *and* poetry is assured: 'I flatter myself that with this book I have brought the German language to its peak of perfection. After Luther and Goethe a third step had to be taken: tell me, old comrade of my heart, whether power, flexibility and euphony have ever been so united in our language... I have the advantage of a more severe and manly stylistic line [than the "undulating" Goethe], without at the same time falling among the ruffians, as does Luther. My style is a *dance*, a playing with symmetries of all kinds and a leapfrogging and mockery of those symmetries – even in the very choice of vowels. Forgive me!' – an increasing number of Nietzsche's letters end with such apologies – 'Forgive me! I shall beware of confessing this to anyone else!' (to Rohde, 22 February).

No real reconciliation takes place – 'That accursed anti-Semitism is the cause of the radical breach with my sister' (to Overbeck, 17 April). Now everything is explicitly related to 'the great task': 'I am glad there are no letters from Naumburg... You may well imagine how the constant repetition of a single process has affected me: [while experiencing] the enormous tension and momentous feeling which encompass the fate of mankind, to have one handful of filth after another thrown in my face!!' (to Overbeck, ca. 18 August).

Brief friendships with admiring readers are invariably followed by rejections. In Zürich a conductor and full orchestra are prevailed upon by Nietzsche to play, for him alone, the overture of Peter Gast's comic opera, *The Lion of Venice* (a disaster). Nietzsche meets Gottfried Keller.

1885

Thus Spoke Zarathustra, part IV, 'a kind of sublime *finale*, not meant for the public (in connection with *Zarathustra* the word "public" sounds to me much like "whore-house" or "common prostitute")'. The book is printed privately, with financial help from von Gersdorff: 'as a matter of fact,' Nietzsche writes to him, 12 February, 'I am forty years old and have never earned a single penny from my numerous books'.

In a long letter to the Leipzig organist and conductor Carl Fuchs (early January), Nietzsche discusses metrical and musical questions in historical terms: 'the decay of a sense of melody...the dominance of discrete parts of the whole, of *pathos* over *ethos*' are diagnosed as the signs of modern 'decadence', a term which Nietzsche proposes 'not in order to reject but merely to find a word for' contemporary culture.

22 May: Elisabeth marries Dr Bernhard Förster.

The arch jokes which, in Nietzsche's letters, so often hide despairing outbursts, are wearing thin; many take the eerie form of dissociation: 'I am being confused with the late Professor Nietzsche of Basle', 'My son Zarathustra will leave you to guess...' 'You mustn't believe that my son Zarathustra is expressing my opinions...'

At times it seems to him that he is fundamentally ill-equiped for his philosophical task: 'If only I had occupied myself with medical, climatological and other such problems *at the right time*, instead of studying Theognis and Diogenes Laertius, I would not now be a half-ruined person' (to his mother, 21 March).

Reading Keller's novel *Sinngedicht* and St Augustine's *Confessions*; to his mother (21 March): 'Incidentally, there is nobody alive today for whom I *greatly* care. All the people I like have been dead a long, long time, e.g. the abbé Galiani [an eighteenth-century Italian economist and wit], Henri Beyle, or Montaigne.'

1886

Beyond Good and Evil, published at the author's expense. A previous publisher, Ernst Schmeitzner in Chemnitz, has done nothing for the sale of Nietzsche's books, keeping no stock of them, sending no review copies or advertising them, 'in brief, my writings from *Human, All-too-Human* onwards are *an-ecdota*';

Nietzsche therefore buys back his copyright. All his books except *Thoughts Out of Season* are now given new introductions (forming a kind of 'history of my development'), and re-issued by E. W. Fritzsch of Leipzig, his first publisher.

Beyond Good and Evil takes up ideas originally developed in Nietzsche's first philosophical essay of 1873, 'On Truth and Falsehood in an Extra-Moral Sense' (published posthumously in 1903). In a letter to Burckhardt (22 September) the theme of *Beyond Good and Evil* is described as 'the contradiction between every conception of morality and every scientific [i.e. biological and physical] conception of *life*', and again as 'that extremely problematic relationship between what is called "the improvement" or even "the humanization" of man, and the aggrandizement of the species of man'. To Overbeck (5 August): 'Perhaps [the book] may help to throw a few beams of light on my *Zarathustra*, which is an *incomprehensible* book because it goes back to experiences which I share with no-one. If only I could give you an idea of my feeling of solitude. There is nobody among the living or the dead to whom I feel related. This is indescribably terrible... The task for the sake of which I live lies clearly before me – as a fact of indescribable sadness, yet transfigured by the consciousness that there is greatness in it, if ever the task of a mortal man was informed by greatness.'

In January, Nietzsche's sister and her husband emigrate to Paraguay, to found a racially pure colony of German settlers.

Nietzsche succeeds in getting a septet of Peter Gast's performed privately at Leipzig: 'the music did not sound good – much too thickly laid on' (to Overbeck, 20 June). Rohde accepts a professorship at Leipzig, relations with him worsen: 'In this university atmosphere the best people degenerate. I constantly sense that even characters like Rohde have nothing to fall back upon except their accursed general indifference [eine verfluchte allgemeine Wurschtigkeit] and a complete lack of faith in their own cause' (to Overbeck, summer). There is no mystery about Nietzsche's breaking with each of his friends (except Overbeck): he will have nothing less than their complete concern. The breaks occur as soon as he suspects 'indifference' to *his* work, 'lack of faith' in the cause *he* has chosen to live for.

1887

Genealogy of Morals: 'moral–historical studies...psychological problems of the most exacting kind – it almost requires more courage to pose them than to risk answering them' (to Burckhardt, 14 November). The dissolving of spiritual and secular moralities into a system of psychological responses is seen as the first step toward a 'revaluation of values'.

24 February: earthquake in Nice: 'Last night, between 2 and 3 o'clock, I inspected (*comme gaillard*) various parts of the city, to see where there was most fear...' (to von Seydlitz). May: Lou Salomé writes to announce her engagement to the Protestant theologian Dr Friedrich Carl Andreas, Nietzsche does not answer. A deeply reproachful letter to Rohde ends: 'I am now 43 years old and as solitary as I was in my childhood' (11 November); to von Gersdorff: '*Who* or *what* I shall be left with, now that I must turn to the main concern of my existence (now that I am condemned to turn to it...), that is now the paramount question' (20 December).

'I have no respect for present-day Germany, even though, hedgehog-fashion, the country is bristling with arms. It represents the most stupid, the most depraved, the most mendacious form of "the German spirit" that ever was.' It was with this ambience that Wagner made his compromise, albeit 'circumspectly and with shameful ambiguity' (to von Seydlitz, 24 February). Yet on hearing the *Parsifal* overture for the first time (to Peter Gast): 'Has Wagner ever done anything better? This music is informed by the highest psychological consciousness and prevision in respect of what it says, expresses, *communicates*, [finding for its message] the shortest and most direct form – reducing every nuance of feeling to the epigrammatic. Music as a descriptive art [reaches here] a distinctness which makes one think of a superbly worked shield. And, finally, [there occurs] in the very depth of this music a sublime and extraordinary feeling, a living experience and an event of the soul which does great honour to Wagner, a synthesis of states which many people, including our "superior" intellectuals, will regard as incompatible: an awful severity of judgement "from on high" which issues from an intimate understanding of the soul and sees through the soul, piercing it as with knives – and hand in hand with this goes a compassion for what has been perceived and judged. Only Dante is comparable, nobody else' (21 January).

Reading: Galiani, the Swiss poet and novelist Carl Spitteler, a commentary on Epictetus, de Tocqueville, *Journal des Goncourt*; he discovers two Dostoyevsky stories ('strokes of psychological genius'); correspondence with Taine. To Burckhardt: 'Everybody has said the same thing about *Beyond Good and Evil*: that they have no idea what it is about, that it is something like "the higher idiocy" – everybody, that is, *except* two readers – yourself, dearest Professor, and M. Taine, one of your greatest admirers in France' (14 November).

Nietzsche's anti-liberalism, his dislike of the egalitarian ideas of 1789 and of Montalembert's *L'Eglise libre dans l'Etat libre* (1863) lead him to reconsider medieval Christian values.

Like Wittgenstein, Nietzsche is forever dissuading 'young people' from 'following him', yet deeply moved by the most modest signs of discipleship. 2 December marks the beginning of his correspondence with the Danish (Jewish) critic Georg Brandes (1842–1927), 'a good European and cultural missionary', and the first university teacher to give serious consideration to Nietzsche's philosophy. Brandes is praised for describing Nietzsche's writings as '*aristocratic radicalism* – with respect, the most intelligent thing I have so far read about myself', and rewarded with an illuminating self-analysis: 'In the scale of my experiences, the rarer, more distant, thinner tonalities predominate over the normal middle ones. As an old musician (which is what I really am) I have an ear for quarter tones. Moreover – and this presumably is what makes my books so dark – I am suspicious of dialectics, even of reasons. More important, it seems to me, is courage – the amount of courage [manifest in] what a man *already* regards as true, and what he does not yet [regard in that light]...I myself have only rarely the courage of what I know.'

The Will to Power. Since 1882 Nietzsche had been planning a systematic summation of his philosophy under this and several other headings, interpreting the bulk of his earlier writings, and especially *Zarathustra*, as an 'ante-chamber' and prolegomena to such a system. He wrote a number of outlines and tables of contents for this system-to-be; perhaps the most viable of them is the one dated 17 March 1887. The work remains a series of disconnected fragments, headings and reflections, some of them the best he has ever written. The order imposed on these reflections by Elisabeth Förster-Nietzsche, adopted by several subsequent editors, though not wholly arbitrary, is only one among several possible; it is the basis of the Kaufmann–Hollingdale translation (New York 1968). Thus the most remarkable paradox of 'the Nietzsche influence' is that the work to which numerous German and Italian fascist ideologists referred as their chief 'philosophical' source does not exist as a book authorized by Nietzsche himself, though all the individual prose items which they quote from *The Will to Power* were actually written by him, his sister having supplied some of the headings and some of the arrangements.

What makes the intended order of *The Will to Power* irrecoverable are Nietzsche's many changes of disposition for *this* book as well as his manner of writing generally. He occasionally boasts of his habit of composing during his walks in the mountains (this is part of his anti-academic pose), as when he claims to have completed each part of *Zarathustra* 'in approximately ten days', 'all *en route* during forced marches' (to Brandes, 10 April 1888). Having filled the *recto* pages of small note-books with disconnected reflections, he then turned the note-books over and filled the *verso* pages in the same way, sometimes scrawling further notes vertically across the already filled pages. Worsening myopia made his handwriting all but illegible to other people, occasionally even to himself; only Peter Gast seems to have been able to read his notes with confidence. However, what Nietzsche wrote down in these note-books are not single significant words or abbreviated sentences or 'notes toward...' (though there are occasional logograms), but finished and for the most part superbly formulated sentences and paragraphs. The way these sentences were to be organized into a book was then indicated by means of ingenious signs and numbers, and finally the fair copy for the printer was written out by Gast or, calligraphically and with great physical effort, by Nietzsche himself. The unabating liveliness of the style – or rather styles – of Nietzsche's books derives in no small measure from the fact that most of these sentences and paragraphs retain the freshness of first formulations. From this unusual mode of composition a number of consequences follow: first, Nietzsche always had a great deal of material in store and more or less ready to be turned into a book in a relatively short time; secondly, the majority of his books do not have the coherence, the textual and structural integrity of the kind one finds in philosophical treatises (e.g. in Kant's *Prolegomena* or Descartes's *Discours de la méthode*) – their coherence is more like (though it is not the same as) that of a collection of aphorisms or poems; and therefore, thirdly, since in the case of Nietzsche's writings it is part of the critic's task to create contexts his author has not supplied, it makes no sense to accuse the critic of 'quoting out of context' or 'picking out purple patches', though it does make sense to accuse him of supplying false contexts. Finally, it also follows that the material that was to go into *The Will to Power* (and further collections now in the *Nachlaß*), though somewhat more fragmentary and less organized, is not fundamentally different from the material that went into the books Nietzsche wrote between *Human, All-too-Human 1* of 1876 and the end of his conscious life. All this helps to explain why Nietzsche never referred to himself as a 'philosopher' without an admixture of irony, and why he most readily thought of himself as 'ein Schriftsteller' and occasionally 'ein Dichter', and of his work as 'Literatur'. More than any other thinker, and in more senses than one, Nietzsche is the writers' philosopher.

1888

The Wagner Case: a Musician's Problem; The Twilight of the Idols (published 1889); *The Antichrist: a Curse upon Christianity* (published 1895); *The Dionysos Dithyrambs* (mainly collected from previous volumes, published 1891); *Nietzsche contra Wagner* (published 1895); *Ecce Homo* (published 1908).

Grave illnesses afflict Nietzsche during his sojourns in Nice and Genoa, but throughout his first stay in Turin (from April till early June) he feels extremely well. Sils Maria (till late September) turns out to be wet, cold and depressing: 'the life-force is no longer intact – the loss of ten years can never be made good – during that time I lived only "on capital" without adding anything, anything new at all' (to Overbeck, 4 July). From 21 September to 9 January 1889 Nietzsche is in Turin.

10 April he writes yet another slightly stylized *vita* to Brandes, ending: 'I am by instinct a brave, even a military sort of animal. Long resistance has somewhat exasperated my pride. You ask if I am a philosopher? But what does that matter!' What he means by this is made clear in the next letter: 'We philosophers like to be mistaken for artists' (to the same, 4 May).

In July there is good news from Elisabeth Förster from the Nueva Germania colony. Numerous letters of this period, including one in praise of the new Emperor, William II, and several in praise of her own good sense and understanding, are partly later forgeries by Elisabeth. In her birthday letter to him (15 October) she asks scathingly whether he too is now beginning to be famous, even though nobody but 'a fine set of riff-raff, a few smart Jews included' believes in him; this phrase, 'Gesindel...Juden, die an allen Töpfen geleckt hätten', remains a trauma in Nietzsche's mind.

Reading: Stendhal and Dostoyevsky, Paul Bourget; Sir Francis Galton; *The Laws of Manu*; a very warm review article on Nietzsche's work by Carl Spitteler appears.

Several dedicatory notes sent with *The Wagner Case* (e.g. to Brandes, 13 September) describe the book as being 'a recreation from my main task'. His old friend Deussen visits Nietzsche (September): 'On a lovely autumn morning [writes Deussen] my wife and I climbed Majola Pass from Chiavenna and soon saw before us Sils Maria, where with a beating heart I met my friend again and embraced him with deep emotion after fourteen years of separation. How he had changed in the meantime! The proud bearing, the springy walk, the easy flow of talk of earlier times – all these were now gone. He seemed to drag himself along with difficulty and to be leaning somewhat to one side, and his speech often became slurred, heavy and halting. Perhaps it was not one of his good days. "Dear friend," he said sadly, pointing up at a few passing clouds, "I must have blue sky above me if I am to collect my thoughts." Then he led me to his favourite haunts. I particularly remember a flat stretch of turf close to a precipice, high above a mountain brook rushing past into the depths below. "Here," he said, "is where I love to lie and where I have my best thoughts." We were staying at the modest "Alpenrose" hotel in which Nietzsche had his lunch, usually consisting of a simple chop or something similar. We went back there to rest for an hour. Scarcely was the hour past when our friend was at our door, inquiring tenderly if we were still tired and apologizing in case he had come too early, etc. I mention this because such exaggerated anxiety and consideration were not previously characteristic of Nietzsche and seemed to me indicative of his present condition. Next morning he took me to his room, or as he said, his den. It was a simple sitting-room in a peasant's house, three minutes' walk from the main road; Nietzsche had rented it for the duration of the season for one franc a day. The furniture was as simple as can be imagined. At one end were his books, most of them well known to me from earlier days, a rustic table with coffee cups, egg-shells, manuscripts and toilet articles in bewildering confusion, which further extended over a boot-jack with the boot standing in it, to the still unmade bed. Everything indicated careless service and a patient, uncomplaining master. In the afternoon we left, and Nietzsche came with us as far as the next village, an hour downhill. Here he again spoke of his dark forebodings, so soon alas! to prove accurate. When we said goodbye he had tears in his eyes, a thing I had never seen before.'

Both Deussen and Meta von Salis now help substantially to cover Nietzsche's printing expenses. Nietzsche writes his letter of thanks 'in the midst of an infinitely difficult and decisive task which, if it is understood, will split the history of mankind in two. The meaning of it, in a word, is the *Revaluation of All Values*. Thereafter many things which were permitted hitherto will not be permitted any more; for major decisions [?] affecting values will have reduced the realm of tolerance to the status of mere cowardice and weakness of character. To be a Christian – I will mention but one consequence – will from now on be indecent' (to Deussen, 14 September).

To von Bülow: 'You have not answered my letter [on behalf of Peter Gast]. I promise you that you will not be troubled by me ever again. I think you are perfectly aware that the foremost mind of the age had expressed its wish to you' (9 October).

Nine days later, a letter to Overbeck shows the first unmistakable signs of madness, and in the same breath contains an astonishingly brilliant interpretation of Germany's contribution to European civilization. After announcing that 'the first book' of *Revaluation of All Values* is ready for the printer: 'You will have no reason to complain of any "ambiguity" [in my treatment of the Germans]. This irresponsible race, which has all the great disasters of European history on its conscience, and in all decisive historical moments always has "something else" on its mind (the Reformation during the time of the Renaissance; Kantian philosophy just at the time when, with great effort, England and France had attained a scientific mode of thought; the "Wars of Liberation" when Napoleon appeared on the scene, the only man so far who would have been strong enough to turn Europe into a political and economic unit) – this race now has "the Reich" on its mind, that recrudescence of petty states and cultural atomism, at the very moment when *the great question of values* is being asked for the first time. Never in all history was there a more important moment. *But who is there that knows anything about it?'*

On the same day, 18 October, he breaks with Malwida von Meysenbug who had reproached him for his attacks on Wagner. And now the process of breakdown gathers speed. In a letter to Gast of 2 December: 'Have just come back from a great concert, fundamentally the strongest impression of my life – my face was constantly grimacing to get over my extreme pleasure, including ten minutes of grimaces to hide my tears'.

To put an antic disposition on

(*Hamlet* 1: 5)

The medical cause of the collapse that now ensues is reasonably clear. It was diagnosed as 'paralysis progressiva' by the doctor to whose clinic Nietzsche was taken – that is, 'tertiary paralysis' if, as is to be presumed, the disease was syphilitic in origin. This, however, tells us nothing about the intellectual circumstances of the collapse, and the significant form it took. In attempting to relate it to the immense creative activity of the last few months of Nietzsche's conscious life, one may as well avoid the vulgar error of judging the products of the mind according to the circumstances in which they were generated. ('The causality under the influence of which a product of the mind has come into being indicates nothing about the value of that product', says Karl Jaspers;[1] what he does not say is that Nietzsche himself, like Marx and Freud, consistently practises the opposite, never hesitating to judge the works of philosophers and writers according to the causes and reasons he sees behind the works.) Whether or not what Nietzsche thought is valuable, or valid, or in its exaltation merely marginal to the human condition, must be determined by what he wrote, not by the state of mind in which he wrote it; the value of his work is neither enhanced nor impaired by our recognition that there is a continuity between the reflections of his sanity and the reflections which accompany his collapse into madness.

The scene of the catastrophe is Turin, the 'royal residential city' he discovers in the late spring of this fateful year.

[1] Jaspers, *Nietzsche*, p. 101.

Everything about it is right – why had he not discovered it years earlier! – its quiet, majestic streets, excellent theatres and noble palaces, its clear skies and fresh Alpine winds, its exquisite colour scheme of yellow and russet. The Italian royal family ('our King and Queen') are present; only the best music is played in the concert halls (Nietzsche mentions Bizet and several composers whose names are now forgotten); the vegetables and *ossobuchi*, the coffee and ice-cream, are of incomparable quality...The elation he has experienced on a number of previous occasions is heightened to a point of no return. Each fragment of his daily life – the modest rented room opposite the palazzo Carignano, the way people open the door for him when he enters a restaurant – all is exalted and celebrated as intimations of his future greatness, no, as the present signs that the great world – every waiter who, unasked, brings him the *Journal des Débats*, every Russian prince who smiles at him and every old crone who sells him a bunch of over-ripe grapes – recognizes him as 'someone very distinguished'. The great world: Brandes, Strindberg, Taine...They, too – like his 'maëstro Pietro Gasti', like the sleek Italian servants whom he will reward one day when he comes to reign in glory – *know who he is*: 'the first and freest spirit of Europe', 'the *only* German writer', 'Nïezsky, the Polish aristocrat', the castigator of Wagner and Germany, of Christianity and the Crucified Himself – the philosopher whose writings will 'break the history of mankind in two', if they have not done so already...There is something movingly, pathetically German about this notion of 'the great world' – the world which he hardly knows except from the pages of the *moralistes*,[1] and which is now on the point of acknowledging him. Or is it? Who is there, in that great world, that believes in him, except 'a fine set of riff-raff, a few smart Jews included'?

Why does the bow snap? Final affirmation and catastrophe are one, and Turin is the scene of both. The immense spiritual tension which, year after year, accompanied his acknowledgement of his 'great task'; which was just bearable while he lived on the margins of the worldly world, in solitude, and suffering endless bodily afflictions; which was the price he willingly paid in the expectation that, the task accomplished, the world would recognize the magnitude of his achievement and of his sacrifice,

[1] W. D. Williams, *Nietzsche and the French* (Oxford 1952), p. 181.

and the world would change – this immense tension can now be borne no longer. The moment of affirmation has come at last, the 'yea-saying to life' has begun, *and nothing whatever happens.* 'Europe will have to invent a second Siberia to which to send the author of this new *tentative* of values!' – yet Europe goes on as though it were unaware of the philosopher and arch-criminal who is plotting the overthrow of all it believes in.

The great task has long since ceased to be merely literary, merely philosophical, a mere matter of 'words, words, words'. Now Zarathustra's worst suspicion has come true: he really is 'only a poet, only a fool', only a philosopher...And so: action is all that is left. But what action? The copies of *Ecce Homo* which go to Bismarck and the young Emperor must be accompanied by a declaration of war (to Strindberg, 7 December); 'the next few years will stand the world on its head: since the old God has abdicated, I shall from now on rule the world' (to Carl Fuchs, 18 December); 'meanwhile I am becoming unbelievably famous. I really think no mortal has ever received such letters' (to von Salis, 29 December); 'Ah, my friend! What a moment! When I received your post-card – what did I do?...It was the famous Rubicon...' (to Gast, 31 December). The last letter of all (posted 5 January but dated 6) is to Jakob Burckhardt. It begins: 'Dear Professor, in the end I would have much preferred being a Basle professor to being God. But I did not dare to carry my private egoism so far that for its sake I should omit the creation of the world. You see, one has to make sacrifices, however and wherever one lives...' It is a bizarre description of the different ways the two men saw their life-tasks, yet it is splendidly accurate. For what, in Nietzsche's eyes, sustains Burckhardt's 'private egoism' and his refusal to make sacrifices is his ability to contemplate the history of mankind with the historian's impartiality and detachment – to see it in an attitude closely linked with the aesthetic.[1] To this attitude Nietzsche is no stranger. He has tried hard to establish and validate it – the paradox of trying hard for an aesthetic validation of the world is central to all he wrote – but again and again he fails: the moral concern prevails, in the work and in this letter too. Its end is as bizarre *and* meaningful as its beginning: 'I have had Caiaphas put in chains, last summer I too was being crucified by German

---

[1] See E. Heller, *The Disinherited Mind* (Cambridge 1952), pp. 68ff.

doctors in a very wearisome way. Wilhelm [the Second?[1]],
Bismarck and all anti-Semites [are to be?] abolished...'

1889

Early January. Nietzsche creates a public commotion in the Piazza
Carlo Alberto by throwing his arms around an old carthorse,
perhaps to protect it from being flogged by its driver. A few days
later he suffers another breakdown and has to be carried to his
lodgings. He sends numerous postcards to various public figures,
those written to his friends are signed 'The Crucified' and
'Dionysos'; one to Franz Overbeck ends, 'At this moment I am
having all anti-Semites shot'. Alarmed by one of these notes, and
by the letter to Burckhardt (5 January), Franz Overbeck hastens
to Turin (8 January), to take Nietzsche under medical escort first
to a clinic in Basle (run by a colleague called Wille[!], whom
Nietzsche is still able to recognize), and then to Jena.

The end

Apart from a few outbursts of frenzy, Nietzsche throughout the
remaining twelve years of his physical life was gentle, childlike
and friendly, recognizing only his daily companions. Occasionally
he conversed on indifferent matters, but never again mentioned
his philosophical work. It was as if the unknown god had used
him and had done with him. Often he would scrawl a few words
on a sheet of paper – 'Friedrich Nietzsche. I was born in
Röcken...' – but the line peters out in a series of meaningless
loops. One of the few testimonies we have of those last years
comes from Franziska Nietzsche, his mother. In a letter dated
Jena, 22 March 1890, which is surprisingly full of solecisms and
difficult to make out, she describes to Franz Overbeck a walk
during which they met an officer who was returning from the
local firing range. She tried to turn back, but Nietzsche insisted
on going up to him. 'Once an artilleryman myself, now a
professor and suffering from overwork', Nietzsche said to him.[2]

---

[1] Or, more likely, Wilhelm Bismarck, the Chancellor's notoriously anti-semitic
    eldest son.
[2] Bernoulli, *Franz Overbeck und Friedrich Nietzsche*, vol. II, p. 324: 'ein Artillerist,
    jetzt Professor und überarbeitet...'

At her request the officer gave Nietzsche his hand before they parted. 'He understood directly', she adds.

After the suicide of her husband in Paraguay, Elisabeth Förster-Nietzsche returned, eventually to set herself up as the jealous guardian of her brother's growing fame and royalties. After their mother's death (1897) she moved the invalid to Weimar. (In the 'Nietzsche-Archiv' which she founded and administered, she was later to receive A. Hitler on his way to Bayreuth.)[1] In the devoted care of an old family servant and under the hideous supervision of his sister Nietzsche lingered on, progressively paralyzed, until his death on 25 August 1900, two months before his 56th birthday. The finest portrait we have of his last years is in chapter XLVII of Thomas Mann's *Doktor Faustus*.

In a memorandum about the possible cause of Nietzsche's final breakdown,[2] Franz Overbeck observes that Nietzsche 'never feared insanity or thought much about it, but what tormented him was the question of whether it was given to him to achieve anything special at all. . . To me it seems quite possible. . . that he did not bring madness into life with him, but that it was a product of his way of life'.[3] And Overbeck confesses that he 'could not entirely resist the thought that Nietzsche's illness was simulated – an impression derived from my long-standing experience of Nietzsche's habit of taking on many different masks'. The objective correlative of these 'masks' is Nietzsche's intellectual and stylistic versatility.

A diagnosis of tertiary syphilis cannot now be seriously doubted. Overbeck's speculation is not an alternative to this diagnosis, but a complement to it. It is based on the plausible premise that, having chosen what was beyond his capacity to accomplish, Nietzsche feared the moment when he would be overwhelmed by the evidence of his inadequacy to his chosen task. In the face of this evidence, which now – at the end of 1888 – takes the form of an increasingly unmanageable convolute of notes and plans and skeleton outlines,[4] his self-criticism does not abate but becomes if anything more radical and destructive. For

---

[1] See Kaufmann, *Nietzsche*, p. 46.
[2] Bernoulli, *op. cit.* vol. II, pp. 215–18.
[3] '. . .dass er sich [den Wahnsinn] zugelebt habe', *ibid.*
[4] Overbeck writes of a trunkful of 'in trostloser Weise angewachsener Wust', Bernoulli, *op. cit.* vol. II, p. 292.

one who at all times was given to strenuousness and self-laceration, and incapable of intellectual compromise, there now arises the need to withdraw from an impossible situation, to 'clown'[1] his way out of it. And if this, or something like this, is what really happened, it need not surprise us that such a mind, heedless and passionate in all its actions and reactions, might then no longer find its way back into sanity. It is not very different from what happened to Hamlet.

[1] Nietzsche sometimes (e.g. *EH* IV/1) called himself 'Possenreisser' and 'Hanswurst'.

2
Life and work

. . .the motive and the cue for passion. . .

(*Hamlet* II: 2)

How is the biography of a philosopher related to an understanding of his work? Aware that there can be no general rule,
Nietzsche envisages two broadly distinct types of thinker:

If one compares Kant and Schopenhauer with Plato, Spinoza, Pascal,
Rousseau, and Goethe in respect of their soul and not their mind
[Geist], one is putting the former thinkers at a disadvantage. Their ideas
do not make up a passionate history of their souls, there is here no novel,
no suggestion of crises, catastrophes, and hours of agony, their thinking
is not at the same time the instinctive [unwillkürliche] biography of their
souls. (*M* §481)

Is this what Nietzsche's writings amount to – the instinctive
biography of his soul? By insisting on that faintly embarrassing
distinction between 'mind' and 'soul', by including Goethe in his
list, and by emphasizing the dramatic character of thought,
Nietzsche is challenging the 'scientific' conception of philosophy
as a cool technical pursuit within a circumscribed range of
affective moods (he will eventually challenge all areas of modern
culture in this way). He does not believe in philosophy as the
pursuit of pure knowledge free from value judgements. On the
contrary: no experience is excessive (the above reflection from
Aurora continues), or too passionate, or too wild to determine
the substance and form of philosophical reflection. 'Everything
that happens' may turn out to be relevant to it,

though of course [he adds, disarmingly] by everything that happens I
do not mean crude outside 'events', but those spasms and strange
adventures to which the loneliest and quietest of lives succumbs – a life
that is unhurried and burns itself out in the passion of thinking.

And this (it may surprise the reader to note) is how Nietzsche
often saw his life: as devoted to thinking, to the delight that goes
with the pursuit of intellectual matters, and to nothing else (*WKG*
VIII/2 p. 114).

35

The change of direction in Nietzsche's argument as well as its heightened diction are characteristic: what began as a general reflection on two kinds of philosophers turns into a personal avowal. Now the validity of such an avowal can hardly be established without some reference to that 'loneliest and quietest life' as it was actually lived, including those 'crude outside "events"', yet we shall find that a little factuality goes a long way with him:

> ...in systems that have been refuted only the personal interests us, for that alone is eternally irrefutable. It is possible to paint a man's portrait in three anecdotes; I try to pick out three anecdotes from each system, and throw the rest to the winds.[1]

Most of Nietzsche's philosophical thinking goes on in just this way, moving swiftly between the intimately personal and the philosophically significant. This indeterminacy is among several aspects of his writings that make him the most literary of philosophers, or rather the one in whom the time-honoured distinctions between literature and philosophy are radically challenged. As a consequence, some critics have denied him the name of philosopher altogether, treating his books as though they were (in Goethe's phrase) 'fragments of a great confession',[2] or (with some encouragement from Nietzsche himself) as an elaborate metaphysical fiction or 'Begriffsdichtung'.[3] Finding that his books do not fit into any previously labelled boxes, some of Nietzsche's earliest critics decided to treat them as part of a cultural–political programme – that is, as an ideology – and this of course was also the procedure followed by fascists, national socialists, activists, vitalists, as well as a whole host of harmless cranks and humbugs. Yet others, exasperated by the gory phraseology of post-war existentialism, in which they found a good many borrowings from Nietzsche, proceeded to disinfect Nietzsche's texts of all taint of 'literature' *and* biography, and to make him sound like an eminently sensible Oxford philosopher with a penchant for Shavian paradoxes. Karl Jaspers's study (1936) ignores the chronology of Nietzsche's writings and presents him as a dialectician whose contradictions

---

[1] *WKG* III/2 p. 297, from the second preface to *Die Philosophie im tragischen Zeitalter der Griechen* of 1873, published posthumously.

[2] *Dichtung und Wahrheit*, book VII.

[3] See Hans M. Wolff, *Friedrich Nietzsche: der Weg zum Nichts* (Bern 1956), p. 53.

are a guarantee of the fundamental truthfulness of his moral–existential commitment; while Martin Heidegger (in his lectures of 1936–41), ignoring the first half of Nietzsche's work, concentrates, tacitly and exclusively, on his last cosmological and ontological speculations. And so, to some extent, does Eugen Fink ([2]1960). He too trusts ontological thinking farther than Nietzsche ever did, and in his treatment of Nietzsche's aesthetics, perhaps in order to redress Jaspers's and Heidegger's virtual neglect, Fink is apt to take Nietzsche's fragmentary proposals for a more rounded achievement than I can see in them. Nevertheless I found his study more disinterested and thus more helpful than any other. Walter Kaufmann's *Nietzsche: Philosopher, Psychologist, Antichrist* ([1]1950, [4]1974) presents the richly illustrated but oddly idealized portrait of a classical German philosopher in the Kant–Hegel–Schopenhauer tradition, a little neater, a little more systematic and a good deal less contentious than...the real Nietzsche? Than the Nietzsche that is to be presented in this study, at all events. Critics with an eye to the pathology of the man who was granted less than twenty years of creative life, have psychologized his every thought to the point where the entire work is reduced to a monstrous solipsism; and in this they have recently been joined by some structuralist commentators, who are apt to leave their bemused readers with the impression that Nietzsche's writings are really about the great difficulty of finding appropriate metaphors for his difficulty in finding appropriate metaphors...Yet it must be added that almost every one of these interpretations, including the most reductive, receives some support from Nietzsche's pen:

It has gradually been borne in on me that every great philosophy so far has been the confession of its originator and a kind of involuntary and unacknowledged autobiography; and, moreover, that the moral (or immoral) intentions in every philosophy have constituted the true vital germ from which the entire plant has always grown...Accordingly, I do not believe that 'an impulse to knowledge' is the father of philosophy; but that, here as elsewhere, another impulse has merely used true (and false) knowledge as an instrument... (*J* 1/6)

(And yet, the chapter in *Ecce Homo*, entitled 'Why I write such good books', begins with the sentence, 'I am one thing, my writings are another thing').

The bewildering variety of these interpretations bears witness to the exceptionally wide range of Nietzsche's own interests, thoughts and reflective moods, and to the equally wide range of influences – often mutually opposed influences – which he has exercised on Western culture throughout the last seven decades.

Yet to anyone not misled by 'deep' theories it is obvious that what Nietzsche has written is more than a self-portrait. It *is* the 'biography of a soul' but, far from there being anything particularly 'instinctive' or 'involuntary' about it, it is a biography that abounds in articulated consciousness of world and time – his time and world, and ours. The work has a broad realistic base: how, otherwise, could it contain those remarkable anticipations of twentieth-century conflicts for which it is praised by some and condemned by others? Nietzsche's is a negative biography, a life lived increasingly in the shadow of the belief that the world as we experience it is the only world there is, and that it is, fundamentally and as a matter of principle, untruthful. (The invoking of 'instinctive' or 'unconscious' motives is, as we shall see, an attempt to cut through this untruthfulness.) Under ever worsening conditions of health, this biography is the story of rejections and resignations, transmuted, whenever possible, into a process of self-liberation: from friends and material conditions and loyalties of every kind; from Christianity and every other piety; from philology and his beloved Greeks (*FW* §340); from the university and every other institution; from Wagner, Schopenhauer, Germany, his family – a liberation from every sustaining belief and, in the end, from the burden of sanity itself. At the age of 19, shortly before leaving Schulpforta, he writes in an autobiographical sketch:

And thus man outgrows all that once embraced him. He does not have to break the fetters – they fall off him unexpectedly, at the command of a god; and where is the ring that will contain him at last? Is it the world? Is it God?[1]

German intellectual history is strewn with such rejections, attempted liberations and metamorphoses: the poet Christian Günther, the playwrights Heinrich von Kleist (*U* III §3) and Georg Büchner, and Heinrich Heine, Nietzsche's own contemporary, are among those who (to quote Nietzsche echoing Baudelaire) tried to master 'the alchemists' trick' of turning 'the

[1] *Schlechta*, vol. III, p. 110.

mud' of their lives into the gold of literature.[1] How is it to be done? What values will survive the fire of the kiln? Jakob Burckhardt, Basle patrician and eventually Nietzsche's reluctant friend and senior colleague at the University, had once faced the same problem: 'Shovelling through the ruins of my recent view of life,' he wrote at the age of 20, with less than his usual elegance, 'I came upon a remedy: my new academic subject!'[2] The history of art, and of the Renaissance, becomes the en-compassing intellectual and moral discovery of Burckhardt's life. Nietzsche hits on no comparable solution, he will never have a 'Hauptfach'. There is no one discipline or method or doctrine he is prepared to settle on, and while every paragraph of his mature work is unmistakably his own, the variety of his styles and masks continues undiminished. There is only the philosophical task – all-consuming, impossible.

The obvious temptation therefore is to read his philosophical writings as compensatory inversions of his biography: as the reflections of the sick man exalting physical health, the intellec-tual waxing ecstatic in praise of the instinctual life and preaching 'the doctrine of weaklings who aspire to be strong'.[3] More than one Pozzo-like critic has portrayed him in this vein, and again it must be admitted that, both implicitly and by his own example in interpreting other thinkers, Nietzsche himself lends some support to these hostile interpretations, yet in most respects they remain both crude and misleading. There is no suggestion of self-identification with 'the Superman' in one who writes, 'But a philosophy such as mine is like the grave – one no longer lives with others' (to Georg Brandes, his first independent critic, 2 December 1887).

What then *is* the relationship of the author's life to his work? Kierkegaard ponders the question in one of his desultory speculations, and the fact that his answer is valid for our enquiry, even though he is concerned with poets and their

---

[1] Cf. Baudelaire's projected epilogue to *Les fleurs du mal*: 'Tu m'as donné ta boue, et j'en ai fait de l'or.' Apart from this collection, Nietzsche knew Baudelaire's essays on Wagner and Heine: cf. his letter to Peter Gast, 26 February 1888.

[2] Quoted from Hermann Heimpel's introduction to Burckhardt's *Weltge-schichtliche Betrachtungen* (Berlin 1960), p. 12.

[3] Miguel de Unamuno, quoted from Michael Hamburger's *From Prophecy to Exorcism* (London 1962), p. 52.

productions, underlines once more the literary aspect of Nietzsche's philosophical undertaking. It is a mysterious relationship, Kierkegaard writes: the circumstances of an author's life are not the cause of the created work, they merely provide the occasion that brings the work into being:

A creation is a production from nothing; the occasion is, however, the nothing from which everything comes...The occasion is the delicate, almost invisible web in which the fruit hangs...Without the occasion precisely nothing at all happens, and yet the occasion has no part at all in what does happen...[1]

(In the *Genealogy of Morals* III §4, Nietzsche puts this less delicately: the artist, he writes there, 'is merely the precondition of his own work, its maternal womb, the soil – on occasion the fertilizer and manure – on which and from which it grows.') Even though they play a greater part in Nietzsche's work than Kierkegaard's delight in paradox allows, the events of Nietzsche's life do not explain why he wrote as he did. They may explain how he came to be a precocious, solitary boy of ten, but they do not explain the boy's passionate devotion to the business of writing – of writing endlessly, publicly and privately, on every conceivable subject. Acute myopia, colic and endless attacks of migraine may explain why the young professor was forced to abandon the traditional forms of essay and learned treatise, but psycho-somatic disturbances do not explain how he discovered that the note-books he did manage to keep could be transcribed for publication, and that they are worth reading. It was a tremendous discovery, and it determined every hour of his life. Writing had for him strong compensatory erotic overtones (which it is the foolish prejudice of French structuralists to identify with sexuality), but so has all creativeness. What distinguishes his books, apart from their intellectual energy, is his passion for shapeliness, balance and clarity *over brief stretches of prose*. He loathed the idea of democracy in all its forms, yet his utmost concern with intelligibility is present in almost every sentence he wrote: that he has been accused of 'obscurantist' and 'elitist' tendencies by Marxist detractors whose wilful obscurities render their own prose inaccessible to all but the smallest circle of initiates, is one of the many ironies that make up the posthumous fate of his work. All assessments of clarity are

[1] *Either/Or* (translation by Walter Lowrie), vol. 1 (Oxford 1946), pp. 191ff.

relative to the task in hand. The yearning for communication and communion without compromise, the ethical ideals without compromise, the self-destructive scepticism without compromise, the monstrous exaggerations issuing in the most accurate insights, the search for the hardest solutions, to be combined with an unending search for effortless joy and equanimity, and the last despairing expedient of all, the disillusioned embracing of the single grand metaphysical illusion – it is against all these exactions that the clarity of Nietzsche's style will have to be considered.

Nietzsche's reputation in Germany after the First World War, and in France and England after the Second, is that of an existential thinker. This is a wide term but not a vague one. It means (among other things) that a particularly close and 'committed' relationship obtains between Nietzsche the man and Nietzsche the philosopher; a relationship as close as that between D. H. Lawrence the man and Lawrence the novelist. Nor is this a gratuitous comparison, seeing how much of the Lawrentian spirit is in fact Nietzschean: 'I have at all times written my works with my whole body and my whole life' – this is Nietzsche writing, not Lawrence – 'I don't know any "purely intellectual problems"...These things you know as your thoughts, but your thoughts are not your experiences' – 'nicht eure Erlebnisse...' (*WKG* v/I p. 644). And Zarathustra, acting here as Nietzsche's mouthpiece (e.g. II § 2), loudly proclaims the message of 'commitment' as the identity of thinking and willing and being, the doctrine of the personal entitlement to knowledge. Why thought that is less 'committed' should be inferior – why Hume's philosophy should be impaired by his preference for backgammon – is not explained.

The dubious nature of this doctrine of heroic commitment will concern us later in our argument. Here we may note that this dubiousness has not escaped Nietzsche himself, as when he reflects on the vulgarity of minds that will take nothing less than the personal witness (replete with sores and suffering) as evidence for the truth of an opinion; mercifully, at the point where such insistence is apt to become a bore he, unlike his disciples, is quite capable of an ironic disengagement – 'But let's leave Herr Nietzsche! What concern of ours is Herr Nietzsche's health?' (*FW*, introd. § 2). Again, he invokes this disengagement when commending *The Will to Power* as 'a book for *thinking* and nothing else – it belongs to those who take pleasure in thinking and nothing else'. Yet this pleasure has no other source than those 'purely intellectual problems' he had condemned as inauthentic...

How 'authentic', then, is this image of the heroic thinker (perpetuated in a hideous bust by Max Klinger, but also in Nietzsche's own Prussian self-stylizations when posing for photographs), how true is this portrait of the 'hermit philosopher' committed with every fibre of his body to his great reflective venture?

In a sense it is not true at all. In the sense with which we must be concerned much of the way, Nietzsche's thinking is a series of experiments 'which I live' (*WzM* § 1041) – some of them tentative speculations, hunches and suspicions which come and go, some of them *in corpore vili*. 'I desire that your hypothesizing should reach no further than your creative will' Zarathustra calls to us (II § 2): are we to think that Nietzsche obeys Zarathustra's command in that notorious reflection in which he rejoices in Galiani's observation that predictions are apt to be self-fulfilling and that 'prevision is the cause of European wars', and then adds, 'Since I do not share the [anti-war] views of my friend, the late abbé Galiani, I am not afraid to predict and therefore conjure up the causes of wars'? The best that we can say of the author of images of violence like 'the blond beast' (*GM* I § 11) is not that he is living out 'the reality behind the words', but that he is conducting experiments in word and ideas, and *trying out* what their effect might be. His brilliant versatility is unthinkable without a dose of histrionics. In his bitter attacks on Richard Wagner, on Wagner's insincerity and religiosity, Nietzsche seems to be looking for art without artifice, opera without operatic effects, for theatre without theatricality – yet he would be the last to deny that there is, not indeed insincerity, but role-acting and conscious deliberation in his own changes of style and modulations of tone and all the other devices which make his prose such incomparable pleasure to read. Besides, where commitment to a chosen task is concerned, who will say whether Wagner's or Nietzsche's is the more intense, the more authentic and heroic? Wagner loved to boast of his suffering. Perhaps there were times when Nietzsche too did not feel the indecency of such weight-lifting contexts, when he did not mind it enough; but then, as

George Eliot observed of the Reverend Casaubon, perhaps Nietzsche too 'had no sense of fellowship deep enough to make all efforts at isolation seem mean and petty instead of exalting'.[1]

However that may be, in another, more comprehensive sense the existential claim *is* true: to his philosophic venture Nietzsche's entire life is dedicated, and every comfort and consolation is sacrificed. Yet a man's capacity for sacrifice is not in itself a value. The experience which divides us from Nietzsche makes us reject a penitential ethic which determines 'the order of men's rank' according to their capacity for suffering (*FW*, end). Nor can strenuousness be a value for us. What we acknowledge is not the heroic stance, not a self-created value, but the strange aura that surrounds Nietzsche's venture. It is an aura of grave, Hamlet-like charm – the charm that belongs to every tragic character. It derives from the knowledge, which Nietzsche shares with Hamlet, of being over-taxed by his chosen task.

Thomas Mann in his Nietzsche-Essay of 1947 speaks of the boy's and adolescent's prim and exemplary normality,[2] the early letters and reports show his eagerness for learning, his immense intellectual gifts, his gentle gravity. The role of destructive critic did not come easily to him, nor the role of stentorian prophet. In doing violence to a world he diagnosed as decadent he had to do violence to his own nature. Did he choose the moment 'when he himself might his quietus make', not with a bare bodkin but with his own heedless mind? Yet he decided to love his fate. Perhaps the moment he chose was the moment when he knew that he had done all it was given him to do.

[1] *Middlemarch*, book IV, chapter 42. For Nietzsche George Eliot is one of those inconsequential (because English) moralists ('Moral-Weiblein') who fail to see that you cannot reject Christianity without forfeiting any right to its moral scheme (*GD* IX §5).

[2] Before he gets to the end of the sentence, Thomas Mann (in 'Nietzsche's Philosophie im Lichte unserer Erfahrung') manages to make Nietzsche sound like Felix Krull: 'Man hat das Bild einer hochbegabten Edel-Normalität, die eine Laufbahn der Korrektheit auf vornehmem Niveau zu gewährleisten scheint.' ('The picture one gets is of a highly gifted, noble normality which seems to guarantee a career of correctness at a level of high distinction.') Nietzsche shared and would have been quick to diagnose Mann's addiction to parody. For another interpretation of the effects of Nietzsche's boyhood on his philosophizing see W. H. Bruford, *The German Tradition of Self-Cultivation* (Cambridge 1975), pp. 173–4.

3

Three 'prophets' of the modern age

To show...the very age and body of the time his form and pressure
(*Hamlet* III: 2)

Friedrich Nietzsche is one among those very few thinkers – Karl Marx and Sigmund Freud are the others – whose influence on our age is undoubted. The influence of their speculative thinking touches on every aspect of our experience: had they not lived, the life of modern Europe would be different. All three were knowers who would be doers – *savants* with a taste for reform and concrete change, thinkers who, for a time at least, turned ideologists. What characterizes their work and distinguishes it from the work of their philosophical predecessors is that it is in no sense disinterested. Their thinking is directed toward the uncovering of an immanent secret – a secret concealed in men's minds; these minds they wished to change, and with them the world. Because they thought of their undertaking as the solving of a *secret*, they saw all opposition to it as a conspiracy: a conspiracy of men with vested social and material interests, thought Marx; of men with vested moral and religious interests, thought Freud; of men who choose to be only half alive and resent the few who live generously and dangerously, thought Nietzsche. They made a number of confident prophecies, yet the full extent of the consequences that attended their philosophical undertaking was not foreseen by them; and this is so in spite of the fact that they took little trouble to separate their findings from their intentions, formulating their forecasts in a language designed to make them come true.

Their anticipations are inseparable from their religious situation. All three were professed atheists who looked on man's belief in God as an historically determined symptom of man's weakness and subordination. They offered to liberate him from that belief, not only by demonstrating its illusoriness, but also by fostering as its alternative various forms of human self-reliance and self-assertion. Characteristically – and here one must go by the style of what each wrote – only Nietzsche shows an

44

awareness of the full significance of religious belief in our Western experience; only he seems to be aware of the gravity of any undertaking designed to replace that belief.

All three began their work, and continued to be sustained in it, by radically rejecting their own intellectual sources: thus the critical aspect of their work is largely indistinguishable from its 'positive', constructive aspect, and their creativity is involved in both. They tended to underestimate what they owed to their age. They were not always aware of the extent to which their own historical situation formed what Nietzsche called 'the horizon' of their thinking, yet for us their greatest interest, though not identical with their historicity, is inseparably connected with it. Take for instance the identification, common to all three of them, of 'scientific' with systematic knowledge, and their preoccupation with a rhetoric and mode of conviction derived from the natural sciences: these, we can see, are characteristic nineteenth-century preoccupations, yet only Nietzsche recognized them as such. (Marx frequently spoke of the need for historical consciousness, Freud tended to see the past archaeologically, only Nietzsche reflected on it at length and practised historical perspectivism, albeit in a sketchy way.)

Their systematic thinking was directed toward, and in turn issued from, a briefly statable leading idea – an *idée maîtresse* by means of which the secret of all that men do is to be explained; and in each case this explanation of *what men do* proceeds by way of an account of *what moves them* to do what they do. None of these three problematic prophets respects the distinction, fundamental to the liberal mind, between what a thing is and how it came to be what it is, though none is eager to apply his stable explanation to his own work.

Each of these leading ideas – viz., motivation through material interest; sexual motivation; the will to power – is said to be the hidden secret in the depths of men's souls. This motivation is, in each case, the progenitor of mind; it is the begetter of value judgements and therefore not subject to them. It is also, by definition, unavailable to a man's 'ordinary', that is motivated and therefore unenlightened, consciousness. For as long as it dominates the mind, each of these leading conceptions excludes, or at least radically devalues, all impartial insight and stable, 'objective' knowledge. Conversely, as soon as 'Erkenntnis' (which in German is always a dynamic mode of knowledge) is initiated, the ensuing explanation becomes an explaining away. These are passionate thinkers. Just as there is something parricidal in their attitude toward the past, so there is something suicidal about their conceptual schemes: each time the thinker is excluded from the thought he has created, the intellectuality that informs his work is devalued or rendered invalid by it.

Is it a coincidence that all three were German? But perhaps we had better ask first, How German were they? The very fact that the question has no single and obvious answer, that it depends on what one means by 'German', provides part of the answer. Marx was an emancipated Rhenish–Prussian–Jewish intellectual who spent most of his life in exile; Nietzsche, a German (Bismarck moustache and all) on any reckoning save his own, claimed Polish aristocratic ancestry, came to think the foundation of the Second Reich in 1871 an unmitigated disaster, and returned to Germany only when his work was done and his mind was spent; and Freud was a Moravian German-speaking doctor of orthodox Jewish background, who would have lived all his life in Imperial and Republican Vienna had not another quasi-Viennese provincial sent him into exile, to die, like Karl Marx, in Hampstead. They are hardly very representative Germans, yet they all belong to one tradition, one Germany of the mind, where (as Nietzsche writes) 'to be a good German is to undo one's Germanness' (*MA* II/i § 323); is to represent by refusing to represent. They have their intellectual roots in a culture whose dynamic quality Nietzsche saw reflected in its very language: whereas 'reality' derives from 'res' and 'realia', a static concept (he argues in one of his more respectable skirmishes with etymology),[1] 'Wirklichkeit' derives from the dynamic 'wirken', 'to affect by working on'.

But it was, for them, a spiritual and intellectual dynamism. At the end of the eighteenth century, G. G. Lichtenberg (on Nietzsche's very short list of favourite German authors) complained that 'They – the English – do the deeds and we provide the literary history of their deeds'; and 150 years later Bertolt Brecht observed that 'With us everything slips all too readily into the impalpable and disembodied – we start talking about a *Weltanschauung* after the world itself has dissolved', adding that

---

[1] See *Die Philosophie im tragischen Zeitalter der Griechen* § 5 (1873); Nietzsche is referring to Schopenhauer's etymologizing.

'With us, even materialism is abstract'.[1] They were pointing to a disposition of mind which Marx, Nietzsche and Freud viewed ambivalently and critically, yet which they fully shared, not least by virtue of their own critical and ambivalent attitude. The culture into which they were born was one which largely ignored social questions; viewed with uneasy distaste the commercial and industrial successes of the world that sustained it; favoured a picture of 'reality' which offered little resistance to fundamental speculation; and looked on intellectual revolution as a substitute for social and economic change. The scheme of values by which this culture was sustained – a scheme not often made explicit, and challenged by all three men – put the highest premium on the life of the mind.

Nietzsche came to dislike the consequences of Germany's victory in the Franco-Prussian War of 1871 because he saw the new Reich as 'the extirpation of the German spirit' and as the politicization and power-seeking of a society of *parvenus*, whereas he believed that Germany's true mission in the world should be non-political and cultic, indeed mythopoeic. The spirit she should follow was to be not the spirit of Sedan but of pre-Socratic Greece. (Incidentally, the love of classical Greece was not the least of the gifts all three men derived from their common native tradition.) Marx found in England the substance of fact on which to draw for his revolutionary philosophical doctrine, while his polemics against the 'classical' English political economists obscure his indebtedness to them; but for the contemporary intellectual life of his adopted country he professed little more than contempt. His belief in the capacity of the human mind to undergo fundamental change, and his belief in the possibility of seeing things – *all* of life, *all* of history, *all* of men's relations with each other and with nature – in a fundamentally new way derive from his early study of Hegel and from his German experience; anti-idealist he may be, yet whatever he may say about the 'material' origin of consciousness, its conceptualizing and generalizing capacity and its world-changing function are for him never in doubt. And it is surely no accident that Freud, seemingly the least speculative of our trio, draws for his re-interpretation of the human mind on that least resistant, least

---

[1] G. C. Lichtenberg, *Schriften und Briefe*, ed. W. Promies (München 1968), J 1195, and Bertolt Brecht, *Kleines Organon* (1953), § 75.

institutionalized and most suggestible of all cultural milieux, the artistically and intellectually inclined world of the Viennese middle classes; for here above all was a setting which encouraged the strange belief that all the necessities to which men in society are prey could be reduced to, and perhaps solved as, problems of the individual mind. It would of course be wrong to minimize the immense development, or perhaps we had better say the immense changes, that took place between 1843, the year Marx left Germany, the 1870s and 1880s, the years of Nietzsche's greatest intellectual effort, and the first two decades of the new century, during which Freud's doctrine saw the light of day; similarly, one would not wish to minimize the diversity in cultural topography of Marx's Trier, Jena and Berlin, Nietzsche's Naumburg, Leipzig and Basle, and Freud's Vienna. Yet equally it is impossible to overlook that middle-class unity of aspirations and intellectual concerns, that complex yet single spirituality which, at the cost of political tutelage and fetishism,[1] created the most scholarly and intellectual culture modern Europe has ever known; and also, as it turned out, the most vulnerable. To all the phases of this history Nietzsche's writings provide a critical commentary.

There is irony in the fact that all three men saw it as part of their programme to prove the illusoriness of morality, to reveal the unreal, derivative status of moral values. To have told them that what informs their thinking is a deep moral concern, would have elicited little but contempt (from Marx), disdain (from Nietzsche), and an ironical shrug (from Freud). Yet this, ultimately, is the most important thing they share: anguish at the fragmentation of men's lives (*Z* II § 20), and a moral care for the future of mankind. Marx's critique of the consequences of the division of labour, Nietzsche's horror of history seen as an endless Golgotha of betrayals and revenge born of resentment, Freud's pessimistic critique of the etiology of civilization – these are signs of their common concern with what had once been called 'the whole man'. This is the end for which the ages of the Superman and of the classless society are conceived. These fabulous constructs of Nietzsche's and Marx's have no equiva-

---

[1] Among the many writings which bear witness to this 'fetishism' is the 1899 testament of Theodor Mommsen, Germany's greatest Roman historian; reprinted in Alfred Heuss, *Thomas Mann und das neunzehnte Jahrhundert* (Kiel 1956), pp. 282–3.

lent in Freud; but then, who has ever heard of an Austrian utopia...

No sooner have we set out the common ground of our three 'prophets' than it becomes obvious that each of the affinities mentioned needs qualifying. Certainly Nietzsche's place in this company is highly problematic. He cannot, and least of all in the heyday of the great metaphysical system-makers, be seriously presented as a systematic thinker. The doctrine of 'the will to power' does not occupy the central position in his thought that the doctrine of motivation by material interest occupies in Marx's scheme, or the doctrine of sexual motivation in Freud's. Nietzsche's notes and plans towards a systematic philosophy belong to the last phase of his active life, the period from about 1882 to 1888. These attempts are important without being decisive, and they remain fragmentary. They are not the crowning achievement of his thinking (it is a bad critic who judges a tragedy merely by its ending), though he certainly intended them as such. The bulk of his work is quite different in intention if not in form. It is not irrelevant to the problem of system: a large part of what he wrote illustrates 'the possibility that "the will to power" might be one particular name for this [i.e. our human] reality' (*Mus* XVI, pp. 46–7). Yet what he wrote is too rich and too varied to be brought under one common rubric – the writer makes rings round the thinker.

Little of what Marx and Freud wrote stands before us as the work of a free intelligence, unembattled, without its harness of system. Each writes, not to induce thought and the freedom of thought, but to convince, even to bludgeon into conviction. Diverse facts are assembled for the purpose of definitions, definitions are compressed into a technical terminology whose chief virtue is 'scientific' stability, and whose chief function is to be available, without further recourse to the world of facts, in the next chain of arguments. Hence the occasional ballast of verbal scree, and Marx's and Freud's tedious habit of referring the reader confidently from one work to supporting passages in earlier works which then turn out to be less than confidence-inspiring. Hence, too, the mastership, the massive strength of their thought, and (in spite of their protests to the contrary) the relatively undistorted influence they have exercised upon their followers.

Nietzsche, however, even though he has a consistent point of view, and even when he is setting down a coherent chain of arguments, is forever beginning anew. Of the three, he is the only one who strives for unlimited consciousness. With this goes the fact that he is incomparably the most literary of modern philosophers (literary *as* a philosopher; not, like Sartre, a philosopher who also writes fictions). His literary debt is European in scope and leads from Montaigne, Pascal and La Rochefoucauld to G. C. Lichtenberg, Gracian's *Oracle*, and Schopenhauer's *Parerga* (his indebtedness to Heine is of a different kind), yet he no more belongs to the aphoristic tradition than he does to that of the system builders. The appearance of new beginnings is part of the literary effect he aims at. Yet at the same time it reflects his unabating care to remain free, not merely from the influence of others, but also from the fetters of his own prejudices, premeditations and rejections – and this concern, in one whose every observation is shot through with value judgements, constitutes a perpetual challenge. In the freedom and variety of experiment lies his real consistency. What he is concerned with is 'only' a speculative freedom, but as such it is the existential condition of a man whose life is given over wholly to speculation (as was Wittgenstein's; as was Rilke's to poetry). This freedom, we shall see, can be both joyous and terrifyingly bleak.

The overwhelming impression he leaves with us is not one of subtlety, or lightness of touch, or richness of reference, or considerateness for his reader (though he is capable of all these), but it is an impression of intellectual energy. To read him is exhilarating, not always for what he says – and least of all when he engages in those painfully self-conscious attempts at Homeric laughter and 'mediterranean' abandon – but for the adventure of sharing the energy, the reflective force manifest in almost every formulation and new thrust at a problem. Another name for this energy might be truthfulness, were it not that his contant questioning is directed not only at the truth of this or that statement or belief (of his own or of other men's), but at the function and value of truth itself.

Nietzsche's is essentially a modern kind of truthfulness. Experiencing the world as a fragmented thing, he conveys it as such; unmasking all notions of 'Being' as mere myths, he settles, not indeed for *obiter dicta*, but for 'reflections', notes, informal witnesses of discontinuous 'becoming'. In this sense he seems more truthful – and more modern – than Marx, who disguised the discontinuities of his thought (which were not so very different from Nietzsche's) by thrusting a system of doubtful coherence and universality over them. Yet Marx's work too remains a torso; it was not he who gave it the name of 'dialectical materialism'. The diversity of Marx's insights, too, is revealed in the sheer unevenness and undirected intellectual energy of his style. His unselfconscious rhetoric – its leaps and strange balances, its unexpected metaphors and violent inversions, the effect of words on the page which do not accumulate to confirm one another but where each articulation displaces and challenges the preceding one[1] – all this is more accurately prophetic of *our* kind of discourse, more *like* Nietzsche's anticipations, than Marxists have ever seen fit to acknowledge. It may seem strange to see the temper of an age manifest in its discontinuities, yet that is how things are with us. For what other age has conceived of the notion that 'the world of the happy is a different one from the world of the unhappy'[2] – a view on which all our 'prophets' are agreed?

It was Marx, not Nietzsche, who was supreme practitioner of 'the will to power'; Nietzsche only described and commended it. Occasionally he likes to strike heroic attitudes, but really he is unembattled, defenceless. We wonder how, questioning and undermining every view, almost as soon as it looks like providing a stable answer – almost *because* it looks like providing a stable answer – a man can sustain thought and life itself; and Nietzsche wonders too:

I do not wish for life again. How have I borne it? Creatively. What makes me bear the sight of life? The view of the Superman who affirms life. I have tried to affirm it myself – ah!   (*WKG* vii/1 p. 139)

(This is written in 1882–3, at the time of *Zarathustra*, the most 'life-affirming' of all his books.)

He certainly believes in the possibility of a system that would not be a betrayal of individual truths, just as he believes, to quote

---

[1] See John Berger's comparison of Herzen und Marx, in *Selected Essays and Articles* (Harmondsworth 1972), p. 85.
[2] Ludwig Wittgenstein, *Tractatus Logico-Philosophicus*, 6.43.

Lichtenberg again, in 'the healthy *savant* – the man with whom thinking is not a disease'.[1] He recognizes such a system as the goal and fulfilment of purposeful philosophical thinking:

> It would have to be something that was neither subject nor object, neither force nor matter, neither spirit nor soul: but shall I not be told that such a thing will resemble nothing so much as a phantasmagoria? I too believe it will – all the better for that! Of course, it must resemble that and everything else which exists or could exist, and not only a phantasmagoria! It must have that dominant family likeness by virtue of which all that *is* recognizes itself as related to it – (*WKG* VII/3 p. 376).

But what he doubts is whether 'the age' is capable of such a system, and whether *he* is, knowing himself to be a part of his age.[2]

This historicizing reversal of the thought is characteristic. Again and again we shall find that what others have seen as a fundamental or 'perennial' problem in epistemology or ontology or logic, he will deflect, or rather dismantle, into a psychological or historical consideration – into 'not yet', or 'no longer', or 'not this man'. His choice, therefore, 'in these circumstances', 'in this brave century of mine' (occasionally '...of ours') is for the freedom of new beginnings and for clarity of expression. It is a question of that reflective energy again: from the most casual notebook entry to the image-studded *art nouveau* rhetoric of *Zarathustra*, he is incapable of obscurity (lapses of taste and mistakes of tone are a different matter). And yet – 'were it not that I have bad dreams...': the impression he leaves is not entirely that of a free man.

The spheres of personal experience, philosophical venture and literary expression all meet in the question of Nietzsche's freedom. He chooses to be as free from the obligations of society (of family, class, nation, profession) as a man can be – a man who retains a deep longing for friendship, for a public, and for disciples, too. He forces the circumstances – including his health, his temperament, the failure of his professional prospects – to force the choice on him. This is his *amor fati*, the experience of life he chooses his philosophizing to be true to and to reflect. And

[1] Lichtenberg, *Schriften und Briefe*, D 240.
[2] For a different interpretation of this reflection see Jaspers, *Nietzsche*, pp. 297–8. Among the many insights I owe to this book is Jaspers's conception of Nietzsche's work as 'philosophizing'.

since this experience has provided him with amazingly little insight into any form of institutionalization – political, social or national – how can the arguments of his books be other than unsystematic, unspecialized and unconfined, a uniquely free venture?

Nietzsche is concerned, not with man's progress through liberty under the law, but with man's freedom. Hence he writes (most of the time) as if the French Revolution had never been, and as if all association were no more than an encroachment on man's selfhood, a threat to what should be his natural assertion of independence from everything outside himself. Unlike Marx and unlike Freud, Nietzsche does not believe that a man's responsibility for what he is can be shifted on to society or explained away by the traumas of childhood – or indeed by any other mechanisms.

And yet, choosing a mode of writing as free from the restrictions imposed by more conventional and more extended literary forms as it is possible for discursive writing to be, Nietzsche's choice is determined by his own situation – or rather his understanding of it: 'The only thing that can nowadays be well made, that can be a masterpiece, is the small thing. Only in that is integrity [Rechtschaffenheit] still possible' (*FaW*, 2nd post-script). Whatever one may think of this 'integrity', it is not to be found in the works of the philosophical builders of Nietzsche's age.

But what is this 'nowadays', this 'fatality of being modern'? What are Nietzsche's bad dreams? He is almost a free man. Perhaps he could be entirely free – he certainly believes he could be – were he not tormented by the thought that 'God is dead', and by the thought that men behave as though they 'had not yet heard the news that "God is dead"' (*Z*, introd.). This is the situation in which 'the great system', ontology itself, is no longer possible; in which all of Nietzsche's reflective life is encompassed – the limits of his freedom. To be placed thus is not his 'Grunderlebnis'; indeed any appeal to a single 'fundamental experience', he is apt to suspect as the ploy of fanatics and demagogues. But that lurid metaphor, 'the death of God', is the horizon that encircles his speculative life, which is his life.

4

Historicizing an idea

tragical – comical – historical – pastoral...

(*Hamlet* II: 2)

I

Nietzsche begins his philosophizing by taking issue with the cultural situation of the German Empire of 1871. Among the components of that curious amalgam of romantic medievalism and Prussian efficiency known as the Second Reich is a strong patriotic concern with the past, supported by a powerful tradition of historical research. When, in the second of his *Thoughts Out of Season* (1874), Nietzsche enquires into 'The Use and Disadvantage of History for Life', the very title of his essay questions one of the cultural axioms of the day – that a knowledge of its own past strengthens the life of a given society. Yet one wishes he had left it to his reader to decide whether or not these thoughts are 'out of season'. For Nietzsche certainly agrees with contemporary opinion that this should be the function of history, and the bulk of his argument is designed to show how the historical consciousness may succeed in its patriotic aim and why it so often fails to achieve it. He seems to have no fear that historical scholarship will be corrupted by what in effect are political ends. Since he makes no distinction between the needs of individual men, of societies and of states, he does not acknowledge 'the historical spirit' as a political factor at all, but sees it as an aspect of the culture of individual men. They alone count. A people or a state is no more than 'the masses' (*U* II §9) led by a few great men.

The enhancement of man as a species is the end purpose of mankind (§9). If this is our assumption (the nature of that 'enhancement' will occupy us later), it follows that whatever will improve the vitality and passion for life of great men is to be commended as the right kind of historical science. And it also follows that academic history's aspirations to comprehensiveness, its preoccupation with an endless accumulation of factual details, and its ideal of cold, impartial objectivity are bound to be in conflict with 'the needs of great men' as they serve the advancement of mankind. Truth is not objectivity but the will to justice (§6), and historical justice is the business of judging the past in respect of its contribution to human greatness. The demand for historical objectivity recedes behind the demand for this kind of 'justice', which can only be dispensed by judges who 'stand above' those who are to be judged. Hence 'the use and disadvantage of history *for life*' are wholly relative to the character of the historian: 'History is endured only by strong personalities – the weak ones are extinguished by it' (§5).

History at its most life-enhancing is seen, in a Churchillian manner, as the story of great men with heroic ideals and a monumental capacity for self-sacrifice in the service of those ideals. Nietzsche presents such men not merely as examples to those who come after them but, more interestingly, as the creators of a spiritual and intellectual atmosphere (§7), of '*the human horizon*' that is appropriate to a given society and without which no society or culture can exist and prosper (§1). This horizon is made up of men's vital beliefs and ideas, and of the myths in which these beliefs and ideas are expressed; and men – or the majority of them – are condemned to sterility, mediocrity and death (and mediocrity, for Nietzsche, is a sort of death) if that horizon, that 'atmosphere' ('Dunstkreis') is destroyed or damaged. Here, as so often, Nietzsche's cultural criticism impinges on our ecological thinking: we may think of his seminal metaphor as analogous to the ionosphere which surrounds the earth and which, if it is damaged or modified, is bound to affect our life in all its aspects. There is no doubt that Nietzsche at all times saw the power of ideas as in no way inferior to that of physical forces, and often as continuous with those forces. Hence our metaphor from modern ecology is not as anachronistic as it may seem: like Hölderlin and Novalis before him, Nietzsche sees the destruction of the physical horizon as directly consequent on the break-up of a system of religious or philosophical ideas.

Two kinds of ideas threaten or destroy 'the human atmosphere': one kind because it is accepted as true, the other because it is shown to be untrue. Among the former is a decadent society's preoccupation with its heroic past (there should be nothing recondite about the idea of past grandeur dwarfing the present and threatening to extinguish the future when we contemplate this idea from the vantage point of England in the 1970s).

But what happens to 'life' when the picture or the ideas of an heroic past are discovered to be untrue? Then the past turns out to be the thoroughly unheroic product of the spirit of vengeance and grudgingness. Human history, permeated by this spirit, turns out to be little more than a series of reactions by the weak and 'underprivileged' who, in a variety of ignoble ways, resist and revenge themselves on those naturally endowed with nobility and strength of purpose; and they do this – their only form of self-protection – by creating a scale of values (or rather 'anti-values') of their own, a morality of their own, which they then impose by means of blackmail on the gods' own aristocrats of body and soul. What happens to the enhancement of 'life' when we discover that this is the origin of *all* morality, and that the idea of conscience too is the product of the spirit of resentment and grudging envy (and this idea too should not be too difficult for us to grasp at the present time, when so many of our political decisions are determined by what was not done in the past)? And what happens, above all, when we discover that the metaphysical and religious beliefs of a society are fictitious, are merely part of its human horizon? Is anything left of the splendours of human history except a tragical–comical spectacle played before an audience of non-existent gods?[1] Nietzsche faces the destructive conclusion that to recognize history for what it is, a fiction, and a fiction for what *it* is, a lie, is to deprive history of its 'usefulness for life'.

Some of these questions take us beyond 'The Use and Disadvantage of History', into the moral–existential books of Nietzsche's middle and last periods. Yet it is proper to mention them here because they are extrapolated from the two fundamental questions which *are* considered in this early essay: Is life possible without the consolations and protection of a belief in God, once that belief has been shown to be part of a myth (§8)? and, more generally, Is there knowledge (of whatever kind) which should not be pursued because it is noxious to 'life', and is it possible to devise rules – 'a doctrine of the hygiene of life' (§10) – whereby to set limits to the pursuit of such knowledge?

[1] G. P. Grant's Canadian Broadcasting Company Massey Lectures, *Time as History* (Toronto 1969) contain an accurate and sympathetic exploration of most of these Nietzschean topics.

These questions occupied Nietzsche to the end of his conscious life. He never succeeded in devising such a set of rules beyond the tautologous assertion that those who possess the spirit of life know by that spirit (or 'by instinct') what not to know. Nor could he ever be rid of these questions by determining to what extent they are merely verbal conundrums, arising from a hypostatization of the concepts of 'life' and 'knowledge', and to what extent they remain real existential problems. But then, in his practice as a philosophical querist, Nietzsche does not heed his own caution. In his reflections no holds are barred, no hypotheses are ruled out of court, no limits are imposed on the historicizing of the beliefs of an age: thought itself – not 'life' – forms the limit of *his* thought.

2

At the beginning of his next work, *Human, All-too-Human* (1878) Nietzsche writes:

> Lack of historical sense is the hereditary defect of all philosophers ...Many of them take man automatically as he has most recently been shaped by the impression of a particular religion or even of particular political events...But everything [that is] has become [what it is]; there are neither eternal facts nor indeed eternal verities. Therefore what is needed from now on is historical philosophizing, and with it the virtue of modesty (*MA* I/i § 2).

And in a note written at the same time:

> What separates us from Kant, as from Plato and Leibnitz, is that we believe only in Becoming – in intellectual matters too; we are *historical* through and through...The way Heraclitus and Empedocles thought is alive once more (*Mus* XVI p. 9).

'Historical philosophizing', then, is one of Nietzsche's two principal methods of examining the beliefs and ideas of a given society, which to him are always primarily the beliefs and ideas of its great men. (The other is the 'psychological method', the method of 'my evil eye', which looks for the hidden motives.) In this respect Nietzsche knows himself and his age to be deeply influenced by the historicizing thought of Hegel (even though he rejects the notion that world history reached its culminating point when he – Hegel – got the Chair of Philosophy in Berlin, *U* II §8). What is 'historical philosophizing'? In what follows I have tried to show the way Nietzsche applies his method to a major philosophical topic. The example I have chosen comes from *The Twilight of the Idols* (1888), where Nietzsche is at his most intellectually vigorous.

In a sketch entitled

'How the "True World" Finally Became a Fable'

and subtitled 'The History of an Error', he presents the history of Platonism[1] in six stages (*GD* III):

1. The true world, attainable for the sage, the pious, the virtuous man – he lives in it, *he is it*. (This is the oldest form of an idea, relatively clever, simple, convincing. It is the paraphrase of the proposition, 'I, Plato, *am* the truth.')

At this first stage, the 'true' or metaphysical world is identical with the world in which men live: not all or any men, though, but only the elect. (The feeling of cosmic oneness – 'he is it' – is also a moral quality.) By saying that the virtuous man *is* that world, and that Plato *is* the truth, Nietzsche wants to stress not only the personal nature of truth but also the availability and attainability of the 'metaphysical' at a certain moment in history; to portray (as Hölderlin had done) an age whose religious 'ideals' are not remote and 'transcendent', but inherent, in-dwelling in men's world. The 'true world' is not a 'Platonic' idea, it has not – not yet – been alienated into the object of a metaphysical doctrine: it is Plato's world, not the world of Platonism.

2. The true world, now unattainable, but promised to the sage, the pious, the virtuous man ('the sinner who repents'). (Progress of the idea: it becomes subtler, more enticing, less graspable – it becomes female, it becomes Christian.)

This 'progress of the idea' Nietzsche sees as anything but positive. At this stage true being or reality (all that is true or really real for mankind) has been pushed out of this world, to the very edge that men can reach. The sensible world is no longer the meaningful world – meaning is 'beyond'. Now, this new situation makes for a correspondingly finer, 'subtler' awareness of the

---

[1] For a different interpretation of the same sketch, see M. Heidegger, *Nietzsche* (Pfullingen 1961), vol. I, pp. 234–42. Heidegger argues repeatedly (and later takes it for granted) that when Nietzsche denies the possibility of reaching 'the truth', he means a metaphysical or religious or Platonic truth (one of the 'eternal verities'). I hope to show (in chapter 10 below) that in certain important contexts Nietzsche means *truth* of any kind.

impalpable and the merely promised, but it also places the idea of the 'true world' as the repository of all stable values in a remote and erotically enticing perspective. This displacement Nietzsche (like Hölderlin before him) identifies with the advent of Christianity, and among its consequences he sees the emergence of a new morality – a morality not of the old aristocratic kind whose devices were 'good' and 'bad', but of a religiously sanctioned, slavish kind, the morality of 'good and evil'. The point of turning 'the idea's' gender into sex seems merely gratuitous, a piece of bad taste. Yet this shift to 'the female' is significant of the way in which, for Nietzsche, the philosophical argument is accompanied by a physiological one, the mental by the bodily, the abstract by the concrete. These stylistic incarnations are often embarrassing. The ensuing embarrassment however heightens one's perception: we recognize them as Nietzsche's attempts to give life to his reflection and to rebut the body–soul dualism.

3. The true world, unattainable, unprovable, unpromisable, but the mere thought of it is a consolation, an obligation, an imperative. (Basically this is the old sun again, but seen through mist and scepticism; the idea has become sublime, pale, northern, Königsbergian.)

'The mere thought of it': in this account of the Kantian ('Königsbergian') re-interpretation of Platonism, the 'true world' is even further removed from the world of the senses. Since (at that point in time) it is that in which the world and all thought is grounded, and therefore not the object of thought, 'the idea' offers 'consolation' for the absence of truth and stability from the sensible world; it offers 'an obligation' to obey the commands which 'the mere thought' of transcendence imposes upon men; and it offers an 'imperative', i.e. the moral law which Kant had conceived as a postulate of practical reason and thus as the only exception to the rule that reason can never reflect upon its own transcendent foundations. The world depicted in this third stage is the cold and bleak Protestant world, which Heinrich Heine had guyed in his funny stories about the choleric Martin Luther and the cold comforts of his Reformation. The dominant mode of this world is abstractness, in which Nietzsche sees the fountain-head of modern science.

4. The true world – unattainable? at any rate unattained. And, being unattained, it is also *unknown*. Therefore not consoling, redeeming,

obligating: for what obligation could something unknown impose on us? (Grey morning. Reason's first yawning, the cock-crow of positivism.)

We are now moving closer to Nietzsche's own age, the post-Kantian nineteenth century which no longer accepts – should no longer accept – the consolations of religiose metaphysics. More than once Nietzsche has 'unmasked' the substitute-religion of German Idealism. (In *Ecce Homo*, XIV §3, he writes: 'On the roll of knowledge the Germans are inscribed with nothing but dubious names, all that they have ever produced have been "unconscious" coiners – an appellation as appropriate to Fichte, Schelling, Schopenhauer, Hegel, Schleiermacher as it is to Leibnitz and Kant: they are all merely Schleiermacher . . .' i.e. 'makers of veils', obfuscators.)

It therefore seems that Nietzsche welcomes this new age with its lack of illusions and first stirrings of an energetic, self-contained rationality: is it not braver, rougher but also more honest than the effeminate eighteenth century, the age of a transcendentally cushioned rationalism (*WKG* VIII/2 pp. 104–6)? Yet there is nothing enthusiastic about the image with which the description of this stage closes.

5. The 'true' world – now an idea that is no use for anything and does not even provide the grounds of an obligation – an idea that has become useless and redundant and *therefore* a refuted idea: let us abolish it! (Bright day; breakfast; return of *bon sens* and cheerfulness; Plato blushing embarrassedly; pandemonium of all free spirits.)

Is this a picture of Nietzsche's own age or of the future? The cobwebs of all transcendentalisms have been cleared away, men may now rely on the testimony of their senses only, reason's battle has been fought and won; more than that: so complete was the victory that no rancour or resentment, no aggressiveness remain. The historicized idea is now superseded by that stage of 'cheerfulness' – or is it 'serenity' itself? the German term, 'Heiterkeit' means either – which, in Nietzsche's later works, figures increasingly as the one and only value with which to oppose the honourable but cheerless 'spirit of gravity'. But if this reflection is what it claims to be – a realistic account of Nietzsche's own age, or at least of the future with its roots in his age; a sketch of the act of liberation that is to issue from Nietzsche's writings – why not stop there and then? Why do 'all

the free spirits' make a devilish noise? Has the historicized idea
not been fully refuted after all?

6. We have abolished the true world: what world has remained? the
world of appearances perhaps?...But no! with the true world we have
also abolished the world of appearances! (Noon; moment of the briefest
shadow, end of the largest error; the zenith of humanity; INCIPIT
ZARATHUSTRA.)

Nietzsche no longer writes 'We have abolished the "true" world'.
The refutation of the Platonic idea is to be followed by a collapse
of the entire terminology of religious and metaphysical antitheses: there is to be neither appearance nor a reality postulated
in opposition to appearance (just so, in *Beyond Good and Evil*, 1886,
when attacking the notion of 'evil', he also sets out to dispose
of that notion of 'good' which had arisen in opposition to 'evil').
At this highest point in the history of man, when the antithesis
between the sensuous and the supra-sensuous too has been
abolished, enters Zarathustra; and with him comes the reign of
the Superman, whose love of the Earth will validate all.

Or will it? A terrible ambiguity clings to the formulation of
that final stage. 'Incipit Zarathustra' echoes 'Incipit tragoedia'
– the opening sentence of the last section of the fourth (and
provisionally last) book of *The Joyous Science* (1882), which in turn
is repeated verbatim as the opening section of *Thus Spoke
Zarathustra* (I, 1883). The 'tragedy' that now begins tells of
Zarathustra's self-sacrifice and descent among the ranks of men
('human, all-too-human the best of them') and by implication
('When Zarathustra was thirty years old...') of Christ's self-
sacrificial descent. If, with that echo in mind, we now think once
more about the sentence with which the sketch of the last stage
opened – 'We have abolished the true world: what world has
remained?' – we see its meaning radically altered. What it
expresses is no longer the joy of intellectual and therefore
existential liberation, but a feeling of deprivation and loss; the
high noon becomes the moment when the sun's merciless rays
pierce every darkness, every nook and corner of ancient pieties
and divine comfort; and Zarathustra, serene teacher of the
doctrine of the Superman, becomes the prophet of doom.

The two meanings of the last stage do not cancel each other
out, they are locked in an ambiguity which remains unresolved.

What is to be the future and the fate of mankind? The serene life of spirits freed from ancient illusions and false comforts, or a world empty of all purpose and meaning, the reign of Nihilism everlasting? Freed from metaphysics, will the world be more joyful? Or was 'the resentment of the metaphysicians against the real' a *creative* act (*WzM* § 579), so that metaphysics became a source of 'reality' after all; and has man, in destroying metaphysics, destroyed his own horizon and his world? Or does the issue depend on what *you* are, on whether 'you become that you are'?

5
Sketch of a book

...yet there is method in't

(Hamlet ii: 2)

However aphoristic, fragmentary and exploratory (rather than systematic, didactic and conclusive) Nietzsche's thinking may be, he chose to address his reluctant public in the form of individual, thematically organized books. Most studies of Nietzsche's work, however, including the present, rely for the coherence of their accounts on a patchwork design of quotations, assembled from several of his writings at once. Provided that in each strand of his thought some consideration is given to chronology, such a procedure need not be misleading. Yet even when these culled excerpts have been given their proper place in his philosophical development, this method cannot convey the actual shape of any one of his books – cannot convey the coherences and disparities, the idiosyncratic turns in his thinking at any one time. To do just this, and to secure something like a cross-section through his thinking, so that several strands of it – the brilliant and the absurd, the subtle and the gross – may be displayed, I shall devote this chapter to sketching out the arguments of a single work only, occasionally rearranging the order in which they occur, but confining my interference mainly to the task of selection and emphasis, and providing a few linking passages between the individual reflections within each section of the book. Even so, the impression should be preserved that this too is a selection, and that other, different arrangements are possible.

I have chosen *Beyond Good and Evil (J)* because it is in many ways the richest and widest-ranging – the most *versatile* – of the books which Nietzsche himself published, and because it shows forth with especial clarity the range of his thinking during its most mature period. All the main themes of his philosophizing are rehearsed here, but the emphasis is on their existential and (begging the question) their moral import; they often cross the threshold of the metaphysical, but they do not stay there. In this sense the book is a launching pad for the grand cosmology-to-be, the metaphysical project of *The Will to Power*.

Beyond Good and Evil was begun in August 1883, at the time of the second part of *Thus Spoke Zarathustra*, and it was not completed until more than two years later, after the summer of 1885. During that summer, to bring to an end a work conceived in the white heat of reflective passion, Nietzsche had added a fourth, less spontaneous part to *Zarathustra* – had added it reluctantly, since he had originally planned a more substantial continuation. *Zarathustra* is his one and only 'mythopoeic' undertaking – *Beyond Good and Evil* contrasts sharply in tone and manner with it. Nietzsche himself considered its immediate sequel, the more 'popular' *Genealogy of Morals* (1887) to be a part ('a complement and a clarification') of the book, yet I doubt whether it is either, seeing how often the later work vulgarizes and caricatures some of the best thoughts of the earlier. The date of the completion of *Beyond Good and Evil*, three years before the mind's end, is significant: the reflective effort ('the greatest since Plato'? § 191) is fully controlled; the fruit no longer hangs in the web of the occasion, yet it is still the time before the decay.

1. Among the *Prejudices of the Philosophers*[1] is the strange claim that the value of 'truth as such' is to be taken for granted and need never be challenged. Values have always been seen in opposition to each other (truth *versus* falsehood; truthfulness *versus* mendacity; selfishness *versus* altruism, etc.), but the possibility that such antitheses are illusory must now be faced. More than that: philosophers must be prepared to contemplate the fact that truth often depends on falsehood (the one growing from the other), and also the possibility that the life-enhancing and life-protecting value of falsehood is superior to the value of truth. Life – or 'the species' – uses no end of instincts and tricks for its protection, and philosophy – 'the search for truth' – is but one of them. In certain circumstances – those of modern Europe, for instance – 'the will to truth' may turn out to be suicidal, a sign of decadence. A crude, plebeian age – the age of 'machinists and bridgebuilders' (shades of Spengler!) – has but a crude, sensuous, tactile notion of truth; the 'pale, grey, cold, conceptual

---

[1] The numbering and titles of these sections are Nietzsche's own.

nets' which the Platonic philosophers threw over the colourful phenomenal world corresponded to cognition in a subtler, more aristocratic age.

Morality – or the 'will to truth' – is the doctrine of the distribution of power among men in accordance with their 'willing' or 'the action of the will'. 'The will' is very far from being the self-evident thing Schopenhauer claimed, and the fact that ordinary linguistic usage designates a variety of psychic phenomena by a single word should not deceive us into thinking that 'the will' is a single thing. On the contrary: command, obedience, a variety of feelings, as well as the material possibilities involved in an action having an effect, are among its constitutive elements. And the 'free will' for which Kant makes extravagant claims is no more than the pleasurable sensation of compelling others without being compelled oneself.

Logic and quantification; the postulate of a thinking 'I' entailed only by the verbal form of 'cogito ergo sum'; or again Kant's synthetic judgements *a priori* (among them the law of causality) – all these are 'necessary falsehoods of the philosophers', inventions masquerading as discoveries, without which life would not be possible.[1] (The question to ask is not: How are synthetic judgements *a priori* possible? but, What are they for?) These philosophical fictions are not entirely arbitrary. 'A strange family likeness of all Indian, Greek and German philosophizing' has developed 'under the rule and guidance of a common philosophy of grammar' grounded in an overall (Indo-Germanic) kinship of languages, which 'finally' depends on common racial conditions and on value judgements which issue from common physiological foundations. But Nietzsche insists that the connection between value judgements and their material foundations is not one of simple physical causality – rather is it expressed in such terms as 'rule [Herrschaft] and guidance'. These, too, are the grounds on which the strong personality acts; beyond this, Nietzsche's alternative to causality remains undetermined. All talk of 'causa sui', 'the free will' *and* determinism, are mythological fictions, 'reifications of concepts'

---

[1] Cf. G. C. Lichtenberg's famous reflection: 'We ought to say, "it thinks", just as we say, "it thunders". Even to say *cogito* is too much if we translate it with "I think". To assume the "I", to postulate it, is a practical need.' (K76 in vol. II of *Schriften und Briefe, ed. cit.* This is 'the id' which Freud borrowed for his conception of 'the unconscious'. See E. Jones, *Sigmund Freud: Life and Work,* III (London 1957), p. 303.

which reveal the personality of the myth-maker, not the real nature of the world. We are capable of valid (as opposed to fictitious) distinctions of values, but the form they take is a series of subtle gradations, a spectrum stretching between the strong-willed and the weak – those who are proud to accept responsibility for themselves and others, and those who replace personal responsibility with 'socialist compassion'. (Here and elsewhere 'socialism' is seen as a thing by definition generalized and abstract, as an anaemic doctrine.) Natural laws, constructed on the analogy of human laws, are interpretations and adaptations of an essentially lawless reality, designed to make that reality tolerable 'to our democratic instincts'. All laws, whether human or natural, are manifestations of a 'will to power', the basic 'text' of which all laws are 'interpretations'. 'The will to power' is the guiding principle of any psychology fearless enough to face the full consequences of its discoveries, among them the possibility that (contrary to the prejudices of the philosophers) hatred, envy, avarice and the craving for power may be necessary and fundamental constituents of 'the total economy of life'. But, Nietzsche asks, is there such a thing as 'the Will'? Is the notion of 'laws of Nature' more than a metaphor, a dim metaphor at that? Here, as in so many other places, an opening move toward a Wittgensteinian critique of language is made and quickly abandoned; Nietzsche will not confide his philosophizing to the single perspective *sub specie linguae*.

2. Who are the *Free Spirits*? Nietzsche's pivotal terms in this section are 'the philosophers' and 'the truth', and these terms receive strong metaphysical connotations. As always, they are defined largely by their opposites.

'The will not to know' is more fundamental than 'the will to knowledge'. Such truth as the philosophers can glean requires no personal witness. On the contrary, all anguished martyrdom in the cause of truth brings out the worst in them – their subtle vindictiveness and grudging nature, their histrionics and secret demagogy. The elect (among men and philosophers) need the strength not merely to endure the solitude to which their task condemns them, but to experience it positively, as a distinction. 'Disgust, surfeit, compassion, and a feeling of isolation' are what they experience in the company of 'the average man', yet it is this 'average man' who must be the object of their study. Disguise and self-conquest, and above all cynicism, are needed to endure his company: indeed, the cynics (men like the abbé Galiani and the less profound Voltaire) *are* 'the average man', but being in addition endowed with self-knowledge and loquacity, they offer 'the elect' a short-cut to the knowledge of the worst in man. (The *presto* of Machiavelli's prose and the *allegrissimo* of Petronius's are the media appropriate to this kind of truth about life, which German prose, with its 'gravity, sluggishness, solemnity' and all its 'boring' styles cannot convey, even in Goethe's hands.) All hierarchically ordered, non-egalitarian civilizations distinguish between the common, exoteric knowledge available to all men (the little man, like his books and churches, is evil-smelling), and esoteric knowledge, reserved for the few. Each offers a different view of the world: the same deed may be contemptible or criminal in the esoteric judgement, and saintly in the common one. The grounds of judgement change: throughout prehistory an action was judged by its consequences; 'in the last ten thousand years' by its causes; and latterly – 'in the age of morality' – by that most chimeric of causes, by intentions. (Elsewhere, M § 208, in his aphoristic vein, Nietzsche writes: 'Let's stop turning causes into sinners and consequences into hangmen!')

However, the moral superstition has had its day: not intentions but, on the contrary, 'the unintended and hidden' grounds of action are what the subtlest and most honest – that is, the most malicious – thinkers must now search for. Equally it will be their task to dispose of such 'merely grammatical' antitheses as subject *versus* object, real world *versus* phenomenal world. The search for black and white, for epistemological certitudes, is a *moral* naïvety. It must give way to a new philosophy, in which descriptions of the world will not fudge but be true to the perspectivist way in which we actually live: 'values', in this new philosophy, will mean what painters mean when they speak of 'valeurs', that is, hues and shades.

What then is the perspective under which we should see the world? If we assume that our world of passions and desires is the only 'reality' there is; and, if, obeying the law of the greatest economy of method, we assume that in the world there is at work only one kind of causality which explains both mental and material processes – what else, then, can the world be (both in its mental and material aspects) but a product of the will, and more specifically of the will to power, whose disguises are legion? Truth – the truth about our world – needs masks. The deeper this truth is, the less dispensable the disguises, the more necessary the defences, denials, self-inflicted calumnies behind which the truth should be hidden; and our interpretations, which are invariably misinterpretations, are the best of its necessary disguises. Truth is supremely hard to get at, supremely costly in terms of the deprivations, disappointments and suffering it entails. But it is to be found in all sorts of unexpected hideouts: 'Pour être bon philosophe,' says Stendhal ('the last great psychologist' of truth-seeking), 'il faut être sec, clair, sans illusion. Un banquier, qui a fait fortune, a une partie du caractère requis pour faire des découvertes en philosophie...' (Nietzsche adores Stendhal's French worldliness, but cannot refrain from imposing on it his own German punctuation.)[1] The philosophers of the future will break with the idea of 'common' general truths and will insist on 'the right to *my* judgement, to which another is not entitled..."Good" is good no more if it has been in my neighbour's mouth'. But not only truth, freedom too must be measured by the difficulty that is to be overcome in attaining it. Freedom from one's own vices and virtues and from all compassion – even for those most worthy of it; freedom from all men and fatherlands – even those in misfortune; from the authority of any one science and method, however promising; from all habits, however comforting; and freedom, finally, even from the vertiginous delights of distance and solitude – these are the goals of the free spirits of today. But they – heralds of the philosophers of the future – are the opposite of those '*libres-penseurs*' and 'eloquent pen-pushing slaves of democracy' who preach the doctrine of 'equal rights for everyone and compassion for all who suffer', the doctrine of safety, comfort, and the happiness of the herd. The free spirits of today and tomorrow will venture their all for what the '*libres-penseurs*' wish to suppress – the highest potential in man, manifest in his joyful assent to rigour, adventure and danger, and that human greatness whose sources are suffering and solitude.

3. *The Essence of the Religious* as revealed in earliest Christianity grew out of the sophisticated, free-thinking and tolerant world of Imperial Rome. It had little in common with the rough-house Christianity of Luther, Cromwell and other northern barbarians

---

[1] Stendhal, *Oeuvres complètes: Journal littéraire*, 18 December 1829 (t. III, Genève 1970), p. 185.

– it resembles Pascal's faith by being a kind of continual suicide of reason. From its beginning Christianity was intent on destroying the self, on sacrificing all freedom, pride and spiritual confidence, and on holding out a 'moral' hope instead – the hope that the self-abasement of spirit and the destruction of the pagan mental habits which goes with that self-abasement should be immeasurably *painful*. Modern men, long since insensitive to the real meaning of Christian terminology, have lost all idea of what such a gruesome and extreme formula as 'God on the Cross' meant to the Ancients with their subtle sense of paradox: a formula which amounts to a revaluation of values without parallel, a grossness of feelings without parallel, the Oriental slave's revenge on 'Roman' Catholicism. However, what the slave was avenging was not the persecution of his faith, but the aristocrats' disdain in all matters of faith and their sceptical detachment from all suffering. (And this critical view of the value of suffering, adopted by 'the slaves', was among the causes of the French Revolution, 'the last of the slave uprisings'.)

'The religious neurosis (or "the essence of the religious", as I call it)' is always linked with three dangerous dietary commandments: solitude, fasting, and sexual abstention. It is not clear (Nietzsche argues) which is cause and which is effect, whether causality applies at all, or whether all these may not have common status as epileptic symptoms. (Schopenhauer's philosophy, culminating in Kundry in Wagner's *Parsifal*, is the latest manifestation of this epidemic, and so is the Salvation Army.) In any event, is it not strange that the religious mind has always attracted so much attention among philosophers? They are fascinated by the closely connected contradictions, the sudden changes from sinner to saint. But these 'miracles' are no more than faulty interpretations and bad philosophy – we speak of contradictions and sudden changes only because we allow our psychology to be overlaid by the false – because moral – value contrasts of black and white, good and evil. The religious mind with its 'miracles' has had its day. Now healthy embarrassment is appropriate: it is time not to refute, but to look the other way, to pass on the other side.

Yet 'the religious neurosis' is the source of a whole gamut of religious sentiments: think of the warm, generous attitude to the gods felt by the Greeks and only later superseded by the rabble's fear of the gods; the peasant-like, importunate faith of Luther, lacking in all southern *delicatezza*; the ecstasy and self-annihilation of the Oriental slave in St Augustine; the coy, repressed pubescence of Mme de Guyon...The Latin races, having an incomparably more intimate relationship with religion than do all northerners, experience unbelief as an assault on their racial vitality. To say, as Renan does,[1] that 'religion is the product of man in his normality' and that 'man is most fully himself [le plus dans le vrai] when he is most religious, when he feels most assured of an infinite destiny', is to express a subtle nihilism inaccessible to the harder, less 'beautiful' and religiously ungifted German soul. That soul experiences belief as an assault on its race and vitality.

In bowing before the Saint, the most powerful men of all ages were paying homage to another, superior will to power. They believed that the supreme negation and anti-nature embodied in the Saint must hide some secret, some great danger – and to bow before *that* was to pay homage to oneself, one's own will to power. But what is that secret? The great ladder of religious cruelty (correlative of 'the religious neurosis') has three main rungs: sacrifice of the first-born and best loved; sacrifice of one's natural instincts and of 'Nature' herself; sacrifice of all that is consoling and of God himself. Now nothing venerable remains save 'stupidity', the stone, the thing hard to attain [das Schwere], fate, *Nothingness*. Beyond the moral pessimism of the Buddha and Schopenhauer, beyond the deeper pessimism which in turn lies beyond the delusion of good and evil, there is an opposite 'ideal': the ideal of the most exuberant and world-affirming man, the man who has not only made peace with what is as it is, but eagerly calls for its endless, unchanging repetition. Repetition – for the sake of...what? For the sake of the god who needs this spectacle, and who is himself this vicious circle of repetition: this (a rudiment, as we shall see, of the doctrine of 'the eternal recurrence') is the dark secret.

Why atheism today? The Jewish Old Testament is the touch-stone of one's ideas of 'great' and 'small'. As the record of men, their world and their discourse, it has a greatness that neither Greek nor Indian literature can match – let alone 'the tiny peninsula Europe' with its pallid intellectuality and its conception of man as a domestic animal. (To have stuck the New Testament – a rococo product – on to the Old and made a 'Bible'

[1] See Ernest Renan, *Oeuvres complètes*, ed. H. Psichari (t. I, Paris, 1960), p. 280.

– 'the book of all books' – of the two is the cheapest bit of book-making, the greatest 'sin against the spirit' of which modern 'literary' Europe is guilty.) All philosophy since Descartes is anti-Christian, a protracted attack on the old concept of 'the soul' under the guise of a critique of a subject-predicate grammar which argued that thinking as an activity entailed a thinking subject. Kant 'must have come close to' the Vedic thought that 'the self' (or 'the soul') was an apparition, not the subject but a mere condition of thinking. God 'the Father' who cannot help, who cannot even communicate his will unambiguously, is refuted. With him vanishes all European theism, but not the religious instinct.

At all times religion required leisure – the sort of aristocratic leisure which implies contempt for work. Men today – the majority of German middle-class Protestants – are too busy and too preoccupied with their work, their fatherland, their newspaper and their family (in that order), to be much interested in religion, especially since they are not clear whether it is meant to be a part of business or pleasure (there must be more to church-going, they think, than that it should make them ill-tempered); but they are not involved enough to be anti-religious either. Academic persons, on the other hand – all those busy, dwarf-like 'workers of the mind' except the theologians, who are a riddle to the psychologist anyway – regard the religious instinct fastidiously and with contemptuous tolerance, and approach it only indirectly, through the study of history.

The deeper we look into the world's mysteries, the deeper the world becomes. Will not our most solemn concepts – 'God', 'sin'. . . – be like the play of children to a future generation, itself eternally child-like? Yet deep insight leads to 'super-ficiality', a true love of the surface of things. Here artists and religious men meet: they both create from fear of an irremediable pessimism, from the fear that man might attain the dark truth of his existence too soon, before he has become strong and hard enough – artistic enough – to endure 'the dark secret', 'the great danger' to his vitality. And so their creations – the multi-coloured play of art, or again the religious fiction called 'life in God' – are creatures of a will to reverse the truth. What is the highest and most exquisite illusion? It is to have experienced for the first time to the full the idea that 'to love man for his own sake only' is stupid and brutish, and to have expressed for the first time the thought that 'to love him for the sake of God' is the sole measure of man's worth and the salt and ambergris of his being.

Thus religion is always a means to an end: to the strong and independent-minded (the true philosophers and free spirits, as well as those chosen and ready to command) it is either a means of reducing opposition to their rule, or (as in the case of the Brahmins) a means of keeping the filth of politics at arm's length; to those who are chosen for eventual rule it is a preparation (asceticism and religiously motivated puritanism encourage self-control, which Nietzsche sees always as the pre-condition of 'the proper exercise of power' over others); and finally, to the vast majority of ordinary men religion offers contentment with their lot, peace of heart and soul, and a radical transfiguration of their world of drabness and suffering. All these are acceptable uses of an illusion. But where religion ceases to be a means and becomes an end, it leads to an unacceptable inversion of vital values. By offering comfort to the suffering, courage to the oppressed and despairing, by protecting the life of the physically and mentally inferior, Christianity has worked for the subversion of the European race. Breaking the will of the strong, pouring suspicion on all earthly happiness and beauty, and subduing the instincts of the highest and most attractive – and therefore the rarest – type of man, the Church has created her own 'highest type': a sublime freak, conditioned in such a way as to *feel* unworldliness and suppression of the life of the senses as the highest values. Not great enough for the task of shaping men creatively, not strong and confident enough to let the law of chance and failure take its course, not noble enough to observe the difference in rank between men, Christianity has imposed its device of 'Equal before God' and bred the European mass animal, well-intentioned, sickly, mediocre...

4. There follows a sequence of aphorisms entitled *Sayings and Interludes*. Some of them continue Nietzsche's anti-Christian argument and the 'moral unmasking' of the previous sections, a good many are anti-feminist, and a few, which illuminate single emotions or their conflicts, recall the French *moralistes* whom Nietzsche admired. But – unlike La Rochefoucauld's – all these aphorisms are grounded in, and constricted by, a single *ism* – a bleak, uncompromising individualism according to which the opinion of the many is invariably contemptible, their company invariably demeaning and an encroachment on the single self,

their actions never more than reactions and always offensive
to. . .? Nietzsche? What is so disappointing about this and other
collections of Nietzsche's aphorisms is that they lack the charm
of disinterestedness and (which is perhaps the same thing) do not
invite further thought, but, by their brusque and occasionally
arrogant formulations, foreclose it. In this they differ, not only
from the work of other aphorists (especially Lichtenberg), but
also from Nietzsche's own more informal reflections.

5. *Toward a Natural History of Morals.* Since the maxim 'Hurt no
man' is taken, unquestioningly, as the basis of all moralities (the
differences between them lie merely in the different ways they
try to justify this maxim), no fundamental enquiry into what
constitutes a moral act has got under way as yet. The moral
theories of the modern age are as gross as its moral feelings are
subtle. Thus men differ not only in respect of the values they
believe in (their 'value-tables'), but also in what they are
prepared to acknowledge as the true grounds of possession.
Where one man is content to possess a woman sexually, another
measures possession by what she renounces for his sake, while
a third – a fiend for candour – feels cheated unless he has proof
that the woman – or the nation – knows him for what he 'really
is'; parenthood, priesthood, the teacher–pupil relationship
are all ways of imposing value-schemes, and thus forms of
possession.

Every morality is a rationalization of fear, a set of safety
instructions on how to live in peace with the most dangerous
aspects of one's self. As such, moral precepts are incapable of
being generalized, yet – absurdly – moral philosophers insist on
couching them in general and 'categorical' terms. Far from being
objective or scientific, moralities are merely symbolic languages
[Zeichensprachen] expressive of individual passions. What they
express is always an enduring compulsion. 'All' European
achievements of the last millennia (Nietzsche finds the grand
generalization irresistible), 'including all "inspired" works', are
the result, not of laissez-faire morality but, on the contrary, of
tyrannies deliberately accepted – the tyranny of metre and
rhyme, of doctrines and dogmas, of social classes and of man
himself. Self-imposed fasting and abstinence – from work as
from making love – heighten and purify the passions: hence the
institution of the boring English Sunday.

There is no 'categorical', i.e. non-teleological moral impera-

tive. 'Thou shalt obey someone for a long time, or else perish
from the face of the earth', is the only true, 'natural' imperative.
The herd instinct – the instinct to obey – has its rationale in that
most radical revaluation of all values ever performed, which was
initiated by the Jews when their prophets identified worldly
riches and power with godlessness, evil, violence and sensuality,
when 'poor' first became a synonym for 'holy', and 'the world'
a word of abomination. This re-valuation is in effect the moral
revolt of the slaves. One of its results is a thorough misunderstanding of 'nature', of beasts of prey and men of prey (the
Cesare Borgias of all ages) as though they were degenerates and
pathological mutants, whereas they are the healthiest departures
from the sickly norm of 'the moral' and 'average' man. Another
result of that revaluation is the herd instinct among Europeans
– a disposition so powerful and by now so 'natural' that even
those who truly rule (rule not by assent but by command) feel
the need to pretend that they do so 'in the service of a higher
power', such as a tradition, a god, or a code of justice. (All
constitutions, Nietzsche adds for good measure, are misguided
attempts to outmanoeuvre those gifted for command by adding
up and arranging the sheep against them.)

Plato is nobler than Socrates. As a composer does with a vulgar
ditty picked up in the streets, so Plato plays infinite variations on
the notorious Socratic themes. Among those vulgarities (which
Plato himself explores but does not believe in) is the Socratic
doctrine that 'the wise and knowledgeable are good', or that 'it
is stupid to be evil'. But Plato's improvisations still leave the
fundamental theological problem unsolved: What is the origin
of values? Is it faith or reason? Is it instinct, or knowledge offered
in answer to the question, Why? What is life for? Socrates,
connoisseur of dialectics, proposed to decide the question in
favour of reason. But being at the same time full of ironic
admiration for those noble Athenian youths he taught – all of
them creatures of instinct because, like true aristocrats, they were
not very good at articulating the reasons that gave birth to their
actions – Socrates sought a compromise: he persuaded his
conscience, against its better knowledge, to make instinctive
decisions respectable by supplying them with reasoned explanations. He knew this was a falsehood, for he had already
diagnosed the grounds of all moral judgements as irrational.
Plato's reflective effort – 'the greatest effort of any philosopher

so far' – was directed to proving that instinct ('which the Christians call "faith" and I call "the herd") and reason have one and the same goal – the good ('which the Christians call "God"'). Yet although 'faith' has been victorious in all moral matters, its victory is worthless. Both faith and knowledge, especially our knowledge of the unfamiliar, are foreshortened by our impatience and lack of proper suspiciousness, by our habit of hasty hypothesizing. Our senses perceive crudely and inaccurately, they eke out their defects with false analogies, poetic inventions and, in short, lies; we simply do not know how much of 'the artist', the maker and faker, there is in us.

As long as a community is in peril and the safeguarding of its existence remains its vital task, there can be no 'love thy neighbour' morality, and what later ages call 'virtues' remain extra-moral valuations; hence the indifference with which a compassionate act was regarded in the heyday of the Roman Empire. Love of one's neighbour is always secondary to, and contingent on, fear of one's neighbour. Once the community is free from external threat, this fear of one's neighbour creates new moral perspectives – the herd morality – which amount to new evaluations: all those strong and dangerous instincts (such as enterprise, foolhardiness, vengefulness, cunning, rapacity and lust for power) on which the community has relied for its protection now come to be condemned as immoral. Now everything that is not average becomes evil; first the lambs and then the sheep are honoured; all severity, toward oneself and toward others, is proscribed; until at last society takes sides against itself and for its despoiler, the criminal... The imperative of the herd morality is to abolish everything that is to be feared. The will and the road toward that abolition is the European idea of 'progress' in an age of decadence.

Such epochs of decadence – late cultures, dimmed lights, the scent of musk – produce a type of man whose ideal is the sated happiness of repose, what St Augustine (himself a product of such a culture) called 'the Sabbath of Sabbaths'. Now it becomes a man's most fervent desire to cease to be the battleground of vital conflicts. His wish that 'the war which is he should at last come to an end', is identical with the wish that *he* should come to an end. Yet occasionally such epochs act as vital irritants on men of powerful and unappeasable instincts. These are the men who conduct the warfare that rages within them with especial subtlety and self-control, producing such magically enigmatic and, to us, all but inconceivable characters as Alcibiades, Julius Caesar, and Frederick II of Hohenstaufen ('in my view the first European'), and Leonardo da Vinci. The same epochal causes account for both types.

A rhetorical recapitulation and a prophecy conclude the section. The herd morality has been validated by Christianity and its heir, 'the democratic movement', thus becoming the dominant morality of modern Europe. Its greatest success is to have imposed itself as the only conceivable idea of morality. Among its supporters are not only the sentimental socialists, the peace-loving democrats and the meek men of religion, but also those pathological hysterics for whom the pace of change in our 'social and political institutions' is not fast enough – the revolutionary ideologists and 'snarling dogs of anarchism'. What the senti-mentalists and the anarchist assassins have in common is the belief in the abolition of all differences (including the difference between master and slave), of all rights (where all are equal, what need of rights or justice?), of all suffering other than pity and sympathy (which includes the ultimate indulgence of 'sympathiz-ing' and 'having pity with God'). For them all, the only acceptable social form, the only hope and redemption, is what they call a 'free society', by which they mean the autonomous herd. But what of those who recognize the age for what it really is – an age of the degeneration and dwarfing of men? who are scandalized by the sheer adventitiousness of all history so far? Their hope and their task is to breed in man the conviction that his future lies in his will; in this conviction the necessary revaluation of all values must be founded.

6. *We Scholars*, or How is philosophy possible today? After they have freed themselves from the shackles of theology and the oppression of traditional authority, modern 'scientists' (men of exact learning) assume the guise of 'positivists' and, presumably in order to exact vengeance for their disappointed scientific ambitions, set out to get rid of philosophy too, until its own self-refutation remains philosophy's only valid task...The modern *savant* lacks all nobility of outlook. A profusion of scientific specialities clutters up his view and unnerves him for the freedom that is the necessary condition of every compre-hensive and confident survey [Überblick, Niederblick] of know-

ledge and life. His are the small, humble virtues of diligent work
and a limited independence of mind, contentment with mediocrity and the desire for a fine reputation. With these virtues,
however, goes an instinct to destroy everything exceptional, and
if he cannot break the taut bow, he can at least unstring it.

To be sure, we are apt to weary of subjectivity and 'its damned
ipsissimossity', but (more important in our situation) we should
not forget that the function of 'the objective man' must always
be subaltern, uncreative and passive; that 'scholar', 'scientist' and
'ideal *savant*' alike can never be more than a mirror and a tool
in the hands of one mightier than himself, never more than his
slave. Forever expectant of events outside himself, forever
waiting, the objective man 'spreads himself gently on the ground,
lest the lightest footsteps and flitting-past of ghostly beings should
fail to leave their marks on his surface and skin'. His own person
he regards as adventitious and incidental, a mere interference.
If, for once, he does think of himself – of his own fate and
torment – his thought instantly wanders off into generality. He
has lost the sense of taking himself and his deprivations
seriously. Leibnitz's 'I despise hardly anything' is his motto,
weakness of will his main character trait. Hence a tepid sort of
scepticism – its symptoms are tentative hypothesizing or the coy
refusal to hypothesize; love of delay and compromise; fear alike
of freedom and commitment – is all the fashion with 'our
savants and other mongrels'. Their weakness of will parades in
all sorts of guises: as selflessness, as 'l'art pour l'art' aestheticism,
as the pursuit of 'pure' or 'disinterested' knowledge... This
scepticism of the weak will fears the radical denial of life
('Russian nihilin'[1]) as much as it fears the whole-hearted assent
to life. It fears above all the spirit of the age to come – Hamlet
himself is prescribed by the physicians of the age as a remedy
against 'the Spirit's ghostly, subterranean rumblings'. But the
opiates – Schopenhauer's 'quietives of the will' – are ceasing to
work, 'the will' – weakest in France, strongest in Russia – cannot
be held back much longer. Not even the idiocies of parliamen-
tarianism and of the daily breakfast paper can hide the fact that
the age of twopenny states and European parish pump politics
is over and 'the age of grand politics' (power politics on a grand
scale) is at hand; 'das Zeitalter der grossen Politik', it may be,

---

[1] Nietzsche forms such neologisms as 'Nihilin', 'Moralin' (occasionally 'moral-
infrei') on the analogy with 'Aspirin' etc.

in which a strong, manly, German kind of scepticism, exemplified by Frederick the Great and Goethe, and characterized by Michelet as 'fatalistic, ironical, Mephistophelean', will come into its own.

The question, Is philosophy possible today? is hardly different from the question, Is greatness possible today? And it is greatness which is present in that manly spirit of scepticism which will move the philosophers of the future. What will they be like? They will have to be more than interpreters of received ideas, reorganizers of the past or (like Kant and Hegel) systematizers of accepted values; they will have to do without such idealist twaddle as 'This...delights me, *ergo* it must be beautiful' or 'That...lifts me up, *ergo* it must be the Truth!'; and they will have to be, not conciliatory and 'philosophical', but engaged in a constant conflict with the values of the world into which they were born. There is nothing perennial about philosophical ideals. In a turbulent age like the sixteenth century the true philosopher had to choose self-denial and mortification of the will for his ideal; in the aristocratic Athens of Socrates he appropriately emphasized the equality of all men; in a weak-willed age like the present he must espouse solitude, aristocratic disdain, and the essential inequality of man – wholeness must be his device in an age of specialization and fragmentation. To be a true philo-sopher – a philosopher of the future – is to be predestined by genetic heritage and breeding alike to discharge, lightly and gracefully, the greatest of tasks and gravest of responsibilities. It is to be a maker of the world's laws and creator of its values, to formulate the meaning and goal of life. To be a true philosopher is to be a man whose will to truth is identical with his will to power. (The effort of Nietzsche's thinking here is toward seeing 'lightness of touch' as a *moral* category; this is what Schiller aimed at, whose cast of mind Nietzsche affected to despise. In his last books Nietzsche will argue the incompatibility of the moral with the aesthetic on the same grounds – that the moral is 'das Schwere' and thus enemy of all lightness of touch and grace.)

7. What, if any, are *Our Virtues?* Do we still believe in that harmless eighteenth-century notion? We are suspicious of all who pride themselves on the subtlety of their moral discrimination, but 'Blessed are the forgetful'. The moral attitude – morality *as*

attitude – has lost all meaning for those of us who are the immoralists of the new century. The world that concerns us and in which we really live is a world of fine nuances and subtle perceptions, of 'almost...', 'yes, but...', 'in these circumstances...', of invisible duties and inaudible commands. What determines our actions is not one morality but a whole spectrum of moral schemes. Moral judgements (we recognize) are the favourite weapons of revenge in the hands of the dim-witted and spiritually underprivileged, those who need God (and are the most ardent enemies of atheism) because they need someone before whom all men can be declared equal. The idea and living example of greatness – of a human spirituality beyond compare – infuriates them. Still, as a concession to them let it be admitted that the highest spirituality is the sum total of *moral* qualities, qualities which have been purified and bred into the highest type of man in the course of many generations. But 'values' are nothing in themselves, they must be subordinated to a consideration of human rank. Take the value of an altruistic action: one man has a right, another the duty to perform such an action, a third cannot (and should recognize that he cannot) existentially afford it – it is the general and indiscriminate commendation, such as 'Altruism is a good thing', which is immoral or, worse than that, in bad taste. And so it is with the only religion that is left to us – the modern religion of pity and compassion. Its true nature is self-contempt and cruelty, it is the cause of the darkening and uglifying of Europe. Man is creature and creator alike. The only pity (charity, sympathy) we know is directed at the creatureliness of man, at his status as an object, and at the physical and social ills which this status entails for him. Modern life is designed to reduce and if possible eliminate such ills and suffering, and this is what makes it and all morality that centres on this notion of pity contemptible, for of such suffering there should be more, not less, in the world. True sympathy – 'anti-pity' – should be, not for man the object, but for man the creator. Weighed down as he is by the inauthentic pity of the creature (of man as the object of creation), modern man fails to rise above himself, fails to accomplish...what he has been destined to accomplish. All virtues are boring, though none so boring as the English, Benthamite ones, whose end-purpose is 'cant, comfort and fashion' and possibly a seat in Parliament. For us the only virtue left is intellectual integrity ['Rechtschaffenheit'], and it too will become boring and stupid unless it is tested against the greatest odds, the most diabolical temptations we can devise. The impulse behind all integrity – as behind all pursuit of knowledge and all compassion, too – is 'the great Circe, Cruelty', for all deep and radical questioning involves hurting and doing violence to 'the fundamental will [that is, the inclination and direction] of the human spirit[1]...each act in the pursuit of knowledge contains a drop of cruelty'.

But what is this 'fundamental will of the spirit'? First, it is not different from the will which, as the physiologists tell us, manifests itself in the self-assertion of all living things, in the appropriation of what is outside oneself, and in growth; or rather in the sensation of well-being that goes with appropriation, growth and increased power. Secondly, this 'fundamental will' is defined and furthered by an opposite movement, a protective mechanism whereby contact with the world and the acquisition of new knowledge are cut short: it comes to be sustained by darkness and willing ignorance, deriving strength from an eagerness both to be deceived (in its knowledge of 'the way things are') and to deceive. The cruelty and hurtful quality of every radical enquiry into 'the way things are' lies in its piercing the comfort of that darkness and ignorance, in pressing the human understanding past the fancy terminology and flattery of *isms* to the point where the true nature of man – man as nature – emerges. (Which still leaves unanswered the question, Why is there a will-to-knowledge? why do we want to know?) Finally there is in each of us 'a granite fundament of spiritual fate', a something that is unteachable[2] – we must recognize that we are fundamentally unteachable – so that in the end the only thing authentic knowledge can lead me to are my own truths.

Two further observations, of unequal interest, conclude this section. If there is anything original about our modern age, it is our talent for clowning, parody and dressing up, for we are the first to use all history as a store-room of costumes: unlike other ages, we are dominated by 'the historical sense'. (Here, incidentally, lies the origin of Spengler's historicism and Mal-

---

[1] 'der Grundwille des Geistes', where (Geist' offers the notorious alternative 'spirit' *or* 'mind' ('intellect').

[2] Note Nietzsche's beautiful and untrue formulation in §231: '...ein Denker ...kann nicht umlernen, sondern nur auslernen...'.

raux's '*musée imaginaire*'.[1]) To appreciate how inimical to every genuine aristocratic culture our 'doubtful taste and avidity for *everything*' really is, we need only imagine the hilarious sensation which that barbaric synthesis of Spanish, Moorish and Saxon elements called 'Shakespeare' would have caused among the friends and patrons of Aeschylus, or the sensation Homer did cause in seventeenth-century France. We have no taste for the achieved thing, for completion and calm perfection, but delight in the fragmentary and infinite, in the dangerous, the surprising and (once again) the cruel.

There follows a long series of unashamedly Schopenhauerian lucubrations on the subject of true womanhood and the disservice done to it by the emancipation movement, on the eternal and unappeasable war between the sexes, on woman's true duties and her lack of intelligence as shown in her failure to provide her man with wholesome meals.

8. What a strange tale is to be told of the *Nations and Fatherlands* of modern Europe! Take the Germans, a nation of the day-before-yesterday and the day-after-tomorrow – a nation without a today, whose true art is music, not literature. To write for a German public in the manner recommended by classical authors – that is, to give one's sentences the rhythm and balance of physiological entities – is to waste one's finest effects on a public which reads with its eyes only. It is like writing for the deaf, which is why most German prose is intolerable to a reader who can actually hear what is written, and why the best German book – Luther's Bible – is the work of her greatest preacher. Not prose but music is Germany's gift to the world.[2] But German music, which was once 'the voice of the soul of Europe' – the old, rococo Europe of the eighteenth century – is, like German politics, moving into an embattled isolation. Mozart, the great European phenomenon, is followed by Beethoven who, like Rousseau, Schiller, Byron and Shelley, gave expression to a revolutionary feeling we can no longer recapture. There follows the even briefer episode of Romantic music (the example here is

---

[1] See William Righter's *The Rhetorical Hero: an Essay on the Aesthetics of André Malraux* (London 1964).

[2] A sceptical reader may be forgiven for coming away with the (no doubt erroneous) impression that music in the Second Reich was at least as much talked about as practised.

Tannhäuser – 'not musical enough' to succeed without the stage),
leaving to one side Felix Mendelssohn ('that halcyon master and
exquisite episode of German music'); and then the process of
isolation and decline accelerates, until it ends with the oppressively
grave and self-destructive Robert Schumann, whose music is the
very opposite of European, is mere 'Vaterländerei'. Nothing
expresses the essence of the Germans so accurately as the
Meistersinger overture with its astonishing mixture of jocosity and
heavy pomp, of archaisms and youthful vigour, of fiery courage
and the shed skins of decadence. In that music's moments of
hesitation, in its hiatuses between cause and effect, its carefully
calculated artistic self-consciousness and in the self-indulgent
enjoyment of its own virtuosity – in all this there is no grace, only
an almost deliberate ponderousness.[1]

One man [Bismarck] has persuaded Germany to abandon her
old virtues of depth and philosophy, to seek a cure for 'the
German disease' of excessive reflectiveness, shyness and paro-
chialism. Goaded by him, the country is at last entering the era
of nationalism, power politics and shallowness. 'Even we good
Europeans' have fits of nationalism, the duration of which (from
a few hours to half a lifetime) depends on the pace of one's
metabolism – small wonder that the nationalistic epidemic
among the Germans seems to be going on and on! Their laggard
digestion and 'true-blue empty German eyes', the way they drag
at their souls and ruminate on every experience, explain their
love of openness and coarse decency; it is so comfortable to let
yourself go, to be open and decent. But all this is cleverness and
deception, and often self-deception, too: the Germans *are* not,
they are forever *becoming*, 'development' is their major discovery
and philosophical *coup*, is the concept which, together with their
beer and music, will germanize Europe. A huge levelling
process, based on the assimilation of physiological traits to a single
climatic and cultural milieu, is taking place all over Europe, and

---

[1] 'Alles in allem keine Schönheit, kein
Süden, nichts von südlicher feiner
Helligkeit des Himmels, nichts von
Grazie, kein Tanz, kaum ein Wille
zur Logik; eine gewisse Plumpheit
sogar, die noch unterstrichen wird,
wie als ob der Künstler uns sagen
wollte: "sie gehört zu meiner Ab-
sicht"; eine schwerfällige Gewan-
dung...' § 240).

'There is in all this no beauty,
nothing of the South or of the subtle
southern clarity of sky – no grace-
fulness, no dance, hardly a will to
logic; on the contrary, a certain
clumsiness, which is actually emphasized as if the artist wished to tell us
that "it is a part of my intention";
heavy cumbersome drapery...'

the German masses, already contaminated through being 'the most monstrous of racial mixtures', cannot hold out against it. This immense 'democratic movement' produces herds of average men and mediocrity *en masse*, draining those who are true to its 'type' of all power and moulding them for slavery. However, it is not a smooth process. There are eddies where it is delayed or obstructed, and it is there that the great exceptions arise – men with leadership qualities as attractive as they are dangerous: 'the democratization of Europe is at the same time an involuntary arrangement for the breeding of *tyrants* – tyrants in every sense of the word, including the most spiritual'. This is why the Germans who are half in this process and half out of it and whose nationhood is more fictional than real, are forever defining themselves and their place in Europe. Is their national genius male or female? Are they receptive, waiting to be fructified, like the Greeks and the French, charged with the secret task of shaping and perfecting what others have created, or are they not rather creators and fructifiers, founders of new orders of life? In love with alien races, lusting after the new, forever tormented by desires for what is not theirs – like the Romans, like the Jews?

'I have yet to meet the German who is well-disposed toward the Jews...Only we artists among the spectators and the philosophers' appreciate what Europe owes to the Jews: the search for infinite meanings, the grandeur and terror of infinite moral exactions, but above all a morality in the grand style – European culture itself has been brought to its fruition and perhaps beyond it, to the point of decadence, by the most sophisticated enticements to life inherent in that morality. Being the purest, strongest and toughest of races, the Jews could rule all Europe if they wished, and especially such racially weak 'nations' as the Germans. But it is clear that they have no such intention and that, on the contrary, they are eager (often embarrassingly eager) to be assimilated and to find a European domicile at last. From this desire other nations should profit, but the Germans are too much taken up with their various idiocies (anti-Jewish, anti-Polish, anti-French; Teutonic, Prussian, Wagnerian, etc.) to notice what great advantage there would be in encouraging their strongest racial elements, the Prussian officer class, to marry Jewish girls, as the English aristocracy is doing.

The plebeian quality of modern ideas, foremost among them

the ideas of the French Revolution, originates not among the Jews but among the English, the dullest, least heroic and least philosophical of races (English religiosity, from the histrionics of Thomas Carlyle to the moralizing rant of the Salvation Army, fares no better). Men of undoubted usefulness, like Darwin, John Stuart Mill and Herbert Spencer, have minds which do not go beyond fact-finding, classifying and the formulating of new rules. (All painstaking accumulation of new knowledge is the task of the mediocre; true creativeness, which is not incompatible with ignorance, and often requires it, lies not in the establishing of new facts but in the embodying of new values and new modes of being.) True nobility of feeling, taste and morals is the discovery and prerogative of the French – not, however, of those masses who attended that epitome of vulgarity, the funeral of Victor Hugo. There is another France – secret, fastidious, decadent – which has made Schopenhauer's pessimism its own, which is enchanted by Heine's lyricism, whose greatest historian, Taine, is a Hegelian, and which is under the sway of the old enchanter, Richard Wagner. Add to these influences psychological curiosity and moral finesse (exemplified by Stendhal), in which the French are supreme, add their unique mixture of Provençal temperament and Northern thoughtfulness (exemplified by Bizet), and you have at last that 'good European' whose coming the Germans are trying to delay by their nationalistic madness and their 'policy of blood and iron'.

What the politicians with their narrow nationalisms and their politics of the moment overlook or try to suppress is that Europe is striving to be one: this grand unity is what, in their best hours, all the 'higher men' of Europe – Napoleon, Goethe, Beethoven, Stendhal, Heine, Schopenhauer... – have desired, this is what, often unknowingly, their art is striving to bring about and express. For they are all artists – the first artists whose imagination is fascinated by the (Goethean) idea of world literature; and they are literary even when, like Wagner and Delacroix, they work in a mixture of several media. But who are these 'higher' men? Engaged in a tireless search for the sublime, connoisseurs of the ugly and the monstrous as well as of the beautiful; up-and-coming plebeians incapable of enjoying a moment of rest (like Balzac); lovers of the dark, the exotic and the contradictory, they are possessed by a work ethic that drives them to the very edge of exhaustion. Audacious and adventurous, they nevertheless end up as victims of the Cross – after the manly, free, German Siegfried comes the Papist Parsifal, reeking of incense – for although they are strong enough to be enemies of established logic and Antinomians, they are not, in the end, strong enough to be Anti-Christ.

Pointing beyond these 'higher men', pointing beyond Europe, too, is the music of the future. We hardly know what it will be like, or whose redemptive dream it represents.[1] Will it be music freed from its northern penance and yet not liable to be withered in the southern sun (the fate of all German music), filled perhaps with some seafarer's lament and with the golden shadows, gentle remembrances and distant colours of a world that will then be no longer intelligible – filled with mere remembrances of a moral world? Will it be music that has forgotten about Good and Evil...?

9. *What is Noble?* How can the species 'man' be improved? Setting out to answer the fundamental question of 'the value of values', the entire section is built round the polarity of moral opposites. (Incidentally, Nietzsche's two kinds of morality relate closely to the 'inner-directed' and 'outer-directed' ethic of recent sociology.)

A caste of barbaric conquerors, merciless because psychically

---

[1] 'Ein solcher Südländer, nicht der Abkunft, sondern dem Glauben nach, muss...von einer Erlösung der Musik vom Norden träumen und das Vorspiel einer tieferen, mächtigeren, vielleicht böseren und geheimnisvolleren Musik in seinen Ohren haben, einer überdeutschen Musik, welche vor dem Anblick des blauen wollüstigen Meeres und der mittelländischen Himmels-Helle nicht *verklingt, vergilbt, verblasst,* wie es alle deutsche Musik tut, einer übereuropäischen Musik, die noch vor den braunen Sonnen-Untergängen der Wüste Recht behält...' (§ 255, my italics).

'A Southerner of this kind – a Southerner not by descent but by faith – must...dream of the redemption of music from [the dominance of] the North and have in his ears the prelude of a deeper, mightier, perhaps more sinister and more mysterious music, a supra-German music which, when confronted with the blue voluptuous sea and the brilliance of the southern sky, will not, as all German music has done, fade out, wither away and lose its colour – a supra-European music which can even hold its own against the brown sunsets of the desert...'

This passage offers a striking example of that mixture of strong figurative metaphors and the terminology of (abstract) moral judgements which is characteristic of Nietzsche's style at the time of *Zarathustra*; in that work, though, the figurative aspect is carried much further.

superior, forms the origin of every society, and only an aristocratic society based on conquest and slavery has ever been able to contribute to the positive development of the species. Without such a hierarchic society – a society of rigid class barriers – there is no 'pathos of distance' toward the lower classes or toward the lower instincts in oneself, and without such pathos (the opposite of democratic camaraderie) there is no culture. An aristocracy, however, is neither a means toward, nor a function of, a social organism. It is, on the contrary, the end-purpose, the meaning and *raison d'être* of every society that is truly living and free from corruption. Since the essence of all life is appropriation, conquest and exploitation – since life itself is the will to power – abstention from conquest, once it has become not merely a casual courtesy among equals but a 'moral principle', amounts to a denial of life and a sure sign of decadence.

All moral systems (we should do well to remember) began as subjective value-judgements, expressions of personal preference, and only later came to designate actions in a would-be objective way; all moral systems either reflect or try to hide the master–slave polarity of society.

(i) *The morality of* [created by] *masters* and rulers is based on an antithesis between 'good' and 'bad', which is here synonymous with 'lowly' and hence 'despicable';[1] it is no accident that the Athenian aristocrats thought of themselves as truthful and of the common people as liars. This is a morality creative of positive values: its notion of goodness results from a feeling of well-being in the enjoyment of abundance and power in excess of need – power not only, perhaps not even mainly, over others but over oneself. The rule of the master morality is the opposite of the Kantian categorical imperative: not an abstract concept determines a man's conduct, but his personal being. In this sense he is 'master of his four virtues of courage, insight, compassion and solitude'. Here a man's motive in helping others is not

---

[1] 'Man bemerke sofort, dass in dieser ersten Art Moral der Gegensatz "gut" und "schlecht" so viel bedeutet wie "vornehm" und "verächtlich": – der Gegensatz "gut" und "böse" ist anderer Herkunft' (§ 260). See also below, p. 194n.

'Let it be noted at once that in this first kind of morality the antithesis "good" and "bad" means the same as "noble" and "despicable", whereas the antithesis "good" and "evil" has a different origin.'

compassion with their weakness but pride in his own strength, and his motto is the Vikings' saw, 'He who has not a hard heart in his youth will never have one in his manhood'. At the centre of the master morality is an act of homage to a self which experiences itself as a creator and arbiter of values, a self which is contemptuous of 'the warm heart' and of all show of 'disinterestedness' and 'selflessness'. The noble mind sides with ancestral tradition and lore, with the dignity and prejudices of the past, against the future and all 'modern ideas of progress', against all plebeian shamelessness of hand and eye. It recognizes the inborn, 'natural' dignity of high rank, and in its recognition shares it. It knows no 'grace', no 'gifts from on high', and no 'on high'.[1] Finally, the master morality encourages fastidious discrimination in friendship, and emotions which develop slowly and are enduring. It justifies arbitrary conduct toward all who are alien and inferior. It looks on duty as a privilege, and enjoins it toward one's self, one's peers and no-one else. Origin determines value: 'love as passion – our European speciality' – is an aristocratic virtue, for it originates among the Provençal knight-poets and inventors of '*gai saber*', the 'joyous science', to whom 'Europe owes so much and almost itself'.

(ii) *The slave morality*, on the other hand, is the response of the oppressed, the suffering and the unfree. It implies, not only suspicion of the virtues of the strong and of their conception of good, but a profound distrust of the entire human situation, including man's chances of happiness. 'Good', in terms of this morality, means 'innocuous', 'harmless' and hence 'stupid', while its antithesis, 'evil', means above all 'dangerous' and connotes hostile power and terror beyond the reach of contempt. Unlike the morality of the masters, this is a morality not of abundance but of utility, expediency and want. Its virtues – sympathy, industry, patience and 'the warm heart' – are all designed to lighten life, for life is experienced not as a joy but as a burden; while the three main vices of the slave morality – it is always guilty of some sort of offensive intemperance, some hole-and-corner enviousness, some act of gross self-righteousness – constitute the essential character of the plebs. As the aristocratic mode of conduct and thought is characterized by devotion, loyalty and reverence, so the slave morality is informed

[1] But see below, p. 105.

by weak compassion (the compassion of those who suffer with
their own kin) and an instinctive yearning for freedom.

Vanity is the slave's attempt to create a good opinion of
himself in others and to share this opinion only when the others
have stamped it with their approval; because it is the master's
nature to create values (not to share approved ones), he finds
vanity hard to understand and tends to ignore it as a motive of
conduct. But common men at all times have measured themselves
and their worth according to criteria designed by others. Even
now, when the mixing of masters and slaves has brought about
a new, democratic order, and when 'the master' in men's blood
urges them to determine their own value freely and independ-
ently of others, men still wait for the good – or bad – opinion of
others (including the Church) so as to have an authority to which
they can submit. And it is 'the slave' in the blood of vain people
that makes them delight in *any* good opinion of themselves, even
if they first had to persuade others into it...: vanity is an
important atavism.

How does the morality of the mediocre arise? An aristocratic
community like Venice or the Greek polis is born in, and
maintains itself against, the least favourable circumstances.
Surviving by virtue of its hardness, uniformity and the simplicity
of its style of life, it becomes, deliberately or by necessity, an
institution for the breeding of men. (This, incidentally, Nietzsche
regards as adequate proof that 'the problem of race' is inescapable: the inheritance of [dominant] ancestral traits he accepts
as absolute fact; education and 'Bildung' are merely attempts to
cover up the unalterable *données* of a man's character; all this
is no more than a restatement of Schopenhauer's theory of
'intelligible character'.) Once fortune begins to smile on such a
community and neighbouring enemies become friends, the
life-giving tension instantly snaps and the discipline of former
ages – which had been the necessary condition of survival – turns
into love of luxury and a taste for the archaic. Now the battles
of competing, explosive egoisms begin to rage, the tropical
burgeoning and the decadence of life destroy the old morality
of the élite, the venerable meanings and goals of the past fade
away, chaos and destruction begin to threaten once more: what
they now endanger is no longer the whole society but the
individual. And those solemn observers and street-corner idlers,
the moral philosophers, begin to preach a new morality. They

note that, while all is decaying and hastening to its end, only the average man, the incurably mediocre, survives and multiplies; and so they preach *his* morality, *his* scale of values and mode of life (which is not easy: they may not admit that they preach mediocrity but must talk of all sorts of virtues and altruisms, they need a dose of irony to help them along).

Mediocrity is the essence of easy communication. For if it is agreed that words are sounds standing for concepts, and concepts are more or less definite pictorial signs for frequently repeated, average emotions and experiences, it follows that words function most efficiently and most quickly when they relate to the most common – that is mediocre – emotions and experiences; and that the need for quick and unambiguous understanding is greatest where the survival of the mediocre is at stake: here the sensitive, the subtle and the fastidious are at a disadvantage. The masses, however, even though their coarseness and capacity for taking punishment are almost unlimited, have a great need for stable, protective communication, especially in situations of distress. The satisfaction of this need is the greatest single moulding force that acts upon them.

The elect few in their isolation find both communication and survival much more problematic. They do not wish to eat out of the same dish as the noisy, plebeian contemporaries into whose company they have been thrown, and so find themselves having to choose between starvation and after-dinner nausea. A psychologist and guesser of the secrets of souls must harden himself to so much vulnerability and destruction, for he cannot avoid the discovery that all history is a charnel-house of the great. Where the cultured masses admire, he *sees* what the truth about human greatness and perhaps about God himself amounts to and prefers to keep silent, lest his discoveries should lead him to the point where 'the Great' turn out to be an object of compassion and contempt. Nothing succeeds like success. In a work of art this includes success in disguising the truth that it is 'the Work' which creates the artist and philosopher, that *they* are its mean little fictions. 'The Work' is the shameful stop-gap of defective being. Look at the great poets – Byron, Musset, Poe, Leopardi, Kleist, Gogol (and Goethe himself)[1] – their childishness, sensu-

---

[1] Nietzsche does not name Goethe but adds (§ 269) with a sententious quaver in his voice, '(ich wage es nicht, grössere Namen zu nennen, aber ich meine sie)'.

ality, their unsteadiness of purpose and the frivolousness of their likes and dislikes, the way they use their 'work' to paper over and compensate for their inner flaws and lack of faith! What torment all this is to the psychologist who has guessed their true nature! Neither pity nor love can help them – it is only woman's superstition that love can do everything. . . Is this what Jesus too believed? His was the martyrdom of the innocent yet imperious heart, the martyrdom of one who wanted to be loved and nothing but loved, by all men, inventing hell for those who would not love him, inventing a God of infinite love who would have mercy on human love because it is so wretched and ignorant. True saintliness, which lives in solitude, is a very different thing: it is the highest spiritualization of that instinct of cleanliness which, to one side of all decency and utility and good will, makes a man confess that he cannot 'endure the smell' of another. And this instinct drives the souls of men out of darkness and gloom into the brilliant light of morning, but also into the perils of solitude.

What determines a man's spiritual rank? A man must live *désinvolte*, beyond good and evil and in the cleanliness of solitude which comes from the knowledge that in the end all community (later Nietzsche will add: and all language) makes common. Not work but faith – whatever is not idolatry of himself but some deep reverence for himself – shows a man's true rank; not the opinions he holds but his way of holding them; not a readily communicable set of fixed 'truths', but ideas as remote as the stars: for the greatest events and thoughts – 'but the greatest thoughts are the greatest events' – take as long to reach us as does the light of the most distant stars, so that many generations live in ignorance of the greatest events of their time. 'How many centuries a spirit needs before it is understood' – that too is a criterion by which rank may be measured. But most of all a man's spiritual rank is his capacity for profound suffering, for it separates him from others (think of the cynicism of such broken souls as Hamlet), and teaches him the supreme value of masks and the self-control needed to welcome misunderstanding. (When one is misunderstood, only vanity suffers; where one is understood, the sufferer is likely to be one's heart.)

The value of psychologists is as problematic as the value of communication and truth: think of the psychologist who, used to debunking every motive, is no longer able to recognize true greatness when he sees it; think of the saint contaminated by the filth of compassion for all that is human, all-too-human. If, therefore, each truth has its appropriate discoverer, and if some truths are dangerous and destructive and others again demeaning, then books may have to be written in order to foster misunderstanding, and hermit-philosophers must hide what they have divined in their long solitary discourse with their own souls. There is something uncommunicative and reluctant in the presence of such hermit-thinkers; a musty smell of the deep blows cold on every passer-by. Every philosophy is a foreground philosophy (says the hermit-philosopher), there is always something arbitrary, and something suspect, too, about the point where a philosopher has stopped in his enquiry, about his decision to pursue this argument but not that. And every philosophy hides another philosophy, for every word is a mask. Morality itself is a fiction, designed to make a man's soul look more appetizing.

A philosopher is one who is constantly experiencing strange, untoward things, who is constantly taken unawares by his own ideas as though they came from outside, as though they were flashes of lightning. 'Shall I be believed?' Nietzsche asks, 'But I insist that I shall be believed: mistrusting the possibility of self-knowledge, I have never thought about myself with any enthusiasm, never thought much of myself...Does this confession betray the species to which I belong? Perhaps it does. But not to me!'

The gods, too, are philosophers, and they share that gift of golden laughter which is a sign of a philosopher's true rank. Closest to the hermit-philosopher is the tempter- and deceiver-god Dionysus, giver of gifts and enricher of men (enriching them only by what is in them already), keeper of secrets and *genius of their heart.* He it is who teaches men to keep still and with their still surface to reflect the sky, to look for nuggets of golden thought amid the dross and the mud; who makes men more open and more tender, and more unsure and vulnerable, too, but full of nameless hopes. And the hermit-philosopher? He is the god's last disciple (for do not our friends protest that there is no god, that there are no gods?), to him the god speaks freely, without masks. Among the many eerie, frightening things Dionysus teaches is his love of the species 'man': a pleasant, brave, inventive animal he finds man, who has no equal on earth. But man (so the terrible god teaches) should be improved, should be made 'stronger, deeper, and more evil – more evil and more beautiful'. And when, frightened by the god's message, the hermit-philosopher repeats these words, the tempter-god smiles as though he had conveyed a courteous compliment – but then, are there not good grounds for believing that the gods have much to learn from us?

P.S. 'The old story! As soon as you have finished your house you notice that you have learned something while building it which you should really have known before you ever began . . . The melancholy of all *completed* things!'

6
The first experiment: morality versus life

...for there is nothing, either good or bad, but thinking makes it so...

(Hamlet II: 2)

I

There is little doubt that Nietzsche would have disliked reading most of the previous chapter. The summaries, contractions and de-metaphorized arguments of which it consists go largely against the spirit and the often expressed intention of his philosophizing. The reader he wished for was one who would think round and extemporize on the themes of his 'aphorisms' rather than attempt to connect them systematically, or at least by themes; who would preserve, and perhaps enlarge on, the particular metaphors from which Nietzsche builds his individual arguments, rather than dissolve them in discursive prose. Yet there is more than one way of reading Nietzsche, and there is good reason why occasionally one should read him through the metaphors and for underlying meanings and coherences. Rather than follow Nietzsche in his distrust of concepts, his reader may wish to enquire into the reasons for this distrust.[1]

In the last reflection of *Beyond* (§296) Nietzsche speaks vividly of his fear that his thoughts, once written down, will lose their freshness and life, and be reduced to 'such heartbreakingly honest and boring *truths*'; looking back over the arguments of the book, he regrets having 'caught only the birds that have strayed and grown weary in flight'; what he has been able to 'paint and write...with all my fifty yellows and browns and greens and reds [were]...not the morning thoughts but their

---

[1] Cf. *J* §16 (and *GM* I §13; *WzM* §371): 'It is a falsification of the facts to say that the subject,, "I", is the condition of the predicate, "think" – an observation taken almost literally from Lichtenberg (*Schriften und Briefe*, vol. II, K76 see also above, p. 65); similarly, the idea of epistemological problems being caused by 'the snares of grammar' which originates in 'the metaphysics of the people' is taken from Lichtenberg *J*2148. Such observations occur a number of times, but Nietzsche does nothing to follow them up or to enquire how they might affect the rest of his philosophizing.

afternoons'; and again he complains: 'we immortalize only that which will not live and fly much longer'. One cannot read this passage (and many similar ones elsewhere) without feeling the stylistic intensity and reflective pathos which accompany these language-conscious and language-critical observations. If the hermit-philosopher's own words have been subjected to such an ironical, deprecating scrutiny, how are our words about his words, our account of his account, to be justified? Is it likely that to the critic of his criticisms Nietzsche will allow a more substantial role than that of a taxidermist or (at most) taxonomist – a handler, in either case, of dead birds?

One's excuse for writing a critical summary comes from the conviction that Nietzsche ignores, or at least underestimates, that tendency in the mind which does not easily tolerate divisions, discrete insights and separate images, but makes for continuity and coherence; and it comes from the further conviction that the systematic view, far from being misleading – inherently and necessarily misleading – is really unavoidable. These convictions are not confined to philosophy. Literature too has to do with continuity and coherence, and Nietzsche defies them in the literary aspect of his work no less than in the philosophical. When it comes to 'drawing out the implications' of a given situation, there never was a temperament less Flaubertian or Jamesian.

Continuity and coherence he is apt to regard as boring, as a betrayal of original insight and authentic experience, as anti-life: from this belief spring his attacks on every convention, including the moral. Thus the importance, for him, of a truly creative morality, as opposed to 'a mere laisser-aller view' (*J* § 188), is not that it should aim at stable precepts or be equally available to all and valid for all – these are the factors which make for mediocrity and its survival – but that, by representing 'an enduring compulsion', a moral scheme should provide the mechanism whereby individual creativeness is first suppressed, then forced into conflict with the established convention and thus, finally, enabled to express itself. Similarly with the rule of law, which (Nietzsche argues) must never become a permanent state. For as soon as it ceases to be a means – a means toward creating 'ever larger units of power' (*GM* II § 11) – and becomes an end, it is bound to imperil the expansion and development, the very life of 'Life'. Instead of the stable rule of law which breeds mediocrity, Nietzsche postulates the rule of the Superman, an embodiment of his protest against established legal, moral and religious convention alike. But again, the Superman is the creature of a sudden, catastrophic reversal of values, not of continuous development but of a moment of grace. Or take Nietzsche's view of conventional historiography. Much of it consists in attacks on contemporary historicism, in praise of the great charismatic leaders of the past, and in defence of an apparently anti-historical notion of originality. All this certainly provides a splendid corrective to academic pedantry and the slow-coach mind: 'That a single man' – we are still in his Wagnerian heyday – 'in the span of an ordinary human life, should be able to put before us something entirely new is sure to infuriate all those who swear by the gradualness of all development as by a moral law' (*U* IV § 1). Yes – but *is* originality necessarily discontinuous and anti-historical? Nietzsche himself has shown that the historical point of view is not always the sign of a false, imperturbable professionalism which refuses to acknowledge anything new under the sun, nor are the single insight and the single living experience – the much vaunted 'Erlebnis' – necessarily betrayed and mummified by being treated in a consequential manner. 'We immortalizers of all the things that *can* be written [alle Dinge, die sich schreiben lassen]', Nietzsche complains, insinuating a tautology where there is none. Why should that which can be written down be an insipid substitute for that which cannot be (whatever that may be), and is it not the nature of every major intellectual undertaking that it alters the frontier between the two? That it consistently pushes back the frontier of the unsayable?

Nietzsche's anti-language observations are no mere poetic enhancements. They are consistent and numerous enough to stand as part of his considered view of things and of his didactic strategy. Are these reflections then, as has often been said, anticipations of the language philosophy of our time, and especially of the work of Ludwig Wittgenstein? It is a question to which we shall have to return. The point that needs making here is that these language-conscious and language-critical observations make no sense unless they are seen against the background of a silent cosmos or world of unworded experiences, to which all utterances are intended – but fail adequately – to refer; and this closely resembles the assessment of language which informs Wittgenstein's first work, the *Tractatus Logico-Philosophicus* of 1922. Both Nietzsche and the early Wittgenstein recognize only that severely restricted (and restrictive) idea according to which language is confined to its naming, designating, 'referential' function. (Whereas Nietzsche will challenge this idea with a few casual observations only, Wittgenstein's later work is expressly designed to repudiate and replace it by an altogether richer and more varied conception.) It is this function which, in Nietzsche's eyes, renders language hopelessly derivative – derivative from some (presumably silent) centre. And, unable as always to forego the value judgement, he turns the linguistic argument into a moral one: since language is a derivative scheme, a mere echo of a world from which it is excluded, it is inauthentic, fictitious, lying. For us too this ascription may act as a bridge to Nietzsche's moral philosophy, of which the concept of authenticity is the pivot. For the view of language of which I have just given a first sketch has its equivalent in the non-linguistic, 'moral' sphere charted in *Beyond* and in his other books of reflections on the nature of morality. Again and again we shall find that, in order to derive a coherent, over-all meaning from them, we must postulate that which the discrete reflections assembled in these books aim to subvert: a realm of the ineffable.

2

'Nietzsche's didactic strategy' – I use the phrase in spite of earlier reservations, conscious of the misgiving with which he views the struttings and ·falsities of the didactic posture. To understand what it means we should recall that Nietzsche, like Plato, begins his philosophical venture as an educationalist (and that, unlike Aristotle, he is not often interested in 'scientific' knowledge for its own sake, but takes pleasure in 'de-masking' the idea of such knowledge). His philosophizing is set in train by a deep discontent with the ways his own academic subject of 'classical philology' is practised, and the purposes for which it is practised in his time, and it is worth adding that this is criticism from a young and acknowledged master of the craft. He then goes on to express a more comprehensive discontent with the University, its defective contribution to the creating of valid ideals and to a renewal of the life of the nation as a whole. His most scathing remarks are directed at the University's unwitting propagation of knowledge as a divisive factor, making for the fragmentation of personality and experience. An early critic[1] (1874) observed that Nietzsche 'is one of those young men who still' – presumably in spite of the military achievements of the Franco-Prussian War of 1870 – 'think of Germany as a huge university, and who believe that every German is a *Privatdozent* or Professor of History'; and therefore, the critic concludes, he – Nietzsche – is 'out of touch with the real life of the German nation'. Nietzsche no doubt would reply that it is precisely this estrangement of the practical sphere from the spiritual– intellectual, the gulf between the aridly theoretical scholars and 'Papiermenschen' on the one hand, and the barbarous, unre- generatedly mediocre general public on the other, which he is criticizing and offering to reform. His critical views, I have suggested, unlike the remedies proposed, often recall Matthew Arnold's; in both cases the remoteness from 'the practical world' is more apparent than real.

Though after his first books Nietzsche's didactic strategy ceases to be explicitly related to concrete institutions and circumstances, it is never abandoned. His frequent protests that men are unteachable are a part of it. Throughout his work his pedagogic intention must be seen as a mode of the philosophical; there is a sense in which his philosophical speculation, even at its most metaphysical, does not stray far beyond the pedagogic pro- gramme. And this programme is, quite simply, the creation of a finer and nobler species of man.

Nietzsche's first published book, *The Birth of Tragedy* of 1872, ends with a call for 'the rebirth of the German myth' which is to lead to a rebirth of German culture and to a spiritually richer, nobler vision of life than modern decadent Europe has to offer. There can be no 'purpose' in history (he writes in the second of those *Thoughts out of Season* which was considered in Chapter 4 and to which the critic just mentioned had taken exception): at any rate, there can be no true purpose which the mere passage of time could accomplish, and no (Hegelian) notion of inevitable progress either. History has no other function than to provide occasions for the generation of greatness, for 'The goal of humanity cannot lie at the end [of time], but only in its highest specimens' (*U* II §9). Again, the Superman – the utopian project

[1] Karl Hillebrand, quoted in: W. Mauser, *Karl Hillebrand: Leben, Werk, Wirkung* (Dornbirn 1960), p. 172.

of *Thus Spoke Zarathustra* – is created as an expression of Nietzsche's concern with 'the whole man', whose enemy is fragmentation of knowledge and petrifaction of experience.[1] And the
elaboration, in his last notes of 1884–8, of a 're-valuation of all
values' in the light of a ubiquitous 'will to power' is still in the
service of the same idea: '...To what extent does a sacrifice of
freedom, and even enslavement, provide the basis for a higher
type [of man]...How may the development of mankind be
sacrificed in order to help a species higher than man to come into
being?' (*WzM* §859). This is not an ideal we contemplate with
much sympathy. To return to our earlier comparison with Marx,
we are not even sure which to think of as the greater evil: to be
haunted by the spectre of injustice (a product of the inequality
of the past) or by that of mediocrity (a product of our egalitarian
present). Nietzsche has no doubt: his insistence that only the
generation of greatness matters is 'the most crucial point of his
philosophy of history and theory of values – no less than the clue
to his "aristocratic" ethics and his opposition to socialism and
democracy'[2] – though whether it is also the most comprehensive
of his philosophical ideas remains to be seen.

To this 'elevation of man' everything is a means and everything
must be sacrificed: this is Nietzsche's 'categorical imperative' and,
incidentally, his reply to Kant's. His view of men's past (that is,
of their great 'historic' moments, to one side of any merely
chronological development); of their present state, conduct and
beliefs (in the age of European decadence and at the point of
its merging into a destructive but liberating nihilism); and of their
future hopes (seen in terms of a bio-psychological notion of
breeding) – all these views are offered, not merely as descriptions
of the human condition, but as parts of an all-encompassing
pedagogic purpose. And the brief autobiographical revelations
– some laconic, others full of an ill-concealed pathos, others
again immoderate and assertive – they too are answers to the
question, How can this individual man, this hermit-philosopher
in the age of decadence and on the threshold of the age of
nihilism, contribute to that global process which may one day
lead toward a radical improvement of 'the species man'?

[1]   This, too, is the concern of Goethe's *Faust*, where Nietzsche found the term
      'Übermensch' (I, line 490).
[2]   W. Kaufmann, *Nietzsche*, p. 149.

3

This statement of Nietzsche's moral, or rather existential, project raises some obvious questions. What kind of 'improvement' and 'elevation of man' has he in mind? What is his idea of nobility? Undoubtedly, the ethos described in *Beyond* and *Genealogy* is consciously archaic. Here, sailing under a Hegelian flag, is its summary. It emphasizes the fact (as it was for Nietzsche)

that the words 'noble' and 'base', although they have been assimilated to moral judgement, did not originally express concepts of moral law, of a prescriptive and prohibitory code which is taken to be of general, commanding, and even supernal authority and in which a chief criterion of a person's rightdoing and wrongdoing is the effect of his conduct upon other persons. The words were applied, rather, to the ideal of personal existence of a ruling class at a certain time – its ethos, in that sense of the word which conveys the idea not of abstractly *right* conduct but of a characteristic manner or style of *approved* conduct. What is in accord with this ethos is noble; what falls short of it or derogates from it is base. The noble self is not shaped by its beneficent intentions towards others; its intention is wholly towards itself, and such moral virtues as may be attributed to it follow incidentally from its expressing the privilege and function of its social status in mien and deportment.[1]

Clearly there is much here that is akin to the military life, and indeed Nietzsche was often sympathetic to it, hoping sometimes that the military virtues might provide a cure for the decadence of the age. Yet the archaic nature of such a scheme was as obvious to him as it is to us. To the question, What are the *new* values, what is the re-valuation that is to lead to them? it does not provide an answer at all.

One thing is clear: he will not be another 'idealist philosopher' who puts his faith in 'the good will' or 'compassion', or indeed in any one single and absolute state of mind. Not only are his arguments anti-idealist in tenor, but his insistence on a positive, creative morality grounded in 'the will to power' (itself more than a state of mind) is a direct challenge to the 'mind-matter' dichotomy on which every idealism is based. This new morality must not be abstract – more than that: it cannot be generalized, for generalization itself, the leveller of all distinction and

[1] Lionel Trilling, *Sincerity and Authenticity* (London 1972), p. 37.

excellence, is its enemy.[1] Its material substance – that is, its concern with power – must not be at odds with its spiritual content, nor are the new moral values to be at odds with the biological values by which the healthy and strong part of mankind lives and should govern the rest; and Nietzsche does not hesitate to push the argument to the point where conventional morality – seen bluntly as the protective device of the 'under-privileged' in body and soul – is simply stood on its head, so that right (moral, legal as well as biological right) should be at one with might.

However, it can hardly be denied that this entire argument is erected on a scant foundation of material facts. The ethnological, historical and sociological views on which Nietzsche bases his moral observations are mostly derived from random collections of data, chance impressions, snippets of information; and the biological knowledge on which he bases his notions of breeding, which are later revised, is rudimentary and seems amateurish; it hardly goes beyond the Darwinian tags current at the time. (His plans, in 1869, for the serious study of chemistry, came to nothing.) But this amateurishness does not prevent him from allowing his suspicions to harden with remarkable speed into convictions, or from accompanying every statement, factual or speculative, with a value judgement: 'In order to live, one must evaluate' (*WKG* VII/2 p. 179).

Of course, there is no reason for thinking that one must be a competent historian, sociologist or biologist in order to philo-sophize about the moral nature of man. But equally one may ask why Nietzsche (all in the course of a few pages) should go out of his way to make detailed but doubtfully reliable observations about, say, 1789, or the utilitarian philosophy of Gower Street, the mentality of the French intelligentsia, the inherited character traits of command and obedience, why he should lean so heavily on notoriously vague words like 'instinct' and 'intuition', and concern himself with a hundred other miscellaneous subjects. To which the brief answer is: because Nietzsche does not want to be an 'idealist' philosopher. Not wanting to argue about such artificial moral conundrums as the undeserved sufferings of the just man or the consequences of pinching a spoonful of jam, he

---

[1] A similar criticism is to be found in Wittgenstein, when he identifies the philosophers' 'craving for generality' with 'the contemptuous attitude toward the particular case' (*The Blue Book*, Oxford 1964, p. 18).

is forever in search of concrete facts and scientific data to serve
as illustrations of a theory which rejects generality as inauthentic.
Because the 'ideal' of nobility is to be *realized*, his moral
philosophy moves between the devil of recalcitrant facts and the
deep sea of an all-encompassing cosmology. He wants to be a
practical philosopher (hence his admiration for Emerson), yet
he rebels against the tyranny of empiricism and 'our dubious
taste for facts'. We return here to the idea of an 'existential
commitment' and to Nietzsche's professed distaste for the kind
of thought W. B. Yeats attacked in lines which conceal one of the
cardinal intellectual superstitions of our age:

> God guard me from those thoughts men think
> In the mind alone.
> He that sings a lasting song
> Thinks in the marrow bone.

We cannot be sure that Nietzsche is aware of his dilemma: after
a couple of pages of superior journalistic gossip (*J* § 251) about
German policy on Jewish immigration and the desirability of
marrying blue-blooded Junkers to clever Jewish girls, he stops
in mid-sentence (not, we feel, a moment too soon) to apologize
for indulging in this sort of chit-chat: 'to think about things that
do not concern me [is] a first sign of being infected by the
political disease'. But how can one discuss political problems
without at least a touch of 'the political infection'? How can one
consider, e.g. 'the European problem of breeding a new ruling
class', even as a philosophical problem, with no more than a few
ethnic anecdotes and observations and a few racial clichés to fall
back on? Despising idealist utopias, he is forever searching for
objective correlatives of his proposed re-valuation, and is
forever dissatisfied with what he finds. As we shall see, the
analogy with his linguistic views provides the pattern: a thousand
diverse utterances make little sense unless they are related to a
silent cosmos of authentic being, a thousand diverse facts make
little sense unless they are seen against some supreme – and
ultimately unstatable – notion of moral nobility. This is the
'pathos of distance' by which his philosophy is afflicted *and from
which it takes its sustenance*. To invoke this pathos on Nietzsche's
behalf is to offer no excuse for his world-historical obiter dicta,
doubtful biology, or his crudities about 'the English', 'the
Germans' or 'the French'. (As for these ethnic discourtesies, what

the English seem to mind most is that he actually ascribes a national character to them; what he says about the drinking and thinking habits of the Germans they mind less; and with all he says about French worldliness and polish they agree.) But the 'pathos of distance' does explain how Nietzsche comes to write such reflections as the sketch of 'the higher man' (*J*§262), which must surely be among the most brilliant anticipations of twentieth-century fauna we know:

At these turning-points of history there often occurs the phenomenon of a splendid, luxuriant, jungle-like upward growth and burgeoning side by side and often interlocked and entwined – a kind of tropical acceleration and competing growth, monstrously wasteful and self-destructive, caused by the diverse egoisms – all turning on each other and as though exploding, all fighting each other 'for sun and air' and no longer able to derive any limit, any restraint, any forbearance from accepted morality. It was this morality itself that has stored up such enormous energy, and bent the bow in such a menacing way: – now it is spent, now it is becoming 'outlived'. Things have reached the dangerous and eerie point at which the greater, more complex, more comprehensive life *lives beyond* the old morality; the individual is forced to make his own laws, his own arts and stratagems of self-preservation, self-enhancement, self-redemption. Nothing but new whys and where-withals; no more common formulas, incomprehension allied with contempt; decay, corruption and the highest desires horribly entangled; the genius of the race overflowing from every cornucopia of good and bad; an ill-omened coincidence of spring and autumn, full of new charms and veils characteristic of youthful corruption still unexhausted and untiring. Here once more there is danger, the mother of morality – great danger, only this time it resides in the individual, in neighbour and friend, in the street, in one's own child, one's own heart, in the most personal and intimate corner of every wish and will: what can the moralists of this new age preach? They discover, these acute observers and street-corner idlers, that the end is at hand, that everything about them is corrupt and corrupting, that nothing can last beyond the day after tomorrow, *one* species of man excepted, the incurably *mediocre.* The mediocre alone have the chance of continuing and of propagating themselves – they are the men of the future, the sole survivors; 'be like them! become mediocre!' is henceforth the only morality that still has any meaning or finds ears to hear it. But it is difficult to preach, this morality of mediocrity! for it can never admit what it is and what it wants! it must speak of moderation and dignity and duty and brotherly love – it will have a hard task to conceal its irony!

Déracinement – the feeling of not being very securely at home in the common world of men[1] – is one of the conditions of social insight and prophecy. In this respect Nietzsche's position is strikingly similar to that of Heine, whom he greatly admired, and to that of the Jews generally, with whom he occasionally identified: it is a compound of familiarity and critical detachment, of acceptance and 'the freedom that distance gives'. It is purchased at great cost to himself: 'I no longer have any idea at all which of my views bring comfort to people and which are hurtful to them', he writes in 1881.[2] From this distance he sets up his man-traps and sleights of hand, and achieves his remarkable anticipations.

Nietzsche does not want to be an 'idealist' philosopher. Nothing is so characteristic of his way of thinking as his lack of interest in the classical problems of epistemology and his habit of converting every epistemological problem into a moral and existential one. The Kantian question, 'What can I reliably know?' is replaced by 'What is it good for me to know? What kind of knowledge is likely to further my will and being, and what kind will harm them? What is *my* good?'

The idealist ethic of knowledge, taken over by our scientists, is to be reversed. It is not man that is to be the servant of truth and knowledge, but truth and knowledge shall be the servants of man. It is not knowledge and the pursuit of it that are absolute, but 'life' and the personal being of those who heed its demands, perhaps because it cannot in the last instance be 'known' and defined. Knowledge is fashioned by man and corrupted by man, and therefore it is perfectly conceivable – this is a situation Nietzsche delights in conceiving – that one kind of person is entitled to one kind of knowledge but not to another. What is this entitlement? What is it that makes one person, and not another, or one nation, or one age, entitled to metaphysical knowledge? Why is the question about the end-purpose of life appropriate to one culture, and the undoing of another?

For Nietzsche there is, ultimately, only one answer to these questions: the will to knowledge is to be identical with the will to power, which constitutes the being of man. There is an

---

[1] J. P. Stern, *Re-Interpretations: Seven Studies in Nineteenth-Century German Literature* (London 1964), pp. 221 ff.   [2] To Overbeck, 23 June 1881.

entitlement to one as there is to the other, and the amount of knowledge any man is to acquire should be commensurate with a man's, or a nation's, strength of will and capacity for life: 'Once and for all, there are many things I do *not* wish to know. Wisdom sets a limit to knowledge, too' (*GD* I §5). The pursuit of knowledge is to be determined, not by what *can* be known and what speculation, experiment and observation can make available (which provides very nearly *our* criteria for the pursuit of knowledge), but by a 'doctrine of the hygiene of life' (*U* II § 10) – a doctrine which, alas, apart from exalting 'life' the indefinable, remains unstated. What Nietzsche does formulate are the rudiments of a theory of *existential* entitlement, and to this we shall turn when considering the third and last of his moral experiments.

The idea of a personal entitlement to knowledge is inegalitarian and unscientific (in the sense that, from Plato's *Meno* onwards, all scientific as opposed to esoteric knowledge is seen as available to all rational men), but it is not an eccentric idea. As against scientific objectivity and the establishing of morally neutral 'laws', Nietzsche invokes the unity of the cognitive and moral aspects of man. Like Goethe before him he would like the quality of a man's knowledge (and, incidentally, also of his art) to depend on the quality of his moral–existential being, and (again like Goethe) Nietzsche hopes to achieve this without invoking a religious sanction. Yet the only analogy to this kind of reasoning is Christ's claim that the Pharisees' knowledge of the law is not enough and that only a certain moral state entitles to insight and judgement ('He that is without sin among you, let him first cast a stone at her', John 8: 7). The moral problem posed by this injunction is surely insoluble without a religious sanction (it is because he invokes divine authority – John 8:15–17 – that Christ claims the right to denounce the Pharisees' *dike*); and the same is true of Nietzsche's argument. Only by endowing 'life' with a quasi-religious, transcendent quality, and only by making man into a god, can he set up man as the measure and his enhancement as the goal of all things and all knowledge – yet of course Nietzsche's avowed aim is to do without all gods and all transcending of the human lot. And here we recognize the recurring pattern of Nietzsche's thought: the compulsion, repeated in one area of experience after another, that makes him group his reflections round an empty space – the space reserved for a grace from on high in a world where there is no grace and no on high either.

Yet if Nietzsche's attempts at rationalizing the idea of a personal entitlement to knowledge miscarry, his demonstration of what happens in the absence of such a 'doctrine of the hygiene of life' should not be lost on us. In a prophetic manner he describes the kind of freak whose knowledge is in excess of his existential capacity. Experienced in terms of moral knowledge, the tragedy of this imbalance is familiar to us: its name is *Hamlet*. Nietzsche however is equally concerned with scientific knowledge. In *Zarathustra* he castigates the papery imagination of intellectuals generally and historians in particular, who wield vast resources of information which in no way corresponds to what they are as human beings. In *Genealogy of Morals* he emphasizes the kinship of 'science' with 'the enemies of life', chief among them the anti-life ideals of asceticism. The possibility of an unlimited pursuit of knowledge, heedless of consequences, is 'unmasked' as the symptom of an age of decadence, and of a life whose defences against its enemies have been undermined. Modern scientists live an unnerving existence in which their knowledge is in no sort of harmony with their world or their personal being (*GM* III §23), and in a later note he adds: 'The fact that science as we practice it today is possible proves that the elementary life-preserving instincts have ceased to function...' (*WKG* VIII/3 pp. 180–1). Even without considering how little Nietzsche knew of contemporary science we can hardly fail to acknowledge the accuracy of the fore-vision. For what he is uncovering here is a set of problems which, buried under the dogma of the absolute value of knowledge, are a good deal more urgent in our age than in his own. Of course, with the experience of fascist anti-intellectualism and cliquishness in our minds, we are bound to regard the idea of differing entitlements to knowledge as shockingly undemocratic: we feel the need to insist on a just and equitable distribution of knowledge as of everything. A critic is not obliged to defend – though he may try to explain – Nietzsche's complete lack of interest in this and all other problems of equity and distribution. My present point, however, is not the political implication of Nietzsche's view, but his innocence of politics. The knowledge and science he talks about are states of mind of individual persons, wholly private phenomena whose social implications are left largely unexplored;

while his notion of 'life', too, alternates between the private and the cosmic spheres, leaving out the social and political world which, Nietzsche believes, is either governed by the individual will or made ungovernable by the democratic mob.

There is nothing dogmatically 'anti-scientific' or romantically 'irrationalist' in Nietzsche's attitude. On the contrary: a large number of observations, culminating in *The Joyous Science* of 1882, suggest that, for a time at all events, he takes pleasure in playing off the impartiality and exactness of the scientific attitude against the obscurantist claims of contemporary religion, and in looking forward to the advancement of science as to a new age of sobriety and enhanced vigour of culture and life. There is no contradiction in this. Science and the pursuit of knowledge are not 'absolutes'. They are approved when they further the cause of 'life' and denounced when they encroach upon it, *not* because they lead to truth, but because they lead to the great life-enhancing illusion called 'truth'. (Pontius Pilate, it appears, is the only real gentleman mentioned in the Gospels, *A* §46.) And if there are truths which destroy life, then this too is part of that cosmic economy – the cosmos not of 'Being' but of 'becoming' – whereby the greater will lives and expands at the cost of the lesser.

Life cannot be defined: to define it would be to subordinate it to reason, its servant. This logical conundrum turned out to have most disreputable consequences. It was handed down from Schopenhauer to Nietzsche, and from Nietzsche to Alfred Rosenberg, to Ernst Jünger in the twenties, Gottfried Benn in the early thirties, and a host of other influential authors. It takes the form of the following syllogism: (1) take x to be a man's intelligible 'character', his 'will', or 'will to power' or 'blood', or indeed anything postulated as *fundamental* to the being of man; (2) take y to be reason, or analytical reason, or criticism, or anything described as degenerate, pallid or hypercritical; then (3) any attempt to define x by y must fail because x is (said to be) the basis, or root, or ground ('Urgrund') of y, and it is clearly impossible to explain or define the fundamental by means of its derivative, the primary by means of the secondary.[1] (The fallacy of the argument derives from the notion of misplaced concreteness, as though x and y had different physical depths.)

Life cannot be defined, yet the claim made on its behalf is supreme: without life there are no values, no knowledge, and

---

[1]   See J. P. Stern, *Idylls and Realities* (London 1971), p. 209.

no 'will to power' either. And so it follows that all these – knowledge, values, the will and personal being of man – must be seen as relative to it. The argument is irresistibly circular: the ideals of nobility are those which further and sustain life, while life is that which is furthered and sustained by the true and authentic – the highest ideals...Can we get no further?

5

Nietzsche is a Protestant philosopher. Beyond truth there is, for him, truthfulness. And we can get at least a little further in our argument by recognizing that the essential 'relativeness' or 'perspectivism'[1] of his moral scheme (and of his other schemes too) is the sign of a mind that is attempting to respond as appropriately – as truthfully – as possible to each new set of circumstances that move into view, and turns the strenuousness of its perspectivism into the supreme value.

There is a family likeness about the answers we get to the question 'What is the value of values?' The value of truth is no more than equal to the value of illusion; the will – the only creator of values – is not a single thing but a series of inclinations determined by a flux of circumstances, the singularity of its name being no more than a linguistic and therefore practical convenience – a useful lie; the value of both esoteric and exoteric knowledge depends on the recipient and on what he makes of it; we perceive crudely and inaccurately, in distorting perspectives, and our language fails to reproduce even the prime colours, let alone the hues and shades, of our experience; the truth is supremely hard to get at and its value is relative to the difficulty of its pursuit, or again to the suffering which that pursuit entails; good is no good unless it is tested against overwhelming odds, value is valueless when it is asserted by another; moral precepts are not precepts unless they are generalized, and they cease to be worth obeying as soon as they are; compassion is weakness in one situation, strength in another; love is an aristocratic virtue, or again a decadent romantic sickness; history is debilitating, or again a source of myth and strength; nihilism is the nether end of decadence, or winter's last throes before spring sets in... There seems to be no end to these apparent or partial contradictions, all of them

---

[1] See, e.g. *WKG* vii/2 p. 142; *J* § 11: 'die Perspektiven-Optik des Lebens'; *FW* § 354.

illustrative of Nietzsche's insistence that man alone (and not fate, or a god, or society) is the bestower of values; that the personal being of man must determine what is valuable, and not the other way round; and that the insights man can achieve are not 'subjective' ('the subject', too, being a mere linguistic convenience), but relative and perspectivist:

It is the perspectivist mode that determines the [world's] character of 'appearance'. As if there were a world left over once you have taken away that perspective! Were you to do that, you would take away relativity!

Each centre of force [e.g. each individual] has its own perspective toward all the rest – i.e. its own particular valuation, its own modes of action and of resistance. The 'apparent world' therefore reduces itself to a specific way of acting upon a world, which emanates from a centre.

Now there is no other mode of action whatever; and 'the world' is merely a word for the total interplay [das Gesamtspiel] of these actions. Reality consists precisely in this particular action and reaction of each individual toward the whole...

No shadow of a right to speak here of 'appearance' remains...The antithesis between the apparent world and the real world is reduced to the antithesis 'world' and 'nothing' (*WzM* § 567).

And this 'nothing', incidentally, is no Heideggerian boa constrictor and annihilator of life but – nothing.

6

But what is life? There is no single topic on which Nietzsche has so lavished his descriptive gifts, and all that can be done here is to give a short selection of his views. It follows no chronology, for the writings of his middle period (*Aurora* of 1881 and *The Joyous Science* of 1882) look toward 'science' for the solution of the riddle of life with a confidence that soon wanes; and the changing views of Nietzsche's last period cannot be said to amount to an intellectual development. Even now, of course, Nietzsche is more concerned with the philosophical advocacy of a scientific point of view than with its concrete application. He is indeed an experimentalist. His posthumously published collections especially (from which many of these observations are drawn) must be read as a ceaselessly enterprising and unabatingly energetic series of experiments in ideas and words.

'Life', then, is a repudiation of all that is sick and near to death, it is cruel toward all that is weak and old in us and around us, a perpetual struggle waged always at the expense of another life,[1] it is impious toward dying and perpetually murderous ('And yet old Moses said: "Thou shalt not kill!"'). Its concern is not with distinctions but with antagonisms. It is not merely beyond good and evil, but also beyond all assent and denial, beyond all distinction of inner and outer, of form and matter, all logical finicking – yet reason and logic are among the fictitious procedures whereby life maintains itself. The assent to life entails the destruction of morality, which is nothing but the 'instinct to negate life' (or, as the Devil remarks to the hero of Thomas Mann's *Doktor Faustus*, 'Life, you know, isn't fastidious, and it doesn't give a damn for morality!').

What is life? It is being different and exercising strong preferences, being unjust and partial and limited; it is full of antagonisms, for 'the agreement of all is a principle hostile to life'; it rests on immoral presuppositions and flourishes in danger; it is not a mere desire-to-survive, but a wanting-to-grow; it is constantly being tested by the greatest possible odds and must maintain itself against the most profound discouragements – indeed it is that testing itself. It is not peace; on the contrary, where the antagonisms of men, classes and nations are appeased, and life's enemies – the sick, the mad, the criminal and the disinherited – are cosseted, there the pith of life declines; it is not happiness, but wherever life is in the ascendant, happiness is instinctive; it is not virtue, though virtue is only the way of life which the strong-willed impose; and its value cannot be assessed, for all assessments must take place *in* life ('and outside', says Wittgenstein,[2] 'you cannot breathe'), but it performs its valua-

---

[1] The following are the sources for the rest of this chapter: 'another life': *WzM* § 369; 'Thou shalt not kill': *FW* § 26; 'assent and denial': *WzM* § 351; 'all logical finicking': *U* III § 4; 'instinct to negate life': *WzM* § 343; 'strong preferences': *J* § 9; 'unjust and partial and limited': *Mus* XIV pp. 269–70; 'principle hostile to life': *Mus* XIV p. 271; 'immoral presuppositions': *WzM* § 461; 'flourishes in danger': *WzM* § 929; 'wanting-to-grow': *WKG* VIII/1 p. 153; 'profound discouragements': *Mus* XIV p. 130; 'vigour of life declines': *WzM* § 864; 'happiness is instinctive': *GD* II § 11; 'assessments must take place in life': *GD* II § 2; *J* § 9; 'valuations through us': *GD* V § 5; 'contenders grow unequally': *WzM* § 642; 'that process alone': *WzM* § 769; 'at odds with consciousness': *WKG* V/2 pp. 401–2; 'taking sides with life': *WzM* § 5461; 'the victory is never in doubt': *FW* § 110; 'value for life that ultimately decides': *WzM* § 493; 'contradictions can be thought': *WKG* V/2 pp. 401–2; 'anti-biological': *WzM* § 864, end; 'falsehood and exploitation': *WzM* § 968; 'life's justification must be sought': *WzM* § 1005.

[2] 'Es gibt kein draussen. Draussen fehlt die Lebensluft'. *Philosophical Investigations* (Oxford 1953), I § 103.

tions through us. Life is the enduring form of all the processes
in which force manifests itself and in which different contenders
grow unequally; it is the attempt to encompass and subjugate as
much as is in its power, and it derives pleasure and a sense of
well-being from that process alone. It is at odds with consciousness: indeed, consciousness is only possible to the extent that it
misunderstands and misinterprets the nature of life – 'the
ultimate truth about the flux of all things [which is life] does not
bear incorporating, our organs for living are programmed for
error...Life is the condition of knowledge. Error and delusion
are the condition of life – I mean the most profound errors. To
know them is not to be rid of them.' Hence 'the history of
philosophy is a secret raging against the presuppositions of life,
against the feelings of value inspired by life, against taking sides
with life'. Because perpetual hostility between life and consciousness is the rule in the world we inhabit, and because in the
struggle between life and knowledge the victory is never in doubt,
therefore 'truth is the kind of error without which a certain
species of being would not be able to live – it is the *value for life*
that ultimately decides'. Yet because 'contradictions can be
thought', Nietzsche experiments with the opposite idea, too,
embracing very nearly the ethos of the modern scientist, and thus
incidentally wiping out most of the arguments I have quoted:

Life has not disappointed me! Year by year I find it truer, more
desirable, more mysterious – from the day when the great liberating
thought dawned upon me that life may well be an experiment of the
knower – not a duty nor a predicament nor a swindle! And as for
knowledge: whatever it may mean for others – a bed of idleness, for
instance, or a road to a bed of idleness, and amusement or an empty
pastime – for me it is a world of perils and victories, where heroic
feelings too have their arena and playground. *Life is a means to
knowledge* – with this maxim in one's heart one can live bravely and even
joyfully, one can laugh joyfully! (*FW* §324)

What is life? Is the preservation of 'the species "man"' among
its concerns? That, at all events, is what we must assume if we
are not to conclude that all our moral and spiritual values are
hopelessly 'anti-biological'. But must we not conclude just this,
seeing that 'the Great Man' is what he is because 'he most
strongly embodies life's most characteristic qualities of injustice,
falsehood and exploitation'; or again that 'It is in its most
terrible, most ambiguous and most deceptive aspects that life's

justification must be sought'? Yet had Nietzsche not written, five years earlier, 'Life has not disappointed me! Year by year I find it truer, more desirable. . .'?

But if life is all these things, what is *not* life? The only thing it is not is *Being,* for if there were such a thing, it would be the arrest of the eternal process of *becoming*; though life exploits even this mendacious doctrine of Being in order to make the idea of an eternal flux endurable (*WKG* v/2 pp. 401–2), for there is no end to the deceptions, chimeras and ruses that life has learned to employ for its own mysterious ends.

There can be no doubt that even though Nietzsche's conception of life as a warlike process owes something to Heraclitus, it owes a good deal more to Darwin and his followers.[1] Why then is his attitude to Darwinism consistently hostile? Why does he call it 'true but lethal' (*U* II §9)?

Both Nietzsche and Darwin ignore the distinction between the many and the one, though for opposite reasons: Darwin to favour the many, Nietzsche to celebrate the one.

His objections are not based on any empirical study of Darwin's own data. They are broadly philosophical in being concerned partly with Darwin's methodological premises and partly with some of his ideological inferences. Chief among these is Darwin's idea of progress: mere survival of the fittest and consequent biological improvements in the strain do not, for Nietzsche, constitute any sort of enhancement of the value and dignity of man. To the question, 'Fittest for what?' Darwin would reply 'For survival', but to Nietzsche this is not a self-evident answer: why should the idea of mere survival provide a more valid teleology than, say, the living organism's 'desire to discharge its force', that is, its 'will to power' (*WzM* §§647, 650)? Similarly, what Nietzsche objects to among the methodological premises is the idea of gradualness as a fundamental scientific norm (this again, to Darwin, is axiomatic), and the idea of a 'law of evolution' which in some blind yet biologically purposeful way is supposed to determine the history of mankind. When Nietzsche claims that 'there are no transitions' (§684/1), he is reducing Darwin's unbroken chain of development to a series of discrete phenomena grouped according to an arbitrary taxonomy. It is not 'growth and reproduction' which are the salient

---

[1] Quotations from *The Descent of Man* (1871) and other references are taken from Benjamin Farrington's *What Darwin Really Said* (London 1966).

'characters' of life as Nietzsche sees it, but individual creation
– spontaneous and perhaps *ex nihilo* – and a random fatality
which we must love since we cannot change it. Darwin's
readiness to ignore the distinction between the biological and
moral aspects of the life of man has its parallel in Nietzsche's
insistence on the psychosomatic unity in which man's most
valuable actions, and 'the will to power' itself, are founded. But
while in Darwinian theory this merging (which constitutes the
evolutionary process) is what makes it possible to re-interpret and
in a sense downgrade the mental and moral as aspects of the
biological ('Darwin has forgotten the spirit – that is English!' *GD*
IX §14), Nietzsche's aim is very nearly the opposite: the
psychosomatic unity *he* postulates is intended to challenge and
discredit the Christian idea of the soul and its disembodied
spirituality by 'revaluing' the physical nature of 'life' and thus
endowing it with all the strength and all the fervour which
Christianity (and other 'backworld' religions) had once success-
fully invested in the domain of the purely spiritual.

Where Darwin sees 'adaptation and development of the
species' brought about by sheer numbers, Nietzsche emphasizes
the odds against the survival of complex living structures –
structures which are valuable in proportion to their being
complex and thus supremely vulnerable (*WzM* §684/2). He is
keenly aware of the catastrophic quality – 'the utter disorder' –
of the history of man. If there is a purpose in creation, it lies not
in the perfection of a natural order but in the autonomy of the
self-determining creative individual – whatever is perpetuated in
the form of a racial or tribal characteristic, by that token
degenerates. The Darwinian hypothesis of an ineluctable law of
biological progress is immoral (in terms of Nietzsche's 'supra-
morality'), the true value of life lies in the chanciness and
indeterminability of all that is exceptional. And yet: if 'the
average type' can be bred, why not its enemy, genius? In the early
eighties, the time of *Zarathustra*, Nietzsche (here following
Darwin) is taken with the Lamarckian theory of breeding
acquired moral and cultural characteristics. What turns him
against the idea is not the suspicion that such an inheritance
cannot be enduring. It is his old conviction (*U* III §5) that the
distance between the self-conscious, self-determining individual
and the rest of mankind is greater than the distance which
separates ordinary mankind from the animal kingdom; this is
his axiom.

Quantity, in Nietzsche's view, almost by definition imperils quality. When Darwin writes (in *The Descent of Man*) that a single man's sacrifice of his own life has no evolutionary significance, whereas 'a tribe [which included] many members who were always ready to give aid to each other and to sacrifice themselves for the common good, would be victorious over most other tribes; and this would be natural selection', Nietzsche passionately believes that, whether or not such biological moralisings are 'true', they are certainly 'lethal' to any idea of what *he* regards as the genuine enhancement of man:

Anti-Darwin. What surprises me most when I survey the great destinies of man is that I always see before me the opposite of what Darwin and his School see or want to see today: that is, selection working in favour of the stronger, the better-constituted, and the progress of the species. The opposite is palpably the case: happy accidents are eliminated, the more highly evolved types lead nowhere, it is the average and below average types which ineluctably ascend to power... That will to power in which I recognize the ultimate basis and character of all change furnishes us with the explanation of why selection does not operate in favour of exceptional and fortunate cases: the strongest and most fortunate are weak when they are opposed by the organized instinct of the herd, the timidity of the weak, the greater number. My total picture of the world of values shows that in the highest values which rule mankind today it is not the happy accidents, the selected types, who have the upper hand; on the contrary, it is the types in whom decadence is rife – perhaps there is nothing so interesting in the world as this unwelcome spectacle... (*WzM* § 685).

Survival, duration, numbers, biological usefulness – these are the enemies of Nietzsche's vision. The only value that matters is excellence issuing from catastrophe and deprivation, and proved in solitude and singularity, in the exception. Apart from that consistent emphasis on conflict, the 'life' that Nietzsche extols has nothing in common with the life which his Victorian contemporary had attempted to explain by giving Biology the purposeful intelligence of a God.

7

The second experiment: authenticity and the 'will to power'

This above all: to thine own self be true

(*Hamlet* 1: 3)

I

'Contradictions,' Nietzsche says (*WKG* v/2 pp. 401–2), 'can be thought', but they yield no coherent insight, for there is no limit to the implications that can be drawn from them. His reflections give us a series of vivid sketches of the moral problems that occupy him, but they provide no answer to that question which he would prefer to rule out of court but to which he cannot help constantly returning – the question whether 'life' is to be regarded as an end and value in itself or as a means to some end; and it is in this sense that 'life', amidst the countless scenes and descriptions he sets up for it, remains undefined and indefinable. As Nietzsche's religious views are centred round an absent deity, as his linguistic theory presents the elements of language in their relation to a silent centre, so his conception of moral values is related to a centre, named 'life', whose status and meaning remain a series of questions.

Yet there is no doubt that a fervent moral concern informs Nietzsche's criticism of the customary morality of 'good and evil' as well as his attempts to go beyond it; and that behind all the contradictions and paradoxes a moral sense, and with it a moral scheme of sorts, does emerge. If 'life' – the being of man in time – does not provide such a scheme, it must be sought in life's chief constituent, the discontinuous and catastrophic will to power, whose moral concomitant is the personal authenticity of man. There is no doubt that here for once Nietzsche is not content with 'an immensely fruitful intuition',[1] but that his aim is a systematic doctrine.

---

[1] E. Heller, 'The Modern German Mind: the Legacy of Nietzsche', in *Literary Lectures presented at the Library of Congress* (Washington 1973), p. 404.

The principle of authenticity as a moral value is stated on a number of occasions, from the time of his essay on Schopenhauer of 1874 (*U* III § 1) to *Ecce Homo* and the last notes of 1888:

What does your conscience say? – 'You shall become that you are.'[1]

Nietzsche takes this formulation from the Second Ode of Pindar's, but leaves his reader wondering whether it may not also contain a half-mocking, half-serious reference to the voice Moses heard in the burning bush, calling 'I am that I am'. However that may be, Nietzsche's meaning with its idiosyncratically religious overtone is clear, and entirely familiar. He is saying that the only absolute imperative a man should obey is that of his inward potential: whatever it is given to a man to become, *that* should indicate the direction, and be the goal, of his intense striving, his will. Authenticity is the deliberate coincidence of what a man is with what he can become. (And this is one way Nietzsche is able to square the ontological circle: Pindar's sentence, in Nietzsche's reading of it, acknowledges 'Being' – the being of man – as the valid ground of 'becoming'.)

As so often, Nietzsche here endows a classical apophthegm of exquisite obscurity with a meaning which is more sensational, and more modern, than the one it had originally. 'Become what you are now that you have learned what you are', Pindar had written (Nietzsche omits to mention 'learning'), and he adds a few lines later, 'But one must not fight against God', seeing that the gods dispense power arbitrarily (whereas Zarathustra tells his friends (II § 2): '*If* there were gods, how could I endure not to be a god! *Therefore* there are no gods'). In the context Nietzsche gives it, and seen as he wants it to be seen, as a moral principle, the apophthegm becomes a validation of the self by the simple – though decidedly strenuous – process of self-realization through seriousness and singlemindedness. To put it in the jargon of yesterday: it becomes the maxim of the doctrine of 'commitment'.

'Commitment' to what? This is a question Nietzsche does not ask; and when his existentialist disciples say, in effect, 'It does not matter: the choice of a gratuitous object or of an absurd task is better than no choice at all', Nietzsche may not agree, but he provides no ground on which to oppose them. 'Become that you

---

[1] *FW* § 270; cf. also *Z* IV § 1 and the subtitle of *EH*, 'How one becomes what one is'. Nietzsche first mentions the Pindaric apophthegm in a letter to Rohde, 3 November 1867; cf. also Kaufmann, *Nietzsche*, p. 159n.

are': this reduplication of the 'I' is emptiness itself. Not only does it not offer any guarantee of the moral quality of the 'I' that is thus being confirmed, but it sets up the quality of 'commitment', its intensity and earnestness, as the dominant *moral* quality and the criterion of good and evil. Of course, it is true to the point of banality that what Nietzsche has in mind is 'commitment' to a valuable goal: 'Your true self...lies immeasurably above that which you usually take to be your self' (*U* III § 1), it being understood (for reasons that will become clear in the next chapter) that 'your usual self' is your social self and therefore inauthentic. But is it not equally possible that 'your true self' may lie immeasurably below 'your usual self', and that society, its conventions and laws, may mercifully prevent its realization? Moreover, if authenticity is *the* dominant moral category, what criteria are left for 'high' and 'low'? Nietzsche rightly ridicules the Victorian hope that a new morality, which has freed itself from a transcendental Christian sanction, should really be very much the same as the morality previously attached to Christianity,[1] yet he does not stop to consider the necessary limits of any conceivable moral (or indeed any other) reform and thus the inevitable overlap between old and new. Like Marxism, his idea of authenticity lives on the Jewish and Christian moral capital he disowns. His remarkable description of 'the great deceivers' shows up the full ambiguity of the doctrine. Read by itself, it must be one of the finest portraits of the religious or political demagogue we have, even more relevant to our century than to Nietzsche's own:

> In all great deceivers a remarkable process is at work, to which they owe their power. In the very act of deception with all its preparations, the dreadful voice and face and gestures, amid the whole effective scenario they are overcome by *their belief in themselves*; and it is this belief which then speaks so miraculously, so persuasively, to their audience...For men believe in the truth of all that is seen to be firmly believed (*MA* I, § 52).

But in what way does *this* 'belief in oneself' differ from the belief Nietzsche commends in the context of 'You shall become that you are'? His moral intention – the intention to expose fanaticism and the histrionics of false belief – in this and similar sketches is not in doubt. In one of the central arguments of *Antichrist*

---

[1] See Bernard Williams, *Morality: an Introduction to Ethics* (Harmondsworth 1973), p. 97 and *WzM* § 243.

(§§ 53–4) he warns us that readiness for martyrdom has nothing to do with the truth of a cause; that men like Savanarola, Luther, Rousseau, Robespierre and Saint-Simon are no better than 'sick spirits, epileptics of the concept'; that strong beliefs are prison-houses of the mind; and that 'to have a conviction or a belief...is...a Carlylism', is not to belong to oneself but to be a means to another man's end. And in the same reflection (§ 54) in which he tells us that he does not like the look, the sinister mien of the fanatic, he also complains that 'men prefer seeing gestures (the fanatic's gestures) to hearing reasons'...Yet what *reason* is there for holding that the alternative to belief, 'the great passion' (*A* § 54) which Nietzsche identifies with the total person, is necessarily good? Why should being a scoundrel be better than acting one? He seems unaware that he is giving us nothing to distinguish the fanaticism that goes with bad faith from his own belief in the unconditioned value of self-realization and self-becoming – that is, from his own belief in the Superman. We for our part are bound to look askance at this questionable doctrine. We can hardly forget that the solemn avowal of this reduplicated self – the pathos of personal authenticity – was the chief tenet of fascism and national socialism. No man came closer to the full realization of self-created 'values' than A. Hitler.

But to say this is not enough. The fascist ideologists were not some obscure flat-earth cranks, nor are the Nietzschean ideas on which they drew as 'untimely' as he liked to think. With the demise of a religiously sanctioned morality and of its successor, the morality of duty, Nietzsche's conception of authenticity – of 'to thine own self be true' – represents a consummation of the secular searching for values which is central to the recent intellectual and political history of the West.[1] Only because it was so central could the totalitarian régimes claim that they were fulfilling the 'authentic' aspirations of intellectuals and 'the people' alike. Their claim was not as false as we like to think.

2

'The will to power', the cardinal concept of Nietzsche's only systematic venture, is intended as the centre-piece of a vast philosophical panorama; to its working-out he devoted the greater part of the last four years of his active life. He presents it as a principle discernible in all nature, in accordance with which

[1] See Lionel Trilling's last essay, *Sincerity and Authenticity*.

a self or 'a centre of power' expands beyond its own boundaries, asserts itself over another and strives to appropriate it.

Before we follow some of its ramifications, it may be helpful to recall the simple, common-sense base of the principle. It is precisely what Dr Johnson has in mind when, 'on his favourite subject of subordination', and in defiance of all Whiggish nonsense, he proclaims, 'So far is it from being true that men are naturally equal, that no two people can be half an hour together, but one shall acquire an evident superiority over the other.'[1] Johnson's 'acquire' points to the dynamic nature of the principle which, for Nietzsche in the throes of his experiment in system-building, has unlimited application.

The will to power is the agency whereby man, 'the weakest, cleverest being' (*WzM* §856), becomes master of the earth, yet it is not identical with life. If for Schopenhauer the 'will to life' was the fundamental principle of all being, Nietzsche challenges this view by arguing that where there is no 'life' there can be no 'will' either (*Z* II §12). 'Life', accordingly, appears as an amorphous, inchoate thing which needs the 'will to power' to impose a direction and purpose upon it. Thus the will to power becomes the impulse behind *distinct* activities, the principle which informs all human relationships and all of man's dealings with nature. Its realization through the course of history, in the rise and fall of worldly and spiritual institutions, provides man with the horizon necessary to sustain life itself, but it is equally to be seen as the motive behind all individual cultural, artistic and religious activity. It is the force at work behind all our valuations, behind the 'perspectivism' of our interpretations of the world, and behind the great philosophical fictions: 'To stamp the character of *Being* on the process of *becoming* – that is the highest will to power' (*WzM* §617, beginning). It is not confined to the human world but, like the 'reflectivity' of Leibnitz's monads, it is to be the principle and the distinguishing criterion of all life whatsoever (though the notes in which he tries to secure scientific foundations for it are embarrassingly amateurish).[2] It is the impulse behind the acquisition, ordering and creation of knowledge, and behind creativity itself. Logic too, including the

[1] 15 February 1766, see J. Boswell's *Life of Johnson* (Everyman edition, London 1938), vol. I, p. 318.
[2] See 'The Will to Power in Nature', a chapter in *The Will to Power* ed. W. Kaufmann, pp. 332–81.

law of contradiction, and our 'forms of cognition',[1] are manifestations of whatever happens to be the victorious form of
willing at any one time, for we are motivated, not by a 'will to
truth', but by the 'will to render the world thinkable' (*Z* II § 12).
In a reflection that is usually printed at the very end of *The Will
to Power* (§ 1067), concluding a dithyrambic sentence whose length
and rigorous syntax are meant to represent its subject in all its
richness and variety, Nietzsche writes:

This world...my *Dionysian* world of eternal self-creation and eternal
self-destruction, this mystery world of twofold voluptuous delight, my
'beyond good and evil', without goal unless the joy of the circle is a
goal, without will unless it is the circle's good will toward itself – do you
want a *name* for this world? A *solution* of all its riddles? A *light* for you
too, you who are the best concealed, the strongest, the most intrepid,
the most midnightly of men? *This world is the will to power and nothing
else besides.* And you too are that will to power, and nothing else besides.

'And nothing else besides?' It is certainly true that as soon as
we try to see human conduct in the light of this single principle,
a multitude of insights opens up. We find that the 'will to power'
is involved in every political activity and (if the confessions of our
scientists are anything to go by) in the sciences as well; it colours
the whole gamut of our feelings and emotions, and is present
in every social and familial context. It is hard to think of a
mundane situation in which it is not present: a quarrel between
two friends about an ascertainable fact; the contest inherent in
every erotic encounter and in the sex-act itself; the functions of
the teacher, the preacher, the boss, the adviser are unthinkable
without involving the exercise of power – but also the roles of the
benefactor and alms-giver of every kind, the man who 'loves to
surprise', who 'gladly forgives', the superior conversationalist
à la Dr Johnson, the man who shames you by his misfortune, let
alone the one who shames you by being on top of the world. Nor
is there any doubt about the 'supra-*moral*' nature of all these
insights. The principle, if applied (as Nietzsche proposes to apply
it) as a critique of our customary notions of good and evil,
enables us to discriminate between different actions according to

---

[1] But this is contradicted by Nietzsche, see *Mus* XIV p. 58, discussed below. The
argument is taken to its ultimate absurdity by H. Marcuse when he claims (in
chapter 5 of *One-Dimensional Man*, London 1964) that 'post-Aristotelian logic'
reflects, and conspires to keep alive, modern technological totalitarian society.

the strength or weakness of the will involved in these actions. The criteria for good and evil which we thus establish Nietzsche considers to be superior to those of a more ordinary kind of morality. However that may be, a superior or 'supra-morality' still remains a scheme for distinguishing between good and evil. And if we now ask what is *not* to be identified as this 'will to power', what in this scheme is a 'non-value', the answer (like the answer to the question, What is *not* 'life'?) will be: all forms of passive response to the expansive nature of the will, that is, all forms of decadence, tiredness and despair. In the human sphere Nietzsche calls this resistance 'Ressentiment', by which he means a reactive grudgingness whose endless, 'eternal' chronicle is all of human history. But to acknowledge the illuminating insights which the principle of 'the will to power' vouchsafes is still very far from accepting it as the total explanatory principle of existence in the world.

For if it really is the monistic explanation Nietzsche proclaims it to be, how are we to account for the sheer variety of the phenomena in which this will 'objectifies' itself – that variety in the detailed descriptions of which Nietzsche excels? Is it really convincing to claim that a man's loving, caring, instructing, finding out and reflecting do not merely involve 'the will to power' but are 'nothing else besides'? It is not difficult to accept 'the will to power' as a disposition of mind aiming at the subjugation of any object outside myself; but if this *object*, this '*Gegen*stand', too, is to be seen as a product of that will, we are back in the Idealist's trap of a solipsistic universe. There is a gratuitousness in the assumption that a man is incapable of pursuing a cause which is not his self – that, in effect, no cause exists in the world – and these are implications Nietzsche would not be willing to accept. But we have already seen more than one argument which leads to consequences at odds with his intentions.

Instead of pressing this logical point, let us turn once again to Nietzsche's favourite mode of thought, the historical: we shall find that here, too, the monism does not work. If there is anything in the recent 'Nietzschean' era that comes close to an embodiment of 'the will to power', it is Hitler's life and political career; and this is so even if we assume (as we have good reason for assuming) that Nietzsche's imagination falls far short of this reality. The abstruse, occasionally absurd and almost invariably a-historical subterfuges Marxist and Freudian interpreters are put to when attempting to isolate the major motive force of politics generally, and Hitler in particular, leave little doubt that Nietzsche's identification of the 'will to power' is a good deal more direct and convincing. The neglect of the analysis he offers us – the unwillingness to believe that the desire for power, destructive power at that, can constitute an independent dominant motive – has led and perhaps still leads Western liberal politicians to underestimate the sheer intensity of the power-political struggle in societies whose legal and constitutional arrangements they like to regard as old-fashioned or primitive. Nietzsche's warnings on this score may be ambivalent – he is, at times, not without admiration for the monster tyrant – but they are warnings all the same, and had they been heeded, the history of Europe in the first half of our century might have been different.

Yet there is in Hitler (and men like him) a destructiveness at work which seems to go beyond any conceivable assertion or expansion of the self, beyond any will to *power*, to the point of a 'will-to-nothingness' which is wholly negative. Is this 'Wille in's Nichts' (*WzM* § 55), which Nietzsche sees rising up at the moment when 'all existence has lost its "meaning"', an extension of the 'will to power' and therefore redeemable by it; or is it an independent principle, rather like 'the Thanatos principle' which Freud invented in the early 1930s? Are there any grounds for thinking that decadence and nihilism are subsequent stages on the road to 'a higher, brighter mankind'? The question, left open by Nietzsche, is of considerable importance for his prognosis for European history.

He conceives the 'will to power' as the heir to Western decadence, but only if it really is the all-encompassing monistic principle of Being can it also be seen as a redemption from nihilism. It is because they saw it as such a monism – as disease and cure alike – that countless German intellectuals embraced national socialism, the ideology which promised 'the will's' greatest unfolding.

We know that this promise was false, that the destructive will can operate as an independent principle, not redeemable by itself. Nietzsche did not know this clearly enough. The charge is not that he did not mind what its fullest consequences might be but that, not recognizing its destructiveness for the unredeemable thing it is, he failed to envisage those consequences clearly enough. This, presumably, is why he allows himself to set off his foresights with expressions of intent. He does anticipate the future – not always, however, as a true prophet, but sometimes as one of its accomplices.

3

The attempt has been made to salvage this 'will to power' for traditional moral philosophy by claiming that Nietzsche conceived of it as 'the will to overcome oneself'.[1] This would place him squarely in the same tradition as St Paul, Spinoza and Schopenhauer, though it would then be hard to see what was so original, or notorious, about his moral ideas. Now it is true that Nietzsche's idea of 'the will to power' does not necessarily take the form of the master–slave relationship, but includes 'sacrifice and service and amorous glances' among its subterfuges (*Z* II §12). Indeed, the 'power' which is the will's goal need not be conceived in any such barbaric ways as the Italian and French fascists and the German national socialists conceived of it (though it cannot be denied that the intellectual superstructure of these political movements is as inconceivable without Nietzsche's ideas as these movements are without their superstructure). It is also true that this 'will' does not necessarily entail the actual physical or psychic destruction of, or encroachment on, another will, since Nietzsche is sometimes content to identify it with 'a feeling of increase and power' which needs no confirmation from overt violence. It does entail a self-overcoming, but only where wantonness, cupidity and the like act as impediments to its full exercise: 'Only the degenerate [regard]...annihilation, castration [and other such violent means] as indispensable', for they are too weak-willed to practise moderation (*GD* 5, §2). But when he writes (*WKG* v/i p. 687) that, contrary to 'what the Germans think', strength need not 'reveal itself in hardness and cruelty' and that it may reside 'in mildness and stillness', Nietzsche is not offering an alternative to the 'will to power', but is on the contrary suggesting that the principle of conquest is no

---

[1] Kaufmann, *Nietzsche*, pp. 200, 248, etc. I agree that 'interpreters of Nietzsche who see men as constantly "overcoming" themselves and rising higher and higher in a long succession of overmanliness miss the key point' (T. B. Strong, *Friedrich Nietzsche and the Politics of Transfiguration*, Berkeley 1975, p. 266).

more confined to a crude show of force than it was to 'the dreadful voice and face and gestures' of the false prophet and demagogue.

Nietzsche (like Freud after him) frequently considers the possibilities and conditions of a sublimation of 'the will' (which he sometimes identifies with 'drives' or 'instincts'), and its transformation into artistic or scientific creativeness. Provided the process of sublimation does not entail a weakening of the original 'drive', and provided there is enough to sublimate (one is reminded of Roy Campbell's 'You use the snaffle and the curb all right,/But where's the bloody horse?'), Nietzsche views this process positively – but again its end purpose is an enhanced self, by which he means an increase in its will to power and thus its capacity for conquest. There is a 'will to truth', a 'will to knowledge', and a will which is instrumental in the creating of values, yet they are all deemed decadent unless they are subordinated to the increase of the self. The purpose of all self-overcoming that is not decadent is the validation of command: every Judaic or Christian 'thou shalt' is to be translated into 'I will'. Self-overcoming in the service of a moral or spiritual law (as in Christian or Kantian morality) or in the service of a common good is rejected and so is the idea of self-overcoming for its own sake: wherever a lower self is overcome for the sake of a higher self, 'wherever there is decline and the falling of leaves, there life is sacrificing itself for the sake of power!' (*Z* II §12).

By designating the 'will to power' as the ultimate good, Nietzsche is not, of course, going 'beyond good and evil'; is not (as he claimed) constructing an 'amoralism'. He is making of that 'will' the principle of a moral doctrine for the enhancement of an elect self as a means to the enhancement of a similarly elect portion of mankind – only Nietzsche is not interested in how the transition from the self to mankind is to be effected, whether there might not have to be some rules to make that transition possible, and whether it were not inevitable that such rules will modify the self and the criteria of its election. But then Nietzsche never is interested in the problem of numbers.

4

But the gravest objection to any scheme or system based on the principle of the 'will to power' is the universality claimed on its behalf, which gives it the inflexibility of a Platonic idea and carries with it a denial of much that is characteristically Nietzschean and existential in Nietzsche's thinking. As soon as the 'will to power' is conceived as a universal scheme, it is worsted by the same destructive paradox as is Marx's 'law of universal history', which is his doctrine of the class struggle and of the determination of the political and cultural 'superstructure' of any society that ever was by its economic 'base'. Both Marx's and Nietzsche's schemes are said to 'produce' history, to make relative all values so produced, and thus to provide a strong refutation of any idea of perennial values. Yet, standing outside all history, the schemes themselves are a-historical. They have ascribed to them that perennial validity and relevance which they were intended to challenge and undermine: they subvert their own criticism. Strangely enough, this is not an objection either Nietzsche or (I think) Marx cares to raise.

5

Here if anywhere is Nietzsche's positive system of metaphysics. It arises at the point where the 'will to power' (which is his greatest single reflective experiment) is identified with value judgements (which are the inveterate consistency of his thinking).

Among a number of possible modes of being, man's being in this, his only world is inextricably involved in valuations: being *is* the setting up of tables of values and judging in accordance with them.[1] They in turn are products of man's willing: manifestations of his 'will to power', they are created by the master, accepted and obeyed by the slaves. Whatever is valuable (because constituted by the strongest will) is true. There is no other truth. Or rather, if *this* truth is illusory, at least it is not doubly so, as are those for which it is claimed that they are deeper, or higher, or more valuable, than 'the world of mere appearances' and the products of the will to power. This world of appearances however is 'the "real" or "true" world', and there is no 'Truth'. But if there is no other truth than that which

---

[1] See Eugen Fink, *Nietzsches Philosophie* (Stuttgart 1960), pp. 127–8.

relates to the things in the world (and they are 'always in relationship'), how can we know that the idea and system of an all-encompassing 'will' are true? How can man, the agent of any one specific 'will to power', know it in its metaphysical totality?

A quandary very much like this was bequeathed to Nietzsche by Schopenhauer,[1] who 'solved' it by postulating in man a unity of perceiving subject with perceived object, and declared this unity to be mystical and all-encompassing. Nietzsche is too honest for such subterfuges. What wrecks his hopes for a grand system and saves him from getting stuck with a monstrous unworkable principle is his intellectual honesty, which is full of the seeds of self-destruction; when it forces him to break his own 'system' asunder, he will not hesitate to do so:

What if *either* the hypothesis of the will to power ceases to be adequate (*WKG* v/i pp. 415–16) because it turns out to be 'a metaphor that can mislead' (*WKG* viii/iii p. 186), a mere reification (*Mus* xvi p. 61) of very diverse phenomena which are better considered separately; *or* the conclusion becomes inevitable that the pursuit of knowledge is an end and principle in its own right, so much so that life itself turns out to be 'a means of knowledge and an experiment of the knower' (*FW* § 324)? Is knowledge one of the agents of the 'will to power', or the will to power one of the objects of knowledge? No answer that Nietzsche gives to these questions remains uncontradicted.

The doctrine of 'the will to power' as it emerges from the convolute of Nietzsche's last notes cannot be accommodated within any non-catastrophic, eudaemonic scheme. Whether its notion of power is subtle or crude, concrete or abstract, it remains a doctrine of conquest and domination. It is certainly not an invitation to self-indulgence in any ordinary sense. At their most consistent, Nietzsche's reflections point in the opposite direction, away from all comfort. And the bleak values which will receive his assent cannot be described as 'a striving and perfecting to transcend and perfect oneself',[2] unless it be a perfecting for death.

---

[1] See *Die Welt als Wille und Vorstellung*, vol. 1 § 18.
[2] Kaufmann, *Nietzsche*, p. 248.

8
Discontinuities

That monster, custom, who all sense doth eat...

(*Hamlet* III: 4)

Neither of the two experiments we have considered so far fulfils Nietzsche's or his critical reader's expectations; neither 'life' nor 'the will to power' provides that all-encompassing principle and moral–existential scheme according to which humanity is to be judged and improved. There is a third possibility, but before considering it we must turn to another question. We have more than once noted the fragmentariness and 'aphoristic' character of Nietzsche's thinking; his impatience with all system and ideology, and his readiness to be bored with expatiation are the price he must pay for the versatility and liveliness of his philosophical imagination. But can we see beyond the signs of his impatience? Our concern in this chapter is with the essential limitation of Nietzsche's thinking.

A number of seemingly disconnected observations will point the way. When Hans von Bülow returned Nietzsche's 'Manfred Meditation' to him (24 July 1872), he described it as the most unmusical and disagreeable composition he had seen in a long while, and then added: 'Are you aware that you are making incessant mockery of all rules of tonal composition, from the higher musical syntax to quite ordinary grammar?' Where in this extravagant Wagnerian fantasy, von Bülow asked, is the Apolline element? The reference is to one of the two central categories of *The Birth of Tragedy* which had appeared earlier that year: and in that work too (as we shall see) the Dionysian – catastrophic – impulse dominates the Apolline principle of coherent form, even though it has been Nietzsche's intention to give equal status to both modes. Again, while as a writer Nietzsche certainly does not disregard 'all rules of composition', his theoretical view of language, like his view of literature, is essentially atomistic: if meaning and value are to be found anywhere (he argues), it is in the single discrete elements, in metaphors and individual moments of truth. Just as the architectonic is the weakest aspect of his own books, so his observations on other men's books (after *The Birth of Tragedy*) tend to be confined to brilliant *aperçus* and single impressions. The category of the single and individual prevails in every argument, even where it seems irrelevant. Both 'life' and 'the will to power', we recall, were seen as principles relating to the being and morality of individual persons only – on the occasions when the ethos of groups is considered, it is seen as wholly at the mercy of the charismatic leader. Nietzsche's consistent preference is clear: he is always for the single man against the herd, for genius against justice, for grace against deserts; he favours inspiration against the rule of rules and professional competence, and the heroic in every form against all that is 'human, all too human'. The catastrophic – non-gradual – perception, the unpremeditated insight and sudden conviction, the flash-like inspiration – these, for Nietzsche, are the authentic modes of knowledge-and-experience. And even though, in the 'positivist' period of *The Joyful Science* (1882), he praises knowledge which matures slowly and convictions which are deeply considered, the very form in which he does it shows that this is not the way *he* works. The method he favours (though he does not always follow it) is to proceed *via* 'single little questions and experiments' (*M* § 547), for these alone (he is convinced) satisfy the exacting demands of the modern scientific era. He attacks historians (in the third and fourth of *Thoughts Out of Season*) for burying great men under a welter of facts, for replacing genuine insights with endless continuities, and for denying that there is genius which does not develop as they develop – slowly, gradually, tediously. 'My way of reporting historical facts,' he writes in a note of 1879, 'is really to tell the story of my own experiences *à propos* of past ages and men. Nothing coherent: some things became clear to me, others did not. Our literary historians are boring because they force themselves to talk about and pass judgement on everything, even where they have experienced nothing (*WKG* IV/3 p. 390). The single experience – 'Erlebnis' – is all.

There is no end of such observations, and they all point to a pervasive limitation of Nietzsche's thinking: it is his consistent neglect of the world 'where two or three are gathered together', his indiscriminate bias against what I shall call *the sphere of association*. And to ignore this sphere, as Nietzsche ignores it, is to offer a misleading account of an important part of our world.

By this I mean that in all his philosophizing he has nothing really positive to say about, and is deeply suspicious of, all those human endeavours – in society, art and religion, in morality, even in the natural sciences – in which single discrete insights and experiences and encounters – single situations – are stabilized and made reliable by means of rules and laws and institutions – by structures – leading to new associations or combinations, which in turn bring about new situations.

There are wholes which are undeniably more than their parts, structures which create stability, or again ossification; repetitions, which create rhythms and boredom. Contexts give meanings which single words do not possess. Systems fill in blank spaces in experience, not always with lies. The nexus which leads from words to actions and from actions to changes in the world around us is almost always unstable, unpredictable, and sometimes none the worse for that. And syllogisms operate, irrespective of the intention placed in their premises: logic works, regardless of the personal being of man.

Nietzsche however believes – the belief informs his choice of reflection and aphorism as his favourite literary media – that the part is greater, or at least truer, less misleading, than the whole.

It sometimes seems as if he regarded all entailment and continuity, which are germane to the associative process, as disconnected from specifically *human* existence, indifferent to the dictates of man's will, and therefore as something inhuman. We cannot be sure. What we do know is that he sees man's search for stability almost always as an arrest of living experience, an inauthentic pursuit, a fear of the rigours of solitude, a failure of independence and courage – as a defection from the heroism of singularity.

Tradition, dogma, formulation itself amount for him to a second order of experience, a spurious, reach-me-down reality. Institutionalization as man's only protection against arbitrariness means little to him. Nowhere is this more patent than in his wholesale rejection of the Christian Church in the world, as though the word of Jesus (which he does not reject wholesale) could get around without 'two or three gathering together in his name'. And if, in traditional Romantic fashion, Nietzsche occasionally vilifies 'the State' and glorifies 'the Nation' (Z 1 § 12), he does so for the simple and predictable reason that he regards the former as the coldest of cold institutional monsters, while in the latter he sees a 'natural' extension of the private self. To enlist him, on the strength of such opinions, either on behalf of the nationalists or of political liberals is equally absurd.

Yet strong political implications follow from this emphasis on 'the sudden', and the isolated 'Erlebnis'. It cannot be denied that this affective rhetoric (rehearsed in numerous metaphors of unbridled violence, strokes of lightning, volcanic eruptions and other such subtleties) was to become central to the ideology of Italian and German fascism and that, with the help of men like Gabriele D'Annunzio and Dietrich Eckart,[1] it would one day be translated from the literary–philosophical sphere into political fantasy, and thence into practical politics. Is it meaningful to make Nietzsche responsible for this process? We must certainly absolve him from responsibility for its last stages. Again the question arises: can lack of prescience be blameworthy? Yet had he discovered a philosopher in a similar predicament, facing a similar charge, it is unlikely that Nietzsche would have exonerated him. There never was a thinker more ready to equate failure of the imagination with moral–existential failure.

'All human error is impatience, a premature breaking-off of method': this aphorism of Franz Kafka's[2] could have been written with Nietzsche in mind, and Nietzsche would have acknowledged the verdict it implies. For what it comes to, in the last resort is that he – Nietzsche – does not believe in his own beliefs enough to be circumspect about the conditions in which they might one day be realized. Yet in voicing this criticism one is hardly doing more than applying what he teaches.

In the dialectic which lies at the core of all human experience Nietzsche always favours the unique against repetition and genius against justice. We may leave to one side for the moment the question whether this is a practicable point of view: what undermines his advocacy and limits his perception is that he hardly admits the presence of a genuine dialectic, of an inescapable human problem. Yet although it is inescapable, the problem is of course not insoluble – indeed, all civilized life depends on its on-going solutions; but then, Nietzsche often writes as though this were enough to make civilization itself suspect and by definition decadent. He loves 'brief habits' and hates 'the tyranny of long-standing ones' (*FW* IV § 295). He sees

---

[1] In most other contexts these two men are not to be mentioned in the same breath.

[2] In 'Betrachtungen über Sünde, Leid, Hoffnung und den wahren Weg', 2.

hell populated by 'courtiers, lawyers, customs-officials...
grocers...and all those the balance of whose work consists in
waiting – waiting until somebody comes and speaks to you'
(*WKG* v/2, p. 547), and he notes that life in the big cities is run
by people who find occupations of this kind much to their taste.
We see his point and agree, instantly and as a matter of course
– who does not vaunt a dislike of customs-officials and grocers?
– yet we hardly know how to support life as Nietzsche did,
outside the reassuring embrace of routine.

The signs of Nietzsche's refusal to come to terms with this mode
of human experience are everywhere. He writes splendidly on
Goethe and shows a more intimate understanding than many
literary historians of the nature of Goethe's poetic genius and
generous humanity. For Goethe's love of custom and habit,
however, for that part of the poet's genius which hallows the
everyday and thereby gives it lasting value, Nietzsche seems to
have no spontaneous understanding at all. In *The Joyous Science*,
the happiest and most equanimous of his books, there is a
passage (IV §334) which suggests the opposite. It reads like a
paraphrase of one of Goethe's most characteristic poems,[1] for it
demonstrates in fine detail the virtues of gradual discovery,
patient familiarization and growing habit which (as Nietzsche
affirms) are involved in 'learning to love', whether it be 'music
or any other things'. Yet there never was a philosopher who had
so little of the habit of patience with things or people. He writes
as one who fervently believes he ought to 'learn to love', but
whose will is at odds with his intentions.

We shall see that art above all is, for Nietzsche, the enemy of
the hebetude of custom and repetition. Among the reasons why
he is so intent on assigning to the aesthetic activity a central role
in human existence is his understanding of it as a mode of
experience which, more than any other, escapes the sphere of
association and lives by the appearance of uniqueness. A good
many of his political remarks, including the early essay on *The
Greek State*, must be seen in this light: as attempts to heroify the
political activity by interpreting it as the highest, Apolline form
of aesthetics and by identifying the political leader with the artist
in human 'material' (*WzM* §975). (And when, incidentally but not

---

[1] See e.g. Goethe's 'Die Metamorphose der Pflanzen' (1798), lines 70–1: 'O,
gedenke denn auch, wie aus dem Keim der Bekanntschaft/Nach und nach in
uns holde Gewohnheit entspross,/...'

surprisingly, men like B. Mussolini took their cue from these remarks, they were not misinterpreting them.)

Nietzsche's disregard of the 'associative' mode does not, as we have seen, prevent him from launching into huge and occasionally questionable generalizations. They are conceived as multiplications of individual instances, not on the level of abstract concepts. Sometimes they are the signs of his impatience, but at other times they seem to spring from his innermost trust that the single case *he* knows, cites and generalizes is the exemplary one – a sort of epistemological *amor fati*. The fact that he is not really intent on conceptualizing his insights is one of his attractions for other writers and artists, and one of the sources of his influence as a 'philosopher of life'. But it also limits the range of his criticism when faced with conceptual problems. To take for example his reflections on causality: perhaps the most important of them is his interpretation of 'our concept of "cause"' as 'our feeling of power [which derives] from the so-called act of the will, and our concept of "effect" as the superstition that this feeling of power is the motive power itself' (*WzM* § 689); similarly, he criticizes 'our inability to interpret what happens except as something that is intended to happen...the belief that all that happens is a doing and all doing presupposes a doer' (*WzM* § 550). Here conceptual criticism turns into psychological suspicions – this is what he calls 'my method of the evil eye'. However illuminating this procedure may be, it also means that a critique of the concept of causality in instances where that concept cannot be related to 'our feeling of power' does not get under way. And the same is true, as we have already noted, of his occasionally brilliant yet rudimentary analytical remarks on language. For when we come to the concluding question of the reflection I have just quoted – 'Is an intention the cause of an event?' – we should expect him to press the enquiry and look for an answer in a critique of the many-faceted nature of language, in the course of which, as Wittgenstein discovers,[1] words (including those which express 'intentions') take on the function of deeds. But Nietzsche leaves it at the question.

His consistent rejection of the sphere of association forms undoubtedly the most important limitation of his philosophical thinking. It is also the most disturbing of his limitations, because it is breached by no dialectic of questions and hypothetical

---

[1] *Philosophical Investigations*, I, §§ 241, 546.

answers, by no speculative experiments. Moreover, in this attitude he is in no way original, in no way 'the unique event and exception' in the culture of his country. Here he belongs to a dominant German tradition which goes back to Martin Luther and perhaps beyond.

Whenever social considerations may legitimately be translated into considerations of personal value and dignity, Nietzsche's full critical understanding is brought into play:

> The machine is impersonal, it deprives a piece of work of its pride, of the individual good and the faultiness which adhere to everything not machine-made – it deprives work of its bit of humanity. Time was when with every purchase from a craftsman one singled out the person with whose signs one surrounded oneself: in this way household goods and clothing became symbols of mutual esteem and personal community – nowadays we seem to live surrounded by anonymous and impersonal slavery. Improvement in working conditions must not be bought too dearly. (*MA* II/2 § 288)

But there are aspects of social life (such as the law, or politics, or economic exchange) which have a dialectic of their own and to which, therefore, immediate personal value judgements are irrelevant. Nietzsche's reflections on these topics show up the bad discontinuity of his thought; here his influence is at its most retrograde. One's criticism is not that he fails to provide what he never attempted – a systematic sociology – but that the view of society *and* of the individual entailed by his reflections on social morality issue in an almost absolute individualism which does not provide an account of the way things are in the world.

Characteristically, almost the only form of government that interests him is rule through a leader's or an oligarchy's absolute exercise of power. But because he does not explore the ways in which even autocratically governed societies are formed and sustained by custom and convention – does not ask how much of the old is bound to survive into the new – he cannot explain rule by command except with the aid of catastrophic 'natural' factors. And since for him, in this context, the 'natural' is an irreducible category (*WzM* § 916), the conception of society that emerges from his observations is not that of a self-contained functional system, but a system that works by virtue of its relationship to something outside itself (it is in this sense that the fascist leader claimed to be and indeed was, and the communist leader is, outside politics). Sometimes this outside force is nature, sometimes it is fate, sometimes it is a present god, or again a *deus absconditus* – yet what Nietzsche intends is the opposite, is a self-contained system of rule. His explicit aim, especially in *Zarathustra*, is to make men self-reliant and self-determining, content with their earthly lot and free from all need of gods, yet the arrangements of social and political life that would be required to institute such an autonomous humanity do not interest him. The 'will to power', conceived as the dominant force at work in such a system, is hypostatized into a natural force which encroaches on human society from outside.

Historical change as Nietzsche sees it is brought about by great men who impose their will on the birth–florescence–decay cycles of whole cultures, and these cycles are conceived on the analogy of plant life. Between the two poles of individual psychology and cosmic or millennial speculation – between the Superman and the doctrine of 'the eternal recurrence of the same' – there seems to be a void; or rather, not a void, but the curiously unreal picture of a society which is both rigid and provisional, and which must be totally transcended. (To take an example from his last reflections on 'the modern age – the age of the degeneration of instinct': It is a sign of this degeneration, Nietzsche writes (*GD* IX §40), 'that one has allowed a Workers' Question to arise' by conscripting 'the worker', by giving him the vote, and by making him class-conscious and resentful of 'the injustice of his depri-vations'...There is no suggestion here that the status of 'one' – whoever that may be – or of 'the worker' is other than preördained; no understanding that this society, seen as a huge decaying organism, is moved by anything other than those forces of 'instinct'; and no suspicion that to ascribe 'instinct' to one social class rather than another is not a self-evident thing to do.)

It is Nietzsche's readiness to follow the fashion of 'social Darwinism' and resort to its explanations of all social change as the result of a life-and-death struggle – again the analogy with fascist ideologies is at hand – which leads to his conception of society as a thing rigid and unadaptable to gradual change. What makes the picture so unreal is that societies seem to move from complete stability (which he always identifies with oppressive inertia) through sudden catastrophe or authoritarian command to total re-formation: but this, we know, is not how societies change.

Perhaps it is misleading to speak as though Nietzsche presented an actual 'picture' of this or that society, real or utopian, for his sketches are never detailed enough for that. What he does is to offer certain moral and ethical exhortations – here is one from each phase of his philosophizing: 'I know of no greater purpose in life than to be destroyed by that which is great and impossible!' (*U* II §9); 'There have been a thousand goals hitherto, for there have been a thousand peoples: only the yoke for the thousand necks is lacking – the one goal!' (*Z* I §15); 'I teach that there are higher men and lower men, and that a single individual can under certain circumstances justify the existence of whole millennia!' (*WzM* §997) – and from such exhortations and invectives he lets us infer the sort of society at which they are directed. Its ethos is always the ethos of the market place – it is by definition unheroic and inherently decadent.

In addressing the heroic individual man as though such a man stood wholly outside the social nexus, Nietzsche ignores some of the most important insights of social thought in his age. Early sociologists, among them Marx and Durkheim, but also Max Weber, have shown at length that the individual self, in any living sense, *even as a self* is already implicated in a system of social and moral conventions; that it is nothing ('the merest vapourings of Idealism', Marx calls it) without having some relationship to this system; that, as E. H. Carr once put it, Robinson Crusoe is an Englishman and a native of the City of York. The recognition that any act of reform or revolution must be understood in relation to 'the full and explicit realization of the idea of society as a definite circumstance, the main condition of individual life'[1] is a commonplace, but it is not part of Nietzsche's reflective horizon. He does not quarrel with the central insight of his age: he does not seem to be aware of it. What he attacks as an aspect of the decadence of his world we cannot but regard as an essential part of the human condition itself.

But is it really true to say that Nietzsche does not sufficiently explore the relationship between social convention and the individual's will to power? After all, it is he who not only asserts but shows in convincing detail the 'genealogy of morals' from clerical prohibition and taboos to moral dogmas; in a famous passage in *The Dawn* (§9) he argues the '*mores*' origin of morality; in *The Genealogy of Morals* he describes the source of guilt feelings and the etiology of 'the bad conscience' and points

[1] Lionel Trilling, *The Opposing Self* (London 1955), p. 176.

to the sadistic origin of most social and spiritual ideals...While we appear to claim that his knowledge of – or at least his interest in – society is inadequate, are we not really proposing a different, rival social morality? If our argument relating to 'the sphere of association' is correct, it follows that Nietzsche's ideas about morality are in an important sense defective and impracticable. Comparison with a more orthodox scheme – less original but more realistic, more like what we know to be the nature of our moral experience – will help us to particularize the defect of his scheme.

In an essay entitled 'Three Strands of Morality', Dorothy Emmet[1] describes the grounds from which moral conduct issues; she calls them, 'custom, reciprocity and Grace'. (1) A good many of the decisions we take in the course of our day are made uncritically and without reflection. It may be a banal point, and it is certainly a point ignored by Nietzsche, that life (in no very august meaning of that word) would come to a halt were it not possible to rely on unspoken, unreflected, unchallenged bits of daily conduct, which are yet part of moral life, that is, of our experience of better and worse, good and evil. Even a self-supporting commune of Californian flower children must either evolve a set of such *mores* for itself or (this is more likely) transplant them from the society they have repudiated. (2) At any point where these *mores* are challenged and cease to be self-evident (Miss Emmet writes), 'a reflection on the mixed set of customs which make up [the first] strand' must set in, and the guide of such reflecting will now be a sense of fairness or, at a more comprehensive level, 'reciprocity'. This is the impersonal morality of rules and regulations and laws, of which Plato speaks in the *Protagoras*: 'Fearing that our race would be quite destroyed, Zeus sent Hermes to take to men justice and reverence that there might be orderers of cities and links bringing them together in friendship.' (3) And there is finally the morality of Grace, 'which is not calculating, however fair and reasonable such calculations may be', and which stands 'for the quest of an elusive ideal good which cannot be contained in any set of rules or be expected as of right'. Involving 'a highly personal kind of behaviour', it is 'the morality of saints and heroes', and of humbler people too.

The relationship of Nietzsche's ideas to this scheme should by

---

[1] In *Essays in Honour of W. J. M. Mackenzie*, ed. B. Chapman and A. Potter (Manchester 1974), pp. 69–80.

now be obvious. He allows no positive value at all to the first, the morality which is ruled by habit and custom. To the extent that he can assimilate habit and custom under the heading of 'instinct', he will emphasize their 'life-enhancing' quality and set them in firm opposition to the second kind of morality, the morality of laws; for the rest he will condemn this morality as inert, unthinking (*MA* I §97) and inauthentic (*M* §455) conformism. '*Dike*', the second kind of morality, he will condemn for its rationalizations, its unheroic protection of 'the weak and underprivileged', its interference with the 'natural' effects of 'the will to power'. It is here, in his attacks on the morality of laws and institutions, that Nietzsche's distrust of everything that makes for stability, especially at the cost of concrete personal choice, receives a sympathetic hearing from those protesting minorities in our midst whose survival is assured by the rules of reciprocity they despise.

Nietzsche is therefore left with only one of the three strands, the wholly personal and 'authentic' morality of Grace, which has no rules and follows no precedents and fears no outcome of its generous ventures. This is to be the morality of the Superman, which flows from a full heart and a clear mind, and a love of the earth. However, since for Nietzsche there is no such thing as Grace, we had better speak of a 'morality *as if* from Grace' which, in his scheme, must do duty for all three strands. Not much demonstration is needed to show that life in the world as we know it governed *solely* by the morality of Grace – which in Nietzsche's utopia turns out to be a single man's fervour – is certain to collapse into anarchy.

It is no accident that Nietzsche's disparagement of the rule of law resembles the anti-legalism of the Gospels. The purpose as well as the end-effect of laws (he argues) is not the protection of life and the elimination of arbitrariness, but the creation of crime and thus of a bad conscience; hence he sees the abolition of law as leading to the elimination of crime (*M* §68): certainly this argument looks, and by its context is made to look, like a Christian paradox. Yet in all this psychologizing there is no recognition that the parables of Christ's defiance of the 'laws' of nature (at the marriage of Cana) and of the laws of equity (in the reward given to the last-hired servant, Matthew 21) have no meaning unless they are set within, and contrasted with, a stable natural and legal order of things; no recognition that there is no freeing from the law without the law.

Continuity is acknowledged as the essence of every morality (*J* § 188), except (it seems) of the scheme that is to emerge from the 're-valuation of all values' (the project which occupied him after 1884). Nietzsche reflects at length on what these new values should be, whether they are to be subsumed under an ethical maxim or whether they are to be part of an aesthetic re-interpretation of the world, and to what new goals they are to lead mankind. But prior to deciding what is to be inscribed on the new 'tablets of values' is the question whether such *new* tablets can be written and put into practice at all; and to the extent that this is an issue, not of individual psychology but of the logic of conversion, Nietzsche is not interested in it. Is it possible for a man to reject one set of values and then decide, with a free mind, on another set? Nietzsche seems to think that a man's freedom of moral choice is unlimited. Yet it is obvious that every decision must be preceded by a moment of indecision: such a moment may occur in the course of all sorts of practical choices and scientific experiments, but can it occur in ethics? No man, other than the lunatic or criminal, is ever in a moral vacuum. And if he were, what could possibly cause him to emerge from it? Not the old values, for they are to be rejected (this is to be a radical 're-valuation'), nor yet the new ones, for on these he has not yet decided... [1] Nietzsche's argument lacks a recognition that any new scheme is necessarily continuous with (even: parasitic on) the existent old scheme, and that this state of affairs is not caused by the turpitude of mankind but is inherent in the process of moral reform. Sometimes he writes as if his 'revaluation' is to be a revelation, though without a revealing god; at other times his arguments remind one of those notorious theologians who professed to believe that the New Testament was not revealed to the people of Israel but to a new race of men... Saul, Nietzsche fails to see, was not any Tom, Dick or Harry.

This, then, is Nietzsche's horizon, the limit of one mode of his consciousness. Why can he not think and experiment outside it? Why does he ignore the 'associative' part of our world? The question seems to have a ready answer: because, in a peculiarly radical, German way, he is preoccupied with attacking those currents of contemporary culture and social thought which

[1] See C. S. Lewis's essay, 'On Ethics', in *Christian Reflections* (London 1967), esp. pp., 48–52.

render his ideal for humanity impossible. At this point the different aspects of the sphere of association fall apart. Nietzsche is reacting against the political ideas of the French Revolution, the societal ideas of Rousseau *and* of the English political economists, the nascent international socialist movement and its belief in progress, at the same time as he is reacting against Schopenhauer's and Hegel's expatiations on single themes and against Kant's idealism, which he 'unmasks' as a systematic undermining of man's faith in his senses and in the earth, their object.

However, an answer of this kind is not just obvious, it is also inadequate. His philosophizing and its limitations cannot be explained in terms of his 'reactions'. Its true and irreducible ground is his image of man, 'unhouseled, disappointed, unaneled' and for these reasons heroic, held out into the void of the circle of endless repetitions. He does not love the world – he loves the earth, but does not want it to last. His deepest and most consistent concern is not with social values of any kind, neither with the swaggering gilded fuss of the leader nor with the blood-and-iron ideology of the man of will, nor with any of our prudentialisms. The value that is left at the end of his moral arguments is the opposite of any conceivable utopia. It is the heroism of deprivation: a strange 'value', we may think, yet part of the discontinuous, catastrophic experience which dominates his outlook and writings. And here (we recall from our earlier comparison with Marx)[1] lies the reason for our feeling that Nietzsche anticipates our world; our familiar landscape of craters and scaffoldings.

[1] See above, p. 51.

9

The third experiment: the God-less theology

This was sometime a paradox, but now the time gives it proof
(Hamlet III: 1)

I

We return to the question which concluded our discussion of 'the will to power': what principle or scheme will yield an adequate description and norm of man's being in the world, will 'bring out the best in him'? What is man's best? If the various experiments described in Chapters 6 and 7 failed to provide an answer, at least they point to the conditions it will have to fulfil.

Certainly such a scheme will be related to Nietzsche's Protestant Christianity, for it is bound to take issue with the religious situation of his age, which is for him 'the age of the death of God', and with the morality of that age, which is for him the morality of decadence. It will look very much *like* a religious scheme (and some of Nietzsche's disciples will regard it as such), yet its religiousness will be full of paradox and riven by conflict. It will make no claims to being perennially valid, but instead emphasize its own historicity and irony – 'the irony that is implicit in the historical approach to a fact of moral culture'.[1] An exclusively private device, it will allow no value to politics or to any of the institutional safeguards men put between themselves and the crack of doom. Although it will contain no moral absolutes or material imperatives ('do this, do not do that!'), yet it must enjoin one way of doing things in preference to others. And finally, while it cannot help being a scheme, *a generalization*, it will strive to keep to the language of 'little facts and inconspicuous truths' (*MA* 1 §3), and to preserve the intuition that 'every action is unique and incommensurable with every other action' (*FW* IV §335).

Does all this not look uncommonly like that 'phantasmagoria'

---

[1] Lionel Trilling quoted by John Thompson in the *New York Review of Books*, 11 December 1975.

which Nietzsche saw at the heart of every comprehensive philosophical system?[1] Besides, considering how much variety and how many living colours Nietzsche imparts to his discrete reflections, why bother about a 'scheme', the mere corpse of embodied argument?

Because, whether we choose to call it a moral system, a *Weltanschauung*, or merely a certain style of moral thought and action, what Nietzsche bequeathed to the new century is a single thing – a single distinct heritage of moral–existential attitudes.

The premise on which this scheme rests anticipates our deep discontent with the industrial world and its values:

What I attack [he writes in the Spring of 1888] is that economic optimism which behaves as though, with the increasing *expenditure* of all, the *welfare* of all would also necessarily increase. To me the opposite seems to be the case: the sum total of the expenditure of all amounts to a total loss: *man is diminished* – indeed, one no longer knows what purpose this immense process has served in the first place. A purpose? A new purpose [ein neues Wozu] – that is what mankind needs. (*WzM* § 866)

If man is to be saved from the inauthenticity and decadence he calls civilized life, his 'new purpose' must be relative to its being supremely difficult of attainment, it must be on the border-line of the unattainable; while conversely, anything that is not attained at such an exorbitant cost cannot be the real thing at all. We may call this Nietzsche's 'morality of strenuousness', his 'dear purchase' or, in a phrase from *Zarathustra*, the morality of 'the spirit of gravity', where the German word, 'Geist der Schwere', conjures up a gamut of physical and mental meanings and connotations, from 'weight', 'heaviness' and 'ponderousness' through 'recalcitrancy' to 'hardness' and 'difficulty'. A man's value, accordingly, lies in his readiness to undertake whatever are to him the most strenuous and least comforting moral and existential tasks, regardless of their accepted moral value. The 'purpose' or salvation of modern man (like 'Grace' in an earlier argument, the Christian term is both inappropriate and impossible to avoid) is to be purchased at the highest, most exacting price he can conceive of; and perhaps it lies beyond – tantalizingly, it may be, just beyond – what a man can pay with

---

[1] See *WKG* vii/3 p. 379, quoted above, p. 52; see also Jaspers, *Nietzsche*, pp. 297–8.

his entire being and existence. The structure of any genuine theology is reversed: instead of a relative personal effort being 'justified' by an absolute end, an existential effort is made absolute so as to 'justify' a relative end. Christian theology is replaced by the penitential theology of a God-less universe.

This, then, is Nietzsche's *experimentum in corpore vili*, the one morality that cuts to the quick. Formulations of it occur throughout all his writings, yet he does not give it a single name or indicate how consistent is the attitude these formulations represent. To take the essay on history of 1874, written when Nietzsche had just turned thirty. After the declaration (see above p. 54) that 'the goal of mankind cannot lie in its end but in its highest specimens', he goes on to exhort his contemporaries:

...find an exalted and noble *raison d'être* in life: seek out destruction for its own sake! I know of no better purpose in life than to be destroyed by that which is great and impossible! (*U* II §9)

– as though its impossibility were what makes his 'ideal' great. Again, in the Wagner essay two years later, he commends the cultural and pedagogic function of Bayreuth and offers its tragic masterpieces as lessons to those who are 'preparing for death in the fight for justice and love' (IV §4), as though only death could validate their cause.[1] Youthful romantic rhetoric? The self-destructive strenuousness of this strange morality never changes. When Nietzsche writes, in 1878, that he wishes his life to reflect 'my views about morality and art (the hardest things that my sense of truth has so far wrung from me)'...;[2] and again a year later, referring to the conclusion of *Human, All-too-Human:*

[it is] purchased so dearly and with so much hardship that nobody who had the choice would have written it at that price...;[3]

when he proclaims, in the 1886 preface to that book,

I now took sides *against* myself and *for* everything that would hurt me and would come hard to me...;

when, in *Beyond* (1886), he writes:

[1] Nietzsche's high pedagogic vision mercifully hides from his view the serviettes and elastic braces with the Master's pictures on them, sold in the streets of this new musical academe of the German spirit.
[2] To von Seydlitz, 11 June 1878.   [3] To Peter Gast, 5 October 1879.

A thing might be true, even though it were noxious and dangerous in the highest degree – indeed, it might be fundamental to the nature of existence that we perish by the full knowledge of it; so that the strength of a human spirit might be measured by how much truth it could be made to bear, or, more plainly, to what extent it needs the truth watered down, veiled, sugared, muffled, falsified...; (§ 39)

when he insists that the main achievement of *Zarathustra* should be seen as

a victory over the Spirit of Heaviness, considering *how difficult* it was to represent the problems with which the book is concerned...;[1]

when, in *The Will to Power* (1887–8), he defines 'virtue' as 'the delight we take in opposition', adding that

I assess the power of [a man's] will by how much resistance, pain and torment it can endure and turn to its advantage...; (§ 382)

when again and again he insists on the need to destroy all forms of positive faith and all comforting certitudes, emphasizing the value of scepticism and of despair itself in the battle against the living death of conformity, spurring himself on:

I must set up the philosopher's most difficult ideal! (*WzM* § 421),

defining that 'ideal' in its full self-destructiveness:

Philosophy as I have hitherto understood and lived it is a voluntary seeking-out of the abhorred and detested aspects of existence...; (§ 1041)

and when, finally, in *Antichrist* (1888) he roundly condemns every idea of a pre-established harmony between truth and happiness (or even plain utility), claiming that

The experience of all rigorous and profoundly disposed minds teaches the opposite. Every inch of truth has to be wrested from oneself. We have to surrender almost everything that our hearts, our love, our trust in life normally cling to. This requires greatness of soul: the service of truth is the hardest service... *Faith makes blessed: therefore it lies...* (§ 50),

we are left in no doubt that 'the experimental philosophy which I live', unlike the other moral 'experiments', represents Nietzsche's most intimate personal undertaking and purpose, and informs every phase of his creative life. Its fullest expression is to be found in *Thus Spoke Zarathustra*, the book on which he pinned his highest hopes.

[1]   To Peter Gast, August 1883.

Who is Zarathustra? Why does Nietzsche choose the Old Persian prophet, Zoroaster, to act the part of Christ in this strange parody of the Gospels? Because Zarathustra is the founder of the earliest dualistic Aryan religion we know – 'he who first saw that the moving wheel at the centre of all things is the battle between good and evil' – and therefore shall be the prophet who proclaims the end of the rule of good and evil (*EH*, last section). After ten years in a mountainous solitude Zarathustra decides to go down among men:

But when he came into the forest, suddenly there stood before him an old man who had left his holy abode to look for roots in the woods...
'And what is the holy man doing in the forest?' asked Zarathustra.
The holy man answered: 'I make songs and sing them, and when I make songs I laugh, I cry and I hum: in this way I praise God. With singing, crying, laughing and humming I praise the god who is my God. But what gift do you bring us?'
When Zarathustra had heard these words, he bade the holy man farewell and said: 'What have I to give you? Nay, let me quickly go, lest I take something away from you!' And so they separated, the old one and the man, laughing as two boys laugh.
But when Zarathustra was alone, he spoke thus to his heart: Could it be possible? The old holy man in his forest has not yet heard the news that God is dead! (*Z* introd.)

This 'death' of the Christian God Nietzsche identifies with the virtual end of the morality of good and evil, and of all forms of idealism. It is for him the cardinal event of modern history and of the contemporary world; we in turn recognize it as co-determining Nietzsche's every important thought (though it is not necessarily the ground of his thoughts). Before turning to *Zarathustra*, therefore, and in order to explain the *pathos* of its message, an account of Nietzsche's objections to Christianity and of his attitude to its founder must be given. That his religious reflections are not neutral, no mere *constatations*, hardly needs emphasizing at this stage. Here more than anywhere else he consciously (*GM* §§2–3) exploits the performative function of prophetic utterance. His intention is not merely to announce the end of religion but by his rhetoric to help bring it about: 'whatever is falling – let's give it a push, too!' (*Z* III §12). Statements of this kind say what they say. And even though the 'murder of God' (*FW* §125) is never done with, even though he must be forever returning to the obsequies, there is no denying that Nietzsche 'the prophet of the modern age' is one of the major sources of European atheism.

Nowhere is it more difficult to avoid the trap of clichés – the *flat* atheist caricature on the one hand, the more fashionable cliché of the 'anti-Christ' who is 'really a Christian at heart' on the other. If I have postponed an account of Nietzsche's religious views until this point in my argument, it was in order to avoid giving the impression that Nietzsche's philosophizing is no more than a series of compensations for his loss of faith in the Christian God; and yet it is impossible to imagine what his reflections would be like 'were it not that I have bad dreams'.

2

What ceremony else?

(*Hamlet* v: 1)

For Schopenhauer, the mid-nineteenth century is 'an age in which religion is almost entirely dead'[1] and when 'the shares of the old Jew are falling'; Heinrich Heine's rhetoric is more dramatic but equally irreverent: 'Our heart is full of terrible pity. It is the old Jehovah himself preparing for death...Can you hear the ringing of the bell? Kneel down, they are bringing the sacraments to a dying God.'[2] These (rather than Plutarch's adage, 'great Pan is dead')[3] are the antecedents of that lurid and notorious phrase used by Nietzsche for the first time in § 108 of the third book of *The Joyous Science* (Spring 1882) and then again, four years later, at the opening of the fifth and last section of that book: 'The greatest event of recent times – that "God is dead", that the belief in the Christian God is no longer tenable – is beginning to cast its first shadows over Europe'. In the books of the early 1880s he presents it as a simple fact of modern life –

Time was when one tried to prove that there is no God – today we are concerned to show how the belief that there is a God could arise and whence this belief acquired its weightiness [Schwere] and importance; and thus the counterproof that there is no God becomes redundant (*M* § 95),

[1] *Neue Paralipomena* § 383.
[2] *Zur Geschichte der Philosophie und Religion in Deutschland* (1852), peroration to book II.
[3] Which Nietzsche may also have known from Pascal (*Pensées*, ed. Brunschvicq, no. 695); see Martin Heidegger, 'Nietzsches Wort "Got ist tot"', in *Holzwege* (Frankfurt 1950), p. 198.

– and rejoices in its consequences. His entire anti-religious and atheistic argument is based on the view, set up and illustrated in countless reflections in the books of the middle period, that the belief in God results in an impoverishment of men's lives; that the compensatory belief in heaven ('the Land of Back and Beyond') reduces the value and dignity of physical existence; that the belief in personal immortality, apart from being intolerably egalitarian (*A* § 43), diminishes the seriousness of men's experience of the irretrievable nature of time by mythologizing time into a spurious perpetuity called 'eternity'; that Christianity preaches a denigration of the life of the senses which amounts to a radical devaluing of the earth as an enemy of everything spiritual, a mere valley in the shadow of death, and leads to a fanatical scorning of men's vital concerns, a contempt for 'what is real in the world'. All that Nietzsche attacks is epitomized in one of Kafka's 'Meditations': 'Nothing exists but the spiritual world. That which we call the sensuous world is the evil in the spiritual.'

In answer to these accusations one might point to the radically Manichean trend of Nietzsche's arguments, whereby he (like Pascal and occasionally Luther) polemically exaggerates the world-contemning nature of Christianity. He has nothing to say in recognition of the joyful, positive nature of that faith of which Christ said, 'My yoke is easy, and my burden is light' (Matthew 11:30). He says next to nothing about the *pietas loci* which (as Hölderlin's poems show) is an essential part of the Gospels as it is of the Christian world picture. He seems to be unaware of the overwhelming debt which every form of Western art owes, not only to the Christian faith, but to the Church in which that faith has its historical being. (This is particularly ironical, seeing that in *The Birth of Tragedy* he provides an eloquent illustration of the relationship of art and religious cult within pre-Socratic culture; though it is not at all ironical, but merely gross, to stress the German and ignore the Christian character of J. S. Bach's music, *GT* § 19). And Nietzsche has nothing to say about the positive meaning of Christ's incarnation (1 John 4:9) as a validation of our mortality. A theology that argues the presence of God in the world does not suit his Manichean view, and is accordingly ignored.

To these objections Nietzsche would no doubt reply that they are irrelevant, for *his* remarks are not concerned with the perennial possibilities of the Christian faith but with its actual contemporary desuëtude. Put in these terms, his charge is more considerable. It is that, in his day and age, the belief in God is dispensable because the presence or absence of faith in men's minds no longer makes any real difference to the lives they lead; worse still:

> What is it that Christianity calls 'the world'? To be a soldier, a judge, a patriot; to defend oneself; to look to one's honour; to seek one's advantage; *to be proud*: every practice of every moment, every instinct and every valuation translated into action is today anti-Christian (*A* § 38).

Can we deny that this is a convincing reading of the signs of the times, Nietzsche's times and ours? And equally convincing, it seems to me, is his explanation of the religious decline. Leaving to one side the Victorian clichés about the conflict between faith and science, he draws from the very denunciation of Christianity a paradoxical acknowledgement of its historical significance. This is the dialectical tension that informs *The Genealogy of Morals* (July 1887). For here he recognizes that 'science' – the body of stable and accurate knowledge to the accumulation of which men devote their lives – far from being the antagonist of faith and of the religious outlook, owes its origins and development to Christian thinking and ideals. Ignoring the scientists' delight in abstraction as a motive and the importance of system as a goal of their work, Nietzsche singles out truthfulness as the basic disposition of mind which informs every uncompromising pursuit of knowledge; and this truthfulness is furthered by the Christian faith and its unique morality. If, therefore, truthfulness is recognized as an essentially Christian virtue, the decline of religion must be seen as the radical consequence of its own religiously inspired morality: 'All great things' – but we must not pretend that Nietzsche always sees Christianity as 'great' – 'All great things perish by their own agency, by an act of self-cancellation' ('Selbstaufhebung', *GM* III § 27).[1] And Nietzsche knows, too (§ 24), that his own heedless pursuit of 'truths' – many of them incompatible with each other, many of them noxious to 'life' – is the opposite of any 'instinct' or 'natural drive'; that it

---

[1] Here Nietzsche himself quotes *FW* § 357 and (at *GM* III § 24), *FW* § 344 to underline the continuity of his thinking. Cf. also Karl Jaspers, *Nietzsche und das Christentum* (Hameln n.d.), pp. 9 and 55.

has nothing to do with the tragic culture of the pre-So[...] in which he sees the epitome of the Greek sense of life [...] it too is Christian in origin. It is no accident that [...] thought is full of Platonic relics: Christian truthfulness is not fundamentally different from the spirit that has informed Western philosophy since the days of Socrates, that decadent proto-Christian and first martyr in the cause of his own questionable convictions (*GD* II).

But what is the *value* of truthfulness? There is nothing unconditioned about it. Like science itself it is never value-free (*GM* III § 24) since it is always in the service of some 'unconscious imperative' and ultimate purpose. The 'will to truth' which informs Christianity (and Western philosophy) is in the service of ascetic ideals – ideals which seek to denigrate and suppress life, to uphold a sickly and degenerate will to power over a healthy assertion of life, at the same time as they oppose art and 'all other forms of illusion' and of 'the will to deception'. Throughout Western history, religion and philosophy have been weapons in the hands of the underprivileged, the envious and the resentful, the unhappy and the self-haters – of all those who are afraid of life and 'wish to be different, wish they were elsewhere' (§ 13): it is they who, being what they are, cannot help turning truthfulness against life, making of it an anti-value.

But is this a convincing conclusion? Nietzsche's arguments (we have seen) are always at their weakest where he offers 'ways of becoming' not merely as explanations but as the grounds of value judgements. For even if it were true that the Christian priesthood is recruited from 'the underprivileged' and the Uriah Heeps (which Nietzsche elsewhere, *M* 60, denies), and even if people could live more happily without religious beliefs, the double inference, that this renders religion worthless and the belief in God illusory, would still be unwarranted. Nietzsche's atheism at this point is 'fixed' and dogmatic: apart from the false inference there is only assertion. He merely denies – he does not attempt to disprove – a loving and merciful God, and Christ as the son of that God; and he axiomatically assumes that the meaning of life must be sought elsewhere. But in saying that because men do not believe in God, therefore he does not exist, 'is dead', Nietzsche is once again caught in the same solipsist–idealist trap in which his doctrine of the 'will to power' had landed him.

What is life for? What is the meaning of life? It is the business of priests and philosophers to answer these perennial questions (which is why other men are prepared to keep them in clover). Their answer so far has been nihilistic. By extolling transcendence they have denied the value of the earth, asserted the death of life, and given value to Nothingness. But then (Nietzsche begins and concludes the argument of the last section of *The Genealogy of Morals* with a sentence taken up by Thomas Mann), it is one of the ruses of 'Life' that 'Men would rather will Nothingness [das Nichts] than not will at all' (§§ 1 and 28).

The task of the new age – the age which follows on 'the destruction of Christian dogma and morality by Christian truthfulness' – is to preserve the spiritual energy which past ages had invested in transcendence, and to re-direct this energy toward an immanent world. (A lyrical account of this proposed validation is contained in Rilke's *Duino Elegies*.) Henceforth the meaning of life is to be sought, not in 'the World Behind and Beyond', but in man and in the earth he inhabits. And when that is done, what then becomes of that 'will to truth' which had once created Christian morality and is now destroying it? The task of the future is to create a philosophy that is no longer in the service of ascetic ideals; to give an answer to the question, What is life for?, that will be compatible with a 'will to truth' which is a source of strength to man. Nietzsche's answer seems clear: 'Let us create men to whom truth is useful' (*WKG* VII/1 p. 484). Yes, but *how do you 'create men'*?

Taking no warning from Greek tragedy – we recall his egregious reading of Pindar – Nietzsche has no fear of hubris (*GM* III §9). His ultimate indictment of Christian belief (the basis of his charge that it is against life and against the earth) is that Christianity does not recognize man as master of the universe. What is wrong with the Christian moral scheme and cosmology is that under them the freedom, authority and knowledge vouchsafed to men are all relative to an alien, outside decree, and rendered intolerable (to Nietzsche at all events) because they are derivative. Therefore, Nietzsche argues, man cannot reach the highest enhancement of his powers until he has destroyed in himself his belief in the divine. Only then will life have a meaning for him and the earth yield up her treasures to him, only then will men and things be given their true substance and weight, and be liberated from the burden of metaphysical lies.

There is a tone of almost cheerful aggressiveness about many remarks in book III of *The Genealogy of Morals*, but it does not last. In the more or less contemporary note-books he calls the end of religion 'the most terrible news': rather than cope with the 'unbearable loneliness' of their new condition (he writes there), men will seek out their shattered God, and for his sake they will love the very serpents that dwell among his ruins...[1] Yet the melodramatic metaphors seem to obscure his vision. Like Freud in *The End of an Illusion*, Nietzsche appears less clear about the human consequences of the end of faith than he is about the need to hasten the coming of that end.

In our world there are two kinds of unbelievers. The majority of our contemporaries in the West take the world's God-less character for granted and are to all intents unconcerned about it, hoping to achieve earthly paradise (if indeed they have a wider view) by attending as prudently as possible to the actual arrangements that keep the world going; and there are others, whose outlook is disturbed – still disturbed – by the memory and an occasional reminder that the world was not always thus. Nietzsche of course – in spite of his denials – belongs to this latter kind. And he wants the brave new world to be populated, not simply by the unconcerned, but by men who, while unconcerned about 'the death of God', will yet be metaphysically, religiously concerned. But what is to be the object of their concern, what is this bladeless knife without a handle, this religious disposition without a God?

Our experience almost a century later, and our most vivid historical insights too, suggest that the liberation Nietzsche hoped for has brought no new freedom. Where men have abandoned their belief in an immortal soul, the destruction they visit on others has become more heedless and complete than it was before; and where they act in the conviction that 'nothing is true, everything is permitted' (*GM* III § 24) – that there is no authority to appeal to – their style of life is more troubled and more sordid than before. Such views are usually thought to imply a lack of 'faith in man' and in his ability to be master of his fate. However, the point at issue is not whether to have 'faith in man', but what, in man, is worthy of faith. Is the greatness of which he is capable best displayed in that self-assertion of Zarathustra's which makes

[1] 'terrible news': VII/3 pp. 144–5, 'loneliness': *ibid.* p. 213, both written in 1885; 'serpents': *Mus* XVI p. 80.

man the measure of all things ('if there were gods, how could
I bear not to be a God?') – or is that greatness more truly evoked
by Paul's exhortation 'that ye present your bodies a living
sacrifice, holy, acceptable unto God, which is your reasonable
service' (Romans 12:1)?

3

The denigration of man's life on this earth and the subordination
of man to God are Nietzsche's two principal objections to
Christianity. The third is his attack on Christianity as scripture
and dogma, and on the Church as an institutionalization of that
dogma; and this attack is set in sharp contrast to a strange eulogy
of Jesus of Nazareth.[1] The argument is conducted in the
posthumously published *Anti-Christ*, written and completed
between 9 September and 15 October 1888.

The title is misleading, perhaps deliberately so, and has little
to do with the name traditionally given to Christ's enemy at
his second coming. More relevant to its meaning is Schopenhauer's use of the word to represent the view that the world has
merely a physical significance: to deny the world its moral
significance (Schopenhauer had argued) amounts to the greatest
and most pernicious error of which the human mind is capable
– such a denial is 'personified as Anti-Christ'.[2] There is little
reason to doubt that this is the meaning Nietzsche invokes in his
title (and occasionally for himself).[3] Thus the book, intended as
the first volume of a grand 're-valuation of all values', proposes
an affirmation of anti-moral, anti-religious and anti-spiritual –
indeed of 'physical' – values, though whether it achieves what it
sets out to do is another question. It is (among other things)
Nietzsche's final rebuttal of Schopenhauer, the end of a life-long
agon.

The book consists of a series of profound insights embedded
in a mixture of vituperation and incongruities: but insights and
incongruities alike derive from a single perspective. I have
described this perspective at some length in Chapter 8. What I

[1] Nietzsche does not consistently follow the distinction, customary in theological
usage, between 'Christ' and 'Jesus'.

[2] See Schopenhauer's *Parerga und Paralipomena*, vol. II § 109; full textual
evidence to support this discovery is given by J. Salaquarda, 'Der Antichrist',
in *NS* II (Berlin 1973), pp. 91–136.

[3] For Nietzsche's self-identification as 'Anti-Christ' see his letter to von
Meysenbug, end of March 1883.

have called the sphere of association is here rejected more
resolutely than ever before: this sphere of experience where, to
quote Matthew 18:20 again, 'two or three are gathered together',
is condemned more scornfully and uncompromisingly than ever
before, and Nietzsche's almost absolute individualism is given
freer rein to shape and determine his historical analysis and
evaluation.

The argument of the last section of *The Genealogy of Morals*,
in the course of which Christianity was identified with truthfulness, is now abandoned; science, defined briskly as the application of 'the healthy conception of cause and effect' (*A* §49), is
seen as the victorious enemy of faith; and Christianity appears
as the denial of all truth, instinctive and scientific alike. It is seen
as a direct descendant of the Jewish theocratic state – at first a
threat to the life of a small, deeply unheroic nation, and then
a powerful weapon in that nation's lethal struggle against the
mightiest Empire and finest political institution of all ages.

Nietzsche's profound regret for the decline and fall of Rome,
and of antiquity as a whole, looks like an exception to the rule,
valid everywhere else, that institutions are the enemy of human
greatness. The powerful pathos of these elegiac reflections at the
end of *Anti-Christ* –

The entire labour of the ancient world *in vain*: I have no words to
express my feeling about something so monstrous...All in vain!
Overnight a mere memory! Greeks! Romans! the nobility of instinct,
taste, methodical research, the genius of organization and administra-
tion, the faith in and *the will* to man's future, the great Yes to all things
become visible as *imperium Romanum*, visible to all the senses, the grand
style no longer mere art but reality, truth, *life*...

– leaves us in no doubt about their seriousness. Such passages
have no parallel elsewhere in Nietzsche's work. Yet what
prompts them seems to be less an admiration for Rome than a
loathing for 'the conspiracy' that destroyed it. For all the
grandeur that was Rome

was not buried overnight by a natural catastrophe, not trampled down
by Teutons and other heavy-footed tribes, but ruined by cunning,
stealthy, invisible, anaemic vampires! Not vanquished – merely sucked
dry. Hidden vengefulness, petty envy become master! Everything that
is wretched and suffers from its own defectiveness, everything that is
afflicted by its own wretched feelings – the whole ghetto-world of the
soul came out on top, all at once! (§ 59)

Christianity, being 'a diseased barbarism that sets itself up as power' (§ 37), is a falsification of everything Christ was and stood for, it is the very opposite of 'the Evangel', 'the good tidings'. Its history is little more than a series of ever cruder misunderstandings of an original lofty symbolism: 'the very word "Christianity" is a misunderstanding – the truth is that there was only one Christian and he died on the cross', and *'from that moment on'* all is lies (§ 39). The pure, authentic vision of a naïve Jesus of Nazareth was corrupted – was dogmatized and institutionalized – by a fanatical rabbi who set out to restore the threatened priestly power and conspiracy of the weak:[1] Paul is the prophet of the new 'Dysangelium'.

The distaste conveyed in this portrait of the first Christian theologian[2] has no parallel elsewhere in Nietzsche's writings, not even in his portrait of Rousseau. While in *The Dawn* Paul was portrayed as the imitator of Christ and, like Christ, intent on the destruction of 'the Law' (§ 68), here he is in every way Christ's opposite: teacher of a nihilistic morality, a Jewish sea-lawyer and upholder of a moribund legalism; his renunciation of the law (Galatians 3:24) is no longer mentioned. He is the inventor of the doctrine of the Cross ('We – the rabble – are all on the cross, therefore we are all divine') and the myth-maker of the Resurrection (a piece of 'rabbinical impudence'), he is the first to appeal to the twin authorities – both equally unreasonable – of tradition and revolution. These (Nietzsche concludes) are Paul's means of securing Christianity's victory over Rome. Now the invective broadens out to include an account of the disastrous consequences of Luther's protest, and the Renaissance joins Rome as a missed opportunity for making 'the Great Life' victorious. The pungent anti-Semitism of earlier historical sketches of *Anti-Christ* is more or less cancelled out by an equally telling anti-anti-Semitism: for two thousand years now victory has been with 'the little Jews' of all nations and races, who have the religious superlatives constantly on their lips, and the sickly smile of the forgiving dévots...

To all this, the portrait of Jesus of Nazareth (§§ 32–4) provides the starkest possible contrast. Nietzsche presents him largely in negative terms: Christ is no teacher, no priest, no prophet even;

[1] Nietzsche ignores the fact that the two letters to the Corinthians are older than any Gospels we possess today. See H. Küng, *The Church* (London 1967), p. 18.

[2] See W. G. Kümmel, *Die Theologie des Neuen Testaments* (Göttingen 1969), p. 123.

he belongs to no state, no culture and no religion or Church; nothing about him conveys the feeling that he is securely at home in our common world; even his words that have come down to us do not really matter – they are not a literal truth but 'merely a sign-language, mere semiotics'. He passes no judgement, is informed by no will to resist or negate, to be angry or to hold anyone responsible. He lives outside all history and all morality. Incapable of denial and negation, he lives outside the world seen as a world of contrasts. Elsewhere this is, for Nietzsche, the only world there is, but here the lure of ontology is irresistible: *Christ simply is.* His 'kingdom of heaven' is not the Church's metaphysical cloud-cuckooland but 'a state of the heart'. Nietzsche is trying to portray one who is living a new kind of innocent life entirely beyond 'the will to power'; living 'the genuine evangelical practice' which, being outside history, 'is still possible even today'. And, as so often, a conscious pun (on 'freier Geist' with its echo of 'free-thinker') reveals Nietzsche's deepest concern:

Using the phrase loosely [he writes, *A* § 32], one could call Jesus 'a free spirit' – he cares nothing for all that is fixed. The word *kills*, all that is fixed *kills*.

It is hardly too much to say that this Jesus, too, is the 'Anti-Christ' of Nietzsche's title.

The central argument of *Anti-Christ* raises three questions which have a bearing on Nietzsche's moral scheme: (1) What is the source of this character sketch? (2) How true is it to the Christ of the Gospels? (3) What is its meaning for Nietzsche?

  (1) It has sometimes been thought that this portrait was inspired by Dostoyevsky's Prince Myshkin in *The Idiot*. What, apart from affinities of character, makes this plausible is that both Dostoyevsky's name and 'the idiot' occur in connection with Jesus within a few pages (§§ 29 and 31) where Dostoyevsky's skill as a psychologist of religion is admired. Yet we cannot be sure that Nietzsche actually read the novel;[1] moreover, it is hard to see why, if he did read it, he should have failed to take issue with

[1] See C. A. Miller, 'Nietzsche's "Discovery" of Dostoyevsky', *NS* II (Berlin 1973), pp. 202–57; and W. Gesemann, 'Nietzsches Verhältnis zu Dostoevskij auf dem europäischen Hintergrund der 8oer Jahr', in *Welt der Slaven* Jg. VI (Wiesbaden 1961), pp. 131–46.

the novel's central theme, Myshkin's emotional inadequacy and disastrous failure. A more likely source (it seems to me) is that age-old German tradition to which Nietzsche refers mockingly in § 53 – the anti-theological and anti-ecclesiastical tradition of 'the Pietists and other Swabian cows'.

The Pietists continue the anti-institutional and subjectivist tendency of the Reformation, and carry it a stage further. In their writings the history of Christianity is presented invariably as a decline, and sometimes as a series of cyclical movements[1] reminiscent of Nietzsche's historical sketches. Each cycle begins with the personal revelation of an authentic prophet – a Christ-like figure who is branded by the world as a heretic because, taking Jesus as his example, the prophet refuses to accommodate his personal witness to the exactions of any church or dogma. No sooner has he entered the world than disciples and enemies alike conspire to negate his example. 'Whatever, from that moment on, is called the Gospel', Nietzsche had written (§ 39), 'was even then the opposite of what [Jesus] lived'. The Pietists do not go so far, they accept the Bible. Yet they too believe that the pristine personal message is corrupted as soon as it is overlaid by doctrine, dispute and worldly interests, the original words becoming ever more rigid, 'more fixed', until an extreme of worldliness and depravity is reached, another prophet arises in the hour of the world's greatest need, and the apocalyptic process begins anew... Church and state and society alike are the authentic prophet's enemies, the letter of the law is dead: not only does the Manichean bias with which the Pietists depicted the worldly world have its direct parallel in Nietzsche's individualism, but there is also a close resemblance between Nietzsche's characterization of a 'gentle Jesus, meek and mild' who knows nothing of guilt and punishment, and their portraits of the saintly 'heretic' and true prophet. It seems likely (though there is no direct evidence) that Nietzsche knew a good deal of Pietist literature from his clerical home. He certainly knew what had survived of this tradition in the works of writers like Jung-Stilling and Schleiermacher. Moreover, he knew the heritage of Pietism

---

[1] As in the most famous and influential of these histories, Gottfried Arnold's *Unpartheyische Kirchen- und Ketzerhistorie* (Frankfurt/M 1700). For a full account of Nietzsche's anti-ecclesiastical and anti-Christian views, see E. Benz, *Nietzches Ideen zur Geschichte des Christentums und der Kirche* (Leiden 1956), which also includes accounts of the influence on Nietzsche's religious views of Schopenhauer and J. Wellhausen (a contemporary historian of Christianity).

which inspired the 'Nazarene' school of painters of his time to make their Jesus figure into a pre-Raphaelite aesthetic creation.

(2) Most readers would wish to acknowledge the justice of Nietzsche's mockery of ecclesiastical worldliness and power, his horror at the Church's use of the sword and the stake in defending its dogmas, and his repudiation of religious practices intended to excuse and vindicate present injustices by the promise of rewards in Kingdom Come. His attacks on the excessive legalism, literal-mindedness and dogmatism of many priests and exegetes, and on the mustiness of much theological thinking, are well founded. Occasionally – what could be more paradoxical in the creator of the 'Superman'? – his understanding of Christian spirituality is as intimate and sympathetic as any Christian apologist's; thus his moving paraphrase of Luke 23:39:

[Christ's] words to the thief on the cross contain the entire Gospel. 'That was truly a divine man, a child of God!' says the malefactor. 'If you feel this,' the Redeemer answers him, 'then you are in Paradise, you are a child of God!'[1] Not to defend oneself, not to be wrath, not to make responsible...

contains *one* important aspect of Christ's teaching, yet much of it is invalidated by the exaggeration of the concluding words:

...not to make responsible...but on the contrary not to resist even the evil one – to love him. (§35)

But the question still remains: how true is the centre-piece of *The Anti-Christ*, Nietzsche's portrait of Jesus? Most readers, except perhaps the Protestant heirs of that Pietist tradition,[2] would agree that it amounts to a radical misinterpretation of the Gospels. When Nietzsche argues that Christ belongs to no religion, he is really saying that religion itself, as 'a particular *social* realization of a relationship to an absolute ground of meaning',[3] is incapable of containing any of the 'new values' of Nietzsche's 'revaluation', that it is a thing of no value. And when he portrays Jesus as one who knows no contrasts and passes no judgements, Nietzsche deliberately ignores the clear testimony of the Gospels:

[1] The passage is omitted from *The Portable Nietzsche* (ed. W. Kaufmann, New York 1973, p. 609).
[2] See, e.g., J. Nolte, *Wahrheit und Freiheit. Meditationen über Texte aus Friedrich Nietzsche* (Düsseldorf 1973).
[3] Hans Küng, *On Being a Christian* (London 1976), p. 89.

If there is any concept which cannot by any conjuring be removed from the teaching of Our Lord [wrote C. S. Lewis], it is that of the great separation; the sheep and the goats, the broad way and the narrow, the wheat and the tares, the winnowing fan, the wise and the foolish virgins, the good fish and the refuse, the door closed on the marriage feast, with some inside and some outside in the dark. We may dare to hope...that this is not the whole story, that, as Julian of Norwich said, 'All will be well and all manner of things will be well.' But it is no use going to Our Lord's words for that hope. Something we may get from St Paul: nothing, of that kind, from Jesus.[1]

But then Nietzsche's portrait of Paul, too, intended as a masterpiece of psychological finesse, is an absurdity. 'Whoever finds Paul repugnant and uncanny,' writes Rudolf Bultmann, 'must find Jesus just as repugnant and uncanny.'[2]

(3) What meaning has this portrait of the Nazarene Jesus for Nietzsche in his search for a system of new values, announced in the preface of *The Anti-Christ*? Nietzsche calls him 'an interesting decadent' and himself 'a conscious decadent' (*FaW*, preface); he calls Jesus, in Dostoyevsky's sense, an 'idiot', and himself 'a fool' and 'a mountebank'. These self-identifications are as transparent as the self-repudiation contained in Nietzsche's caricature of Paul. It is as if Nietzsche had deliberately endowed the portrait of Jesus with all the irenic and unstrenuous qualities he himself does not possess – all the qualities of being from which he knows himself to be forever excluded; and as if his portrait of Paul were weighed down by all the gravity of judgement and mental turmoil to which he, Nietzsche, feels himself eternally condemned. These are no more than biographical speculations, yet they point in the direction of those 'new values' which were to form the grand finale of his philosophical undertaking.

What they were to be we cannot know for certain, but it seems obvious that something of these values is present in Nietzsche's portrait of Jesus. It is as a gentle, poetic denial of almost everything Nietzsche has stood for – the doctrines of 'life' and 'the will to power', the ideals of embattled authenticity and of the morality of strenuousness – it is as a wish-fulfilment and absolution from a lifetime's exertion and oppressive consciousness of sin, like a figure from a poem by Georg Trakl, that this Nazarene Jesus stalks through the pages of *The Anti-Christ*,

[1] C. S. Lewis, *Christian Reflections* (London 1967), p. 153.
[2] Quoted from W. G. Kümmel, *Die Theologie...*, p. 227.

bypassing the book's vituperations, its contrasts and contradictions. As a sentimental farewell to the strains and stresses of reflection? No, as an 'aesthetic phenomenon'.

4

But howsoever thou pursues this act,/ Taint not thy mind...
(Hamlet 1: 5)

Thus Spoke Zarathustra is Nietzsche's most sustained attempt to free himself from the clutches of negation and 'mere criticism'. Its form consists of a number of parables and oracular pronouncements richly garnished with natural imagery; these are at first organized round a few episodes from the prophet's life, but soon the sequence of story or continuous argument is abandoned, and what takes its place is a unity of concern. With its oracular phrases and archaicizing turns the work overtly aspires to being a rival to 'the greatest book in German' – Luther's Bible translation; it often reads like a pastiche of it. Unlike Richard Strauss's musical fantasy, it has no unity of poetic structure to encompass it, relying for its strong effects on lyrical landscape sketches, Blakean vignettes and polished aphorisms. In a remarkable passage which he paraphrased from Paul Bourget's *Baudelaire* of 1883 (and which he intended as part of his 'case against Wagner'), Nietzsche asks:

What is the mark of every literary decadence? It is that life no longer dwells in the whole. The word assumes sovereign power and escapes from the sentence, the sentence spills beyond itself and obscures the meaning of the page, the page gains life at the expense of the whole, the whole is no longer a whole...

Nietzsche heightens Bourget's laconic observation into a vehement indictment:

Ah, but that is a metaphor for every style of decadence – each time it amounts to an anarchy of atoms, a disintegration of the will...And the whole? Composed, calculated, artificial, an artefact![1]

Instinct, inspiration, the lucky throw of the dice – anything, on Nietzsche's scale of values, is better than 'an artefact'. Yet, given his preoccupation with the symbol, the *mot juste* and the

---

[1] *FaW* § 7; the borrowing from Bourget is noted in Ernst Bertram's remarkable study, *Nietzsche, Versuch einer Mythologie* (Berlin 1929), pp. 253-4.

aphorism, given the book's unabating consciousness and self-consciousness, it cannot be doubted that Nietzsche–Bourget's 'style de décadence' describes the style of *Zarathustra*.

Can the book be read without embarrassment – the sort of embarrassment one feels when faced with D. H. Lawrence at his 'prophetic' worst? A few of the image-studded allegories, parables and dithyrambs resist translation into discursive prose, but it is impossible to think of a reader who would not feel compelled to attempt such a translation. Yet in giving the book its form and style, Nietzsche was not following a sudden whim. In the first paragraph of *The Birth of Tragedy* he insists on the superiority of all concrete and figurative modes of expression over abstract conceptual arguments, and at the end of that book he calls for the creation of a new mythology as the necessary condition of a renewal of German national life. These requirements are realized, after a fashion, in the philosophical fiction Nietzsche created at the height of his intellectual powers eleven years later; though whether *Zarathustra*, said to have been in the knapsack of every German student-soldier in the Great War, contributed to the national rebirth in the way Nietzsche hoped, must be left an open question.

Its story, such as it is, is soon told. After ten years in a mountain solitude Zarathustra decides to 'go down' among men to bring them his message. He finds them in the market-place, watching a tight-rope walker perform his act. The man falls – not a devil but his companion has made him lose his balance – and, mortally wounded, is carried by Zarathustra for a day and a night, and finally buried in the forest. Thereafter we follow Zarathustra, preaching to his disciples, returning again to his solitude, descending for a second and third time...A forest, a ship, a mountain meadow and the desert are the settings, and Zarathustra's animals – the lion, the eagle, the snake – his most faithful companions.

Can there be a modern mythology? Can a myth be deliberately created? A myth without gods, perhaps; but a myth without people? In view of the explicitness of Nietzsche's undertaking it is relevant to note that he lacks a sustained mythopoeic gift (like Richard Wagner's), and that the book is weakest in its presentation of human beings and encounters. Here a comparison with the Bible is most damaging to it. The prophetic or parabolic nature of Christ's sayings does not impair their simple appropriateness to each individual person he addresses, and it is this appropriateness which is missing in *Zarathustra*. We hear of Zarathustra's friends and companions, of his deeply-felt need for communion with them, but they never arrive; it is only his uncomprehending disciples and his enemies – it has escaped the critics' notice how many of the men this 'Yea-sayer to Life' meets are his enemies – who make their shadowy appearance on his horrid alp. Nor is Zarathustra himself more than a sublime abstraction:[1] the enemy of all mediocrity and comfort, the proclaimer of moral paradoxes and hurtful truths, the disappointed lover of mankind, the prophet of a metaphysical vision beyond good and evil...: he is any of these things, but not a living character. Nietzsche can impersonate Zarathustra, not create him. We must not, however, make too much of this literary failure. Once we recognize that Nietzsche has created no persons and no genuine dialogue, and that monologue is Zarathustra's main form of discourse, we are free to read the book for what it really is: not a myth at all but the belated descendant of an eighteenth-century philosophical fiction. Its complex and consciously composed form first hides and then reveals something of that philosophy of strenuousness, of that 'spirit of gravity' which (as I have argued at the beginning of this chapter) represents Nietzsche's crucial 'moral experiment'.

What is Zarathustra's message? He is the prophet of certain values – ideals of attitude, disposition and conduct – to which Nietzsche gives the collective name 'Superman'. The Superman is open toward the world and its vicissitudes; trusting in others and in chance; in him the cardinal vices of lust, lust for power, and egoism are transformed into positive values; and he is in love with the earth, with his own fate, with his own life, and ready to sacrifice that life for...life as lived by those who are open toward the world and its vicissitudes; who trust in others and in chance...Based on the premise of a God-less world, the Superman thus embodies the enhancement of man's untrammelled will to power under the quasi-religious dispensation of 'the eternal recurrence of the same'. The enemies of Zarathustra and of his message are the frivolous and corrupt 'last men' – the Fellini crew of decadents he first meets in the market place; the sophisticated modern intellectuals – the 'higher men' whom

[1] The phrase is Ernst Bertram's, see *Nietzsche*, p. 255; cf. also Fink, *Nietzsches Philosophie*, p. 118.

Nietzsche portrays at length at the end of *Beyond Good and Evil*; and 'the underprivileged' ('die Schlechtweggekommenen') whose motives are envy, grudgingness, and fear.

A framework of qualifications – phrases like 'not yet', 'for this man only', 'but at this time' – emphasizes the relative character of the values whose advent Zarathustra proclaims, and this relativism determines the dialectic of his parables and maxims. This dialectic is enacted in three stages: 'a → not-a → A'. Here are some examples of it from the first part of the book: the passions and all the conventional values, including love of one's neighbour, are condemned, but they are approved of if they spring, not from deprivation, but from a superabundance of personal being; chastity is commended – to him who finds it easy to practise; pity is condemned as debilitating if it is intended to eke out a defective self, but it is valuable if it springs from a feeling of superiority; prayer is right 'for you but not for me'; war is a valuable test of man *if* its motive is hatred (the emotion of a full heart), not contempt – 'a good war' justifies the cause for which it is fought; the gods are condemned, the only god worthy of man's veneration is a dancing god; justice should be for all men save the judges; you call yourself free, but 'are you one of those who had the right to escape from the yoke? Many there are who threw away their last worth when they threw away their servitude'; and 'many there are that have become too old even for their truths and their victories – a toothless mouth no longer has the right to every truth'.[1] There is (as Thomas Mann observed) more than a touch of Oscar Wilde about many of these formulations.

This dialectic in three stages (a → not-a → A) is the characteristic form of Nietzsche's thinking, not only in *Zarathustra*, but wherever a 're-valuation' is to be undertaken; and that, in a sense, is the aim of all his works from *Human, All-too-Human* onwards. (1) A *description*, usually hostile but immensely illuminating, of an accepted value or concept or personal trait forms the first stage (e.g., pity shames both the pitier and the pitied). (2) There follows a *rejection*, for reasons which are usually surprising, and which derive from a projection of the original value beyond its usual range (pity strengthens the weak, destroys the strong: *ergo*

---

[1] One of the acutest of these paradoxes on the text of Titus 1:15, 'Unto the pure all things are pure', is untranslatable: "Dem Reinen ist alles rein...den Schweinen ist alles Schwein" (*Z* III § 12/14).

destroys 'life'). (3) A *re-interpretation* of the original concept and
an eloquent *acceptance* of it in its new form ('true' pity, making
the strong aware of their strength, strengthens 'life'). The
rhetoric of his descriptions and advocacy is an inseparable aspect
of the dialectic – it is this that makes Nietsche so eminently a
literary philosopher.

This dialectic is put in the service of the book's anti-
transcendentalist purpose. Again and again Zarathustra calls for
an enhancement of man's creativeness in a God-less world whose
inhabitants are ready to accept, and even rejoice in, their own
mortality. The function of the will to power is to turn chance into
intention; to create values ('the voice of value-giving is the voice
of the will to power'); 'to make things thinkable' yet not to arrest
them in their movement, in their 'process of becoming'; the
function of the will is above all to affirm – 'be in love with' – the
earth as the source of all living things. For is not man's soul his
body? The soul can certainly be nothing that is the body's enemy.
Not death or suffering demean man, but stasis and that
annihilating despair in whose sight all appears senseless and void.
What is irredeemably evil is 'all this teaching of the One and the
Plenum, the Inert, the Sated, and the Imperishable' – this alone
'is evil and injurious to men'.

   But why, we wonder, do the paeans to the Superman's love
of life, too, become so quickly paeans to sacrifice and death? Why
is the vocabulary of decline – the 'going down' and 'going under'
and the 'shattering' impact of thought and experience –
prevalent over the vocabulary of assent? It is as though
Nietzsche were afraid to set up too readily and too soon the
positive values of graceful ease and harmony and joyful *amor fati*,
for no sooner do they look like being realized in concrete terms
than they are rejected as not the right values after all. The
dominant key of the book – 'Ah, but not this, and not that... and
not yet!' – is intended as a qualification of false absolutes, yet it
is more like an intimation of doom. It is hard to see where the
unqualified *positive* aspects of the Superman, and of the morality
of strenuousness he embodies, might lie. In its negative aspects
– its emphasis on self-sacrifice, renunciation of what is agreeable
and qualified acceptance of 'ascetic ideals' – this morality looks
much closer to Christianity than Nietzsche would have us
believe; and this has led many writers – Thomas Mann among

them – to see in it the authentic form of Christian morality in our time. Yet it needs no great theological perspicacity to recognize that only a deeply confused age could place its faith in a Christianity without Christ and a Christian morality without redemption.

Nietzsche allows himself no way out of the radical negation. Whatever the will creates is there to be destroyed and overcome – all values, and man himself, must be destroyed and overcome: 'Whatever I create and howsoever I love it', Zarathustra proclaims, 'soon I must be its and my own love's enemy – thus my will commands'. All conquest, including self-overcoming, is for the sake of new, higher values and further conquests of the will to power; and these in turn must be overcome for the sake of yet higher values, a yet greater will to power – to what end? We seem to be involved in an infinite spiral, analogous to Hegel's self-realization of the spirit. When Marx decided to translate this process into political theory, he tried to make it palatable simply by decreeing that it was finite and that it would reach its goal in a generation or two. And Nietzsche? There never was a philosopher less intent on making his metaphysics palatable. *He* decrees that the process shall be infinite, circular and intolerable: an infinite repetition of the same.

5

'The will' – any act of willing – is wholly directed toward the future. Whatever else it may accomplish, it cannot reverse the flow of events, undo what has been done, 'it cannot break time and time's covetousness', unless...Is there a condition that would make the will sovereign over the past as well as the future? 'The Riddle and the Vision' (*Z* III § 2) – at once the most moving and the most lurid of Zarathustra's parables – describes that condition and in doing so places the world of the will under a metaphysical sanction – a 'theology' of the eternal return.

A long road, steep and rough with scree, has taken Zarathustra high into the mountains. A dwarf – the spirit of gravity – on his shoulder has made his progress difficult, but now they have come to a gateway and when Zarathustra sits down to rest, the dwarf jumps off his shoulder. The name inscribed on the gateway, Zarathustra explains to the dwarf, is 'the Moment'. Here at this gateway, he continues, the two tracks meet: the one, lasting an eternity, goes back into the past; the other, another eternity, leads into the future.

'Do you think, dwarf, that these two tracks contradict each other, eternally?'

'All that is straight lies,' the dwarf muttered contemptuously, 'All truth is crooked, time itself is a circle.'

'Oh spirit of gravity,' I said angrily, 'do not make things too easy for yourself. Or I shall leave you here crouching, lamefoot – was it not I who carried you all this way up?'

'Behold this moment!' I continued. 'From this gateway, called the Moment, a long, eternal road leads backwards – behind us lies an eternity. Must not whatever can run have run along this road before? Must not whatever can happen have happened before, have been done before, have run this way before? And if everything has existed before, what then do you think of this moment, dwarf? Must not this gateway too have been here before? And are not all things so firmly knotted together that this moment draws all future things after it? And so – itself too? For whatever can run down this long road must run again.

And this slow spider which crawls in the moonlight, and this moonlight itself, and I and you in the gateway, whispering together, whispering of eternal things – must we not all have been here before? And must we not come again and run out, along that other road, ahead of us, along that long, ghostly road – must we not eternally come back?'

'...und ich und du im Torwege, zusammen flüsternd, von ewigen Dingen flüsternd – müssen wir nicht alle schon dagewesen sein?' It is the high moment of Nietzsche–Zarathustra's vision.

Yet is it more than a philosopher's dream, the image of his metaphysical 'Sehnsucht'? It is the minimal theology of the age he identifies as God-less.

The thought of the eternal recurrence and its implications, Nietzsche tells us, came to him with the rush of a sudden inspiration on the shores of Lake Silvaplana, 'six thousand feet above man and time' (*EH* x § 1), and there is no reason to doubt the overpowering nature of the experience. Nevertheless, the thought (as Nietzsche himself emphasized) is pre-Socratic in origin, it had occupied him in his first Basle lectures of 1872,[1] and he had taken issue with its Pythagorean formulation early on in the second of his *Thoughts Out of Season* (§ 2) of 1874; at this point he still regarded it as an absurdity. It becomes 'his'

[1] *Die vorplatonischen Philosophen* in *Mus* IV p. 352; see also Kaufmann, *Nietzsche*, p. 317.

idea only when, recognizing it as the pattern of human history, he imposes his own value judgement on it. At this point the myth, which in early Greek cosmology had served as an image of divine harmony and as a guarantee of man's auspicious fate under the gods, assumes the opposite function, intimating the senselessness of all existence.[1] Nietzsche's interpretation is bound to be negative as soon as he 'historicizes' the myth – as soon as he places it in an historical context.

This (to one side of Heidegger's insistence) is the point at issue: the roots of Nietzsche's version of 'the doctrine of the eternal recurrence of all things' do not lie in any ontological speculation, but in his criticism of contemporary ideology; that is, in that later section of 'The Use and Disadvantage of History' from which I have already quoted, where he meditates upon 'the goal of mankind'. Attacking the fashionable idea of progress, Nietzsche argues that this goal must lie in mankind's 'highest specimens', and that these may occur, and recur, in every age:[2] the past must contain them, but so must the present and the future. And if we assume that the past stretches backward into infinity, it must contain not only 'the highest specimens' of mankind but *all* of mankind – all that has ever happened and all that can ever happen, including 'the gateway called "the Moment"', where the past ends and the future with *its* infinity begins.[3] *And all meaning* – all truth, value and significance – *must lie in this process* of 'eternal' iteration, or else nowhere at all.

But still we have not explained how the will becomes sovereign over the past. The answer must depend on what value Nietzsche decides to impose on his myth: is it to be the source of supreme hope or of total despair? This arbitrariness is irremovable. Looking from the gateway into the future, we see the will reigning supreme: we see the future, and all eternity, undetermined but determinable by our will, and therefore the past too (a replica of the future) wholly determinable by it – the seedbox of hope; looking backward into the past, we find that nothing is determinable, all is determined, including the future, again a replica of the past – a seedbox of black despair.

[1] See Karl Löwith, 'Nietzsche nach sechzig Jahren', in *Gesammelte Abhandlungen* (Stuttgart 1960), p. 138.
[2] See above, p. 54. Nietzsche does not actually say that they occur and recur etc., but he ridicules the clown who denies such a view of history.
[3] See Fink, *Nietzsches Philosophie*, chapter 3 §4.

Supreme hope or total despair? Nothing in between will do. We recall that it was the dwarf – personifying, like Wagner's Alberich,[1] the spirit of gravity – whose words, 'Time itself is a circle', first proclaimed the doctrine of the eternal recurrence, though he had been mocked by Zarathustra for not seeing its implications. And Zarathustra can only elaborate what the dwarf has said, he can only bring out the annihilating, nihilistic aspect of the Janus-faced myth. The recurrence is to be absolute, the identity of the indiscernible replicas is to be complete:

I shall return [Zarathustra proclaims], with this sun, with this earth, with this eagle, with this snake – *not* to a new life, or a better life, or a similar life:...I shall return always to this self-same life, in the greatest and in the smallest things, that I may teach again the recurrence of all things, ...that I may speak again the Word of the great noon of the earth and of men, that I may again herald the Superman to all men. (III § 13)

'Let us think this thought in its most terrible form: existence as it is, without meaning and goal yet inexorably returning, without a finale issuing in nothingness: "the eternal recurrence"' (*WzM* § 55). Waking from the swoon into which the thought has sent him, Zarathustra sees a shepherd struggling with a black snake that had crawled into his mouth and bitten fast into his throat – man struggling with the doctrine in its annihilating aspect – and, 'Bite! Bite its head off!' Zarathustra calls to the shepherd. 'And the shepherd bit as I had called to him to do, he bit with a will, spewing out the snake's head a long way and jumping up: no longer a shepherd, no longer a man, but one changed, radiant, laughing. Never yet on earth did a man laugh as he laughed'. But for Zarathustra, when he himself undergoes the vision,[2] the other aspect prevails:

Alas, the man will ever return, the little man will ever return! Once I have seen them both naked, the great man and the little man; all too like each other, all too human even the greatest!

All too little, the greatest! – that was my weariness of men! And eternal recurrence of the smallest too! – that was my weariness with all existence! Alas, disgust...

[1] See S. L. Gilman, *Nietzschean Parody* (Bonn 1976), p. 114.
[2] John Stambaugh (*Nietzsche's Thought of Eternal Return*, Baltimore and London 1972, p. 42) observes that when Zarathustra himself has the experience – and not just the 'vision' – of the eternal recurrence, he does not seem to remember the earlier scene with the shepherd.

6

The 'doctrine of the eternal recurrence' is determined by the physical properties of the image chosen – Time as a path intersected by the gateway of the Present, with Past and Future equally reified. The image ceases to support the parable and (to paraphrase Nietzsche's remarks on 'the style of decadence) assumes sovereign power over the argument as a whole. Therefore to enquire into its truth and logical cogency must seem as odd as to enquire into the truth and logical cogency of the bird motif in Act II of Wagner's *Siegfried*. The truth of such poetic myths or motifs is their function in the whole to which they belong. That whole is not a positivist's or materialist's 'Weltanschauung'. In extolling 'the earth' and 'the world' as man's only true home, and in calling the body 'man's true soul', Nietzsche at the same time acknowledges and extols man's disposition to transcend himself and his condition, to see himself 'as a transition and a going-under'. But this tendency in man must be given a clear goal, his consciousness – part animal, part metaphysical – must have a clear object: it is the earth as the absolute end of his existence. In other words: the doctrine is designed 'to take the place of metaphysics and religion' (*WzM* § 462), *to be* a metaphysics and a religion (it is, significantly, called an '*eternal* recurrence') but of a negative kind: to offer not consolations for wrongs endured and rewards for virtues practised, but to be a test: 'Who can endure the thought of the eternal recurrence?' (*Mus* XIV p. 187)

The implications of Christian eternity are described → it is rejected → a new conception of 'eternity' is set up: here, once again, is Nietzsche's three-stage dialectic. And this new 'eternity' is not, as some have argued, a contradiction of the idea of the Superman, but the proving of his worth. So powerful is to be his love of life, so intense his passion for it, that even when life is perpetuated into infinity in all its greatness and triviality; when these, too, the great and the trivial, come to be seen, devastatingly, as of one kind and then are to be repeated again and again, *ad infinitum* and *ad nauseam*, without change, without improvement, without added meaning or significance... if all this, carried on into eternity, is to be the 'meaning' of life, and yet the Superman is to assent to it, give it his active approval and the stamp of his love – then indeed he has proved himself in the most strenuous test which his creator is capable of envisaging, then he has cleansed himself of all false and consoling beliefs, of all spurious comfort and superstition, and is left with a 'faith' that is likely to make all willing, all our vital powers, shrivel up in horror. Then he has exposed himself to the merciless rays of the midday sun, the sun that throws its harsh light into every corner of experience; that leaves no hidden comfort in the dark caves and picturesque grottoes of the old religion. (Camus re-interprets the Sisyphus myth and singles out as the one moment of true worth and dignity the moment near the peak of Sisyphus's mountain, the moment when he knows that another push will send the rock rolling down again and thus he will have to start again on his task of pushing it uphill. At this moment Sisyphus decides that he will go on. The meaning he is capable of creating lies in this action. He wills the rest. Not blindly, not unaware of the consequences, not hopeful for a different outcome, he yet wills the ineluctable course of events. The past and the future are one.)

What Nietzsche is trying to put into words is 'a vision of the world *sub specie aeterni*' – the world as a self-contained, deeply meaningless whole – and this vision I take to be ineffable and thus unassailable. Yet we cannot for long contemplate the image which is designed to express the vision, or think about the concept behind the image, without being struck by its inherent contradictions. It is certainly not empty nonsense, yet it does not make coherent sense either. Let us leave aside the question of how such a recurrence is possible, accept it as a metaphysical *donnée* (in the same way as we accept the single occurrence of the world), and confine ourselves to its function as a moral-existential test. The image of 'the great man and the little man' is as moving as it is profound, but what is to make 'the eternal recurrence of it' frightening and nauseous? First, it cannot be simply the repetitious nature of the recurrences themselves, but our awareness of their repetitiousness. This awareness must be cumulative and therefore each time different, each time more acute than the last: neither the experiencing self nor the experience can ever be 'exactly the same'. (And if they are 'exactly the same', then obviously they cannot be distinguished and are all one anyway.) But, secondly, repetition entails horror and accidie only if it is accompanied by an awareness of a repeated failure to reach something better, perhaps even some grand metaphysical goal

– in any event a good that is outside the world which is to be eternally repeated (for if it were inside the world, it would be part of the repetition, unchanging). But this again involves a destructive contradiction, for the image serves a doctrine which is designed to scotch all thought of anything 'outside' – any kind of eschatological ideal, of which the Christian ideal is, for Nietzsche, the only conceivable paradigm. We must conclude that, even as a moral–existential test, the doctrine functions only on the premise of a pseudo-Christian eschatology; but such an eschatology remains unexpressed, for it is destructive of the purpose for which it was set up in the first place – the purpose of expressing a vision of the world as a self-contained, deeply meaningless whole. (It does not make the world meaningful, it only fails to make it a self-contained whole.) With this kind of failure to make sense we are familiar from previous arguments. Each time, transcendence is to be rejected for a moral–existential purpose by an authority that bases itself on transcendent grounds. This is where Nietsche's three-stage dialectic runs into the ground.

Of course, there is another possibility, which I shall call 'aesthetic': that is, to accept the repetitions – joyfully, or at least equanimously, and to rejoice in the spectacle of all that happens without worrying about whether it has, or has not, an ultimate meaning. In these terms, however, there are not only no grounds for despair or disgust, there is no need of either eternity or recurrence.

Immense ontological edifices have been built on the site of Nietzsche's idea of the eternal recurrence. Even more than in other parts of his philosophy, his few remarks have been taken as intimations of an entire cosmology. It is a vision which aspires to being a doctrine (Nietzsche himself repeatedly calls it '*die Lehre* von der ewigen Wiederkunft des Gleichen'), a theory about the ends of life dictated by an intense personal experience and transfixed into an image, conveying a feeling (to us a deeply familiar feeling) about life, but hardly capable of conceptualization. It is, as Heidegger and others have observed, the culmination of Nietzsche's entire philosophical venture. But since (unlike Heidegger) I have taken Nietzsche's moral–existential concern to be the heart of that venture, I have throughout presented the ontological aspect of Nietzsche's thinking, including his speculations on the idea of the eternal recurrence, as ancillary. Nietzsche's concern as I have described it here takes the form of a God-less theology to which only the function of the idea of the eternal recurrence – its value as a moral–existential test – is important.

This 'theology' is Nietzsche's main bequest to the new century. With its heroism of strenuousness, its scepticism of all traditional solutions, its radical rejection of all grace and ease, its occasional pride of despair and its validation through suffering and sacrifice, it became the dominant ideology and 'table of values', of Germany at all events, in the era *entre deux guerres*. It inspired, indeed obsessed, the writings of her greatest literary men and philosophers. From it derives that scrupulousness with which some of these writers anticipated and tried to oppose the monstrous political solutions proposed in that era, whose hallmark was cheapness and brutal simplicity, and which won the day. Yet there is another aspect to this 'heroism of strenuousness': it is also the ground shared by enemies. Reading the literature of national socialism – Rosenberg's book, the speeches of Hitler, Himmler, Goebbels, the poems of countless party hacks (a penitential task if ever there was one), one can no longer ignore the way the rhetoric of all these pronouncements plays on the need for sacrifice, on the exacting yet self-validating nature of the struggle, on the perils of the road ahead, and on the value of authenticity seen as one man's commitment to his supremely hard (and preferably distasteful) task; and as one follows Hitler's career, too, it becomes evident that its apogee lay, not in the years of his great triumphs, but in those last years of strenuousness when he succeeded in identifying his defective self with a nation and a whole world at war, under the device not of conquest but of destruction.

It is no great merit for us to be able to see what neither Nietzsche nor the next generation quite foresaw: that in a situation of lawlessness, with every restraint undermined and 'everything permitted', the idea – accepted as unqualified value – of a validation of man through his own supreme effort, coupled with the allurement of heroic defeat, would lead to horrifying abuse. In estimating the extent of Nietzsche's influence, we must bear in mind that its concrete political consequences were confined to prewar Germany and Italy and, to a lesser extent, war-time France, whereas only its literary and philosophical aspects took root in England. The reason for this is obvious. Men like George Bernard Shaw and H. G. Wells, D. H. Lawrence and W. B. Yeats did not live in a society on the verge of anarchy. What prevented them from turning their literary ideas into political realities was the social *donnée* of their lives – an as yet unbroken national tradition of decency, inertia and institutionalized freedom; a tradition which Nietzsche viewed with little more than contempt.

To the patient reader of this study it will hardly come as a surprise to learn that the morality of strenuousness with its theological overtones does not go uncontradicted in Nietzsche's writings. There are occasions when he attacks it as a distortion of 'the joyful science' about man, as lacking all grace and Mediterranean equanimity, all love of surfaces and *finesse*. As early as *Human, All-too-Human* (1880) he ridicules the notion that 'strenuous effort in search of truth is supposed to determine the value of that truth', and that '"truths" are really nothing more than a sort of gymnastic apparatus on which we are supposed to exercise until we are worn out – a morality for athletes and champion gymnasts of the mind' (*MA* II §4). And in the *Zarathustra* chapter entitled 'The Spirit of Gravity' (III § 11) it is the opposite of such truths – the light and effortless virtues and the grace of flying which are praised and which Zarathustra calls his own. Is there an escape from that spirit, a liberation from that morality? *Thus Spoke Zarathustra* leaves the question open. It is a highly conscious work, yet only occasionally, as if by poetic accident, does it reveal the full object of its author's consciousness, the search for redemption from conflict, from black and white contrasts and judgement... Where is such freedom to be found? Suppose 'the world', 'the whole', were really without 'depth', not serious as the eternally recurring world understands seriousness, no more than a game, a sport of the absent gods?

10
'*Only as an aesthetic phenomenon...*'

I could be bounded in a nut-shell, and count myself a King of infinite space;
were it not that I have bad dreams.

(Hamlet II: 2)

What is aesthetics? What is the function of the aesthetic in the world? For Nietzsche it is a full mode of experience: not the trimmings of life[1] but a total re-enacting of it in a different medium, the whole of life (we might say) 'de-pragmatized', done over again in a lighter substance. Or is the aesthetic even more than that? A full *alternative* to morality, even perhaps to the morality of the will to power? A redemption of our being and our world? The validation of something in itself fragmentary? From his first Basle lectures of 1869 to his last jottings these questions accompany Nietzsche's moral–existential thinking, sometimes merging with it, then again drawn up in conscious opposition to it – aspects of that enigma which never ceases to fascinate him: How seriously, in our moment of history, are we to take life?

I

The young classical scholar's brilliant first book, *The Birth of Tragedy from the Spirit of Music* (1872), was violently attacked on its publication, it destroyed his credentials as a university teacher, and is still regarded by some as a cuckoo in the nest of classical scholarship. Our concern is with the way in which it contributes to Nietzsche's aesthetic project and thus to the dichotomy that determines his philosophizing.

Like Schopenhauer before him, Nietzsche sees the fullest embodiment of the aesthetic in music. He follows scholarly tradition by placing the origin of tragedy in the chorus, though for him the important thing is not its message but its dithyrambs; he sees the chorus, quite literally, as the crowd of satyrs accompanying Dionysus, the god of the vine and of ecstasy, on his drunken revels through the forest. In their ecstasy and in the

---

[1] See Nietzsche's 1871 Preface to *GT*, dedicated to Wagner.

dirge they sing, the satyrs and their god are one: they are a single, undivided expression of the impermanence and desolation of human existence. This 'ground of all experience' is like the earth that was without form and like the darkness that was upon the face of the deep. It stands for and *is* a single, fundamental human disposition, involving as yet no division between self and the world.

This one-ness is broken as soon as men come to know, and to reflect upon, their ephemeral state. In the wake of the satyrs King Midas roams through the forest, seeking Silenus, Dionysus's companion and foster-father, who is hiding from him. At last the mortal king catches the elusive god and forces him to speak, to tell him the most devastating of all truths: 'You want to know what life is about?' Silenus asks. 'The best is out of your reach, for the best of all things is not to have been born, is not to be, to be nothing!' (*GT* § 3) Faced with this knowledge, men become self-conscious, sober, reflective, filled with tragic apprehension. Now they make it their task to hide the terrible knowledge from themselves and from those who watch their revels, and they do this by turning their apprehension of the truth into an ecstatic show, a drama; however, by 'drama' Nietzsche means not an action but an episode or scene – even 'a fundamental mood' – of great pathos (*FaW* § 9). The origin of this pathos in music (analogous to the origin of many lyrical poems in a musical mood) connects drama with a non-verbal, chthonian world which Nietzsche considers more authentic than the world of words and mere 'literature'. It is of the essence of the show which the chorus enacts that it should both preserve the pathos of their new knowledge and make that knowledge bearable, and the god who helps them to fashion it into a bearable – indeed a beautiful – form is the sun god Apollo.

The vitality and importance of art is confirmed by Nietzsche's insistence on its psychosomatic parallel: as Dionysus is the god of chaos, fruitfulness and *ecstasy*, so Apollo is the god of ordered form and of the *dream* seen as the silent re-casting of life. Tragedy is born at the conjuncture of these two fundamental impulses, to which Nietzsche gives the names of their tutelary deities, the Dionysian and the Apolline. What the artist, its creator, experiences is

...the whole divine comedy of life, including the inferno...not like mere shadows on the wall – for he lives and suffers with these scenes

– and yet not without that fleeting sensation of illusion. And perhaps many will, like myself, recall how amid the dangers and terrors of dreams they have occasionally called out to themselves in self-encouragement and not without success: 'It is a dream! I wish to dream on!' (§ 1)

The formulation is among the most accurate and beautiful in Nietzsche's work, but it is as precarious as the moment it describes. As yet, the image-making faculty is not contrasted with consciousness, or indeed self-consciousness. The art thus characterized may not be the art of classical Greek drama that Nietzsche is about to describe, but it fits a work like *Die Meistersinger* or modern, post-Nietzschean drama to perfection. Appealing to a common psychic experience – or, at least, an experience he considers common and which is certainly not eccentric – Nietzsche draws from it the view that drama is both dream and consciousness of dream. But this positive evaluation of consciousness is not maintained. The next step in the argument, in the later sections of *The Birth of Tragedy* and then in the second of *Thoughts out of Season,* will be the exaltation of a healthy, creative life at the cost of all self-conscious and merely intellectual knowledge of the world, followed by Nietzsche's strange paeans to the unconscious, 'the natural' and 'the instinctive' as authentic modes of experience. (I have already suggested that we cannot blame Nietzsche for the ghastly company in which this enthusiasm for authenticity in its various forms was to land him in our time, when he could no longer 'prevent people from doing mischief with me' (*EH* IV § 10). Yet we must marvel at the paradox, for which we have lost the taste, whereby this most intellectual and conscious of modern thinkers invokes values to which he is himself a stranger.)

The *basso continuo* of Nietzsche's dialectic, then, is to maintain the interplay between two fundamental modes of knowledge-and-life which encompass his view of tragedy: its Dionysian foundation and the Apolline order imposed upon it. The distinction has its roots in Schopenhauer's dichotomy of the World as Will and the World as Idea; it is related to Aristotle's distinction of matter and form; its chief ancestor is Schiller's dichotomy of the 'naïve' and the 'sentimentalisch' modes of poetry. It has its place among the three or four truly memorable arguments in the history of aesthetics. Its epitome is mastered energy, its poles are chaos and epic harmony. When the Dionysian element rules, ecstasy and inchoateness threaten;

when the Apolline predominates, the tragic feeling recedes. Of the two, the Dionysian remains the fundamental, but the balance in the great works of tragic art is subtle and easily upset. Changes in this balance provide Nietzsche with the data of a rudimentary literary history. The balance is achieved for the first time in Aeschylus, and then again in Sophocles; by the time Euripides comes to dominate the literary scene, the Dionysian element is attenuated and at last all but completely suppressed, and (in *The Bacchae*) the thwarted god himself takes his revenge.

The predominance of the Dionysian element in the masterpieces of Greek tragedy points to a set of ideas with which we are already familiar: it implies, first, that for Nietzsche intuition and ecstasy are the only authentic modes of artistic creation; it implies, secondly, an interest in the genealogy rather than in the structure of a work of art – an interest which is so strong that it wholly determines the evaluation of the work; and it assumes, finally, an unreflective belief on the part of the playwrights' public in the germinal episodes or myths from which tragedy is fashioned, a belief which the poets share with their public. What these myths represent is not the mimesis of a plot (not, as in Aristotle's famous opening sentence, 'the imitation of an *action*'), *but the articulation of a fundamental mood*, or what we would call a style of life. Throughout Nietzsche's aesthetic writings it is this conception of a mood or life-style which is his dominant concern. Here is the conundrum again:[1] this 'Lebensgefühl' is, for him, more fundamental than rational argument, because it is its source.

The decline of Greek tragedy begins where creative ecstasy is suppressed and has to give way to cold calculation. Now the old myths cease to be experienced as parts of an ecstatic religious ritual and become objects of rational analysis, and the gods and their stories come to be judged according to the prosy maxims of reasoned justice. And (by a characteristic historicizing turn of Nietzsche's philosophical imagination) this development of Greek tragedy emerges as a paradigm for every other cultural development, including the decline into decadence and degeneration he sees taking place around him.

Nietzsche's choice of a biological metaphor is revealing. Art is one of the ruses of life, tragedy has always had a vital function: to protect men from a full knowledge of the life-destroying doom

---

[1] See above, p. 106, and J. P. Stern, *Idylls and Realities*, p. 209.

that surrounds them, and at the same time to refresh their zest
for life from tragedy's own dark Stygian sources. The degeneration of tragedy at the hands of Euripides and of the ugly,
artistically ungifted Socrates means that it can no longer fulfil its
vital function. The new literary forms – Platonic dialogue and
Aesopean fable – are effete parodies of the tragic sense of life,
which in their superficiality and optimism no longer acknowledge
the reality of the abyss of suffering. Through these forms has
been jeopardized that instinctive feeling of awe and apprehension without which the life-blood of every culture runs into the
sand. For true culture (Nietzsche argues) is only possible within
that narrow boundary where knowledge is manageable yet all
that threatens life is not trivialized: an area bounded by a 'not
yet' and a 'no longer'. The 'not yet', pure want, is the stage where
the Dionysian song dominates to the extent of making
articulation and individuation impossible (articulation of inchoate responses till they become myth, and individuation of
responses till they become individual characters who enact the
myth). And the 'no longer' is the prosy stage of rationalism, when
the myths are accounted for in discursive and abstract terms;
explained in rational–causal terms; and thus explained away.

What are the conditions under which that narrow space
between 'not yet' and 'no longer' comes into being? Can it be
deliberately created? When, in the last sections of *The Birth of
Tragedy*, Nietzsche writes his great panegyric of Richard Wagner
as the man who will 'recreate' the cultic and mythical situation
of Sophoclean tragedy, the deeply problematic nature of his
undertaking becomes clear. He is not so much explaining the
origins of Greek drama as re-enacting the classical unity of the
'aesthetic' with a cultic vision – a unity which is to encompass the
whole life of a nation; and what he is seeking is a concrete,
objective correlative to this vision in the world around him. He
finds it – or he thinks he finds it – in Richard Wagner, the most
richly gifted of his contemporaries. He is anxious to attribute to
Wagner's art the same cultic quality which he – Nietzsche – saw
in the great tragedians of Greece. Wagner is delighted to oblige.
The break comes, *not* because Wagner repudiates the role of
modern mystagogue, but because (as Nietzsche discovers) he
cynically exploits it.

There are battles which are lost. Who could fail to sympathize
with Nietzsche when he invokes 'the rebirth of a German myth'

or when he writes, 'Without a myth every culture loses its healthy, creative natural power. Only a horizon enclosed by myths gives unity to a whole cultural movement' (*GT* § 23)? Yet the fact that Nietzsche's critical observation is no less relevant to the condition of our culture than it was to his, does not make his plea for the birth of a new myth less pre-posterous. The vital need of the age (he is saying) is for a new kind of innocence, an archaic state of cult and culture, for a sophisticated breakthrough into unsophistication. At least, we have learned that studied instinctiveness is humbug, and that whatever is wrong with our culture, it is not excess of consciousness. (And if Richard Wagner failed to fulfil Nietzsche's hope for a national rebirth, we can see that it was what Italian fascism and German national socialism aimed at, and in a sense achieved, albeit with ends in view which were very different from those that Nietzsche *or* Wagner ever envisaged.)

Is this, then, Nietzsche's aesthetics? We had better pause here and take our bearings. Tragedy, embodying the aesthetic, receives its justification as a protector of life, almost, we might say, as a biological principle, an *élan vital*. Art becomes one among the many ruses which life employs in its service, for its own further-ance and protection. Everything, in this vein of Nietzsche's thinking, offers itself as a sustenance of life, is subordinated by life and made subservient to its indefinable goals. From the psychosomatic analogy of dream and ecstasy which Nietzsche had used in *The Birth of Tragedy* he moves to the coarse-grained view (e.g. *GM* III § 8) which turns all aesthetic considerations into questions of a man's taste, itself a function of his physiological condition. And since, under the influence of 'social Darwinism', Nietzsche is apt to see all biological facts in terms of achievement and failure, degeneracy and health, of *yes* and *no*, his attempts at a systematic physiology of art (*FaW* § 7) are bound to subvert all autonomous aesthetic arguments. Is this – an aesthetics which slithers into an ethics of physiological or bio-psychological values – the end purpose of Nietzsche's reflections? A number of his disciples – D. H. Lawrence and George Bernard Shaw among them – believed that he was aiming at something like this, but they were misled by their own prepossessions. This is not an end purpose at which Nietzsche's thinking can rest. For if being a prompter and protector of life is the purpose of art, what then is the purpose of life?

2

Nietzsche's speculations on the physiology of taste are intended as a challenge to traditional idealist aesthetics. From Kant and Schiller onwards the aesthetic object had been singled out as the goal and focus of a disinterested attitude, the aesthetic state as a state of equanimity, of 'pure contemplation', so as to counterbalance all those activities and states of mind which have as their aim the pursuit of material values, practical achievements, and vital and moral considerations. Schopenhauer's philosophy of art (which is the subsuming of his entire philosophy) is the culmination and completion of the Kantian aesthetic – and Nietzsche attacked it as such even at the time when he still regarded Schopenhauer as his great teacher and exemplar. Selflessness, disinterestedness, for Nietzsche, are not virtues but merely the shamefaced acknowledgements of a small, defective self:

Since Kant, all talk of art, beauty, knowledge and wisdom is sullied and made messy by the concept of disinterestedness. *I* regard as beautiful (historically speaking) all that which, in the most revered men of an age, assumes visible shape as the expression of what is *most worthy* of reverence. (*Mus* XVII p. 304)

The peremptory tone of this reflection reminds us of several others on the borderline between statement of fact and exhortation: we must create men to whom the truth will be useful (*WKG* VII/1 p. 148); a man's knowledge may not extend beyond his will to power (*J* §211); his thinking and his action should be one (*Z* 1 §5). In all such reflections Nietzsche calls for a reconciliation of two concepts set up in opposition to each other and intended to define one in terms of the other: truth in terms of usefulness, knowledge in terms of the will to power or of 'a hygiene of life', art in terms of human reverence – the objective in terms of the subjective. These are his 'positive' proposals, his pedagogic strategy. All are indicative of his desire that value should be determined by nothing but the personal being of man, but this desire brings the spectre of solipsism in its train. For Nietzsche knows that there is truth which is lethal, knowledge which comes only when the will to power is assuaged, thinking which goes beyond action, and (reluctantly) great art which does not express whatever is 'most worthy of reverence'.

Moreover, who are 'the most revered men of an age'?

Consensus – the opinion of the mob – will not tell us. Are they the men with the superior will to power, those who most joyfully assent to life? The histrionic Wagner is not one of them, nor are 'some of the greatest names in art', including Goethe, for there is 'an actor at the heart of every artist' (*Mus* xv/ii p. 334), and do not the actor and the comedian represent the sum of spuriousness and inauthenticity (*FaW* § 11)? It is clear that since Nietzsche is not prepared to consider a work of art as independent of the character of its creator, the aesthetic mode can never be made independent of the moral. From first ('Lest the bow should snap, there is Art', *U* iv §4) to last ('We have Art lest we should perish of the truth', *WzM* §822) the aesthetic is to be in the service of life – can it also act as a redemption from life? Again and again we feel his intense desire to free the world from the yoke of all moral schemes, including his own morality of the will to power – it was this desire (we recall) which produced the Nazarene fiction of a gentle, unjudging Jesus. Overwhelmed by the ubiquity of conflict and strife, Nietzsche seeks a corner of the world – but with him it can never be less than a total view of the world – that would be free from all conflict and free, above all, from the everlasting business of judging: 'It would be terrible if we still believed in sin: no, whatever we shall do, in countless repetitions, it will be *innocent*. There is no guilt if the thought of the eternal recurrence does not overwhelm you, no merit if it does' (*WKG* v/2 p. 394). Well then – since 'God is dead' and we no longer believe in sin, has not the reign of innocence come? Even in his most euphoric moments Nietzsche does not believe this. Once again, therefore, he moves from statement of fact to exhortations: if 'God is dead', the artist will be god and Nietzsche will proclaim his theodicy:

Only as an aesthetic phenomenon is the world and existence eternally justified.

Three times this strange sentence occurs in *The Birth of Tragedy*, hardly connected with the contexts in which it appears. But since it was written down at least fifteen years before the opening of the last book of *The Joyous Science*, in which 'the death of God' is announced for the first time, is there any indication that this experience of 'a God-less world' casts its shadow over his first book too? It is difficult to answer the question with assurance. Certainly there is no mention of this anguished, wholly *modern* recognition, either in the book's main historical argument with its bright and enthusiastic rush of images and scenes from classical Greece, or in its final sections, where Wagner is invoked as the mythopoeic bard of the new age. Yet the quasi-religious strain to which Nietzsche draws attention in his prefatorial self-criticism of 1886 is certainly present in the book, nowhere more so than in this disconnected sentence: in the word 'eternal', in the totality ('*only* as...') of the claim, and in the 'justification', the God-less theodicy. Man's judging activity is not repudiated (as it will later be in *Anti-Christ*, his last completed work), but it is to be conducted from a different, all-encompassing point of view. Now the entire world and all that we do in it is seen as a sort of game or play, a spectacle for the gods if there are any gods to watch it:

Around the hero everything turns into tragedy, around the demi-god everything turns into satyric drama; and around God everything turns into – what? Maybe the 'world'? (*J* § 150)

The world's gravity and seriousness – its tragic dimension – is rendered weightless (as time is rendered endless in the idea of the 'eternal' recurrence) – weightless, yet infinitely more memorable than it had ever been in its aesthetically unredeemed state. Only in this form does the world become what Nietzsche wants it to be: the worthy object of a limitless, total affirmation. And in this idea of an aesthetic theodicy the eternal recurrence, too, seen as an unending game or spectacle (*WzM* §§ 1066–7), receives its final 'justification'.

Nietzsche loved the image of the snake: the beginning and the end of his philosophizing close in a circle. The aesthetic validation of the world – in *The Birth of Tragedy* it is merely an exhortation and a hypothesis – is taken up again in the panegyrics to Dionysian creativeness at the end of *Beyond Good and Evil*[1] and in the last notes to *The Will to Power*. It is in these notes that the unconditioned assent to the single moment of happiness is identified with Dionysus, the god of chaos, fertility and the enhancement of life through the threat of death (§ 1032); here the world is celebrated as a dancing god, or again as a child; and here too (§ 1039) Nietzsche at last records the self-critical, self-destructive truth that only those who are possessed by the spirit of gravity ever yearn for the ideals of lightness and grace,

---

[1] See above, p. 91.

and go out in search of them. Dionysus now becomes the name of that divinity which, transcending any narrowly aesthetic idea, transforms and 'eternally justifies' the world of suffering; the Dionysian is that tragic mode of being and view of life whose source is not weakness and decadence but 'an excess of force' and vitality (*GD* x §4). Dionysus now seems to stand for all creation, everything...But does it matter by what name that limitless affirmation which Nietzsche desires above all things is to be called, what emblematic figure he chooses for 'that long, that tremendous light- and colour-scale of happiness to which the Greeks gave the divinity's name' (*WzM* §1051)?

It does matter. As long as Nietzsche calls his ideal of affirmation 'Dionysus', he is still involved in the world of conflict and strife. Dionysus still acts as a judge of men, shaming us in our velleities and deprivations (§1051). While he has an antagonist, the assent he commands cannot be total. And indeed, as Nietzsche tells us in these last notes, written in the summer of 1888, there *is* a rival deity. Its name is no longer Apollo (the Apolline is now subsumed under the Dionysian), but Christ.

But is Dionysus as Nietzsche sees him really Christ's antagonist? Intuitively aware of the close tie between the one whom the Maenads tore limb from limb and the one who was crucified, the poet Hölderlin had united both in a single elegiac vision. Nietzsche thrusts them apart:

Dionysus versus 'the Crucified': there you have the antithesis. The difference is not in respect of their martyrdom but of its meaning. Life itself, its eternal fruitfulness and recurrence, involves torment, destruction, the will to annihilation. In the other case suffering – 'the Crucified as the innocent one' – serves as an argument against this life and as a formula for its condemnation. Evidently, what is at issue is the problem of the meaning – Christian or tragic? – of suffering. In the former case it is to be the way toward holy being, in the latter, being itself is holy enough to justify an enormity of suffering...The god on the cross is a curse on life, pointing to a redemption from life: Dionysus torn to pieces is a promise of life – it will be eternally reborn and return again from destruction. (§1052)

We can see why Nietzsche, the declared enemy of Christian eschatology, wishes to widen the gulf between his two deities. And yet: there can hardly be anything more Christian, anything closer to the mystery of the man-and-God on the cross, than Nietzsche's Dionysian justification of the world, of which he says that it transfigures the world's suffering without robbing it of its reality; and there can hardly be anything less 'aesthetic'.

Is there then no end to the conflict, no end to judging? If the god Dionysus does not vouchsafe it, what will? In one of the chapters he wrote for his unfinished *Philosophy in the Tragic Age of the Greeks* (1873), Nietzsche had meditated on Heraclitus's apophthegm, 'The Aeon [time] is a child, playing draughts; a child's is the kingdom', which Heidegger interprets, 'Being within the Whole is governed by innocence'. This is certainly Nietzsche's meaning: freedom from guilt and responsibility – the end of all judging – but also freedom from the burden of consciousness mark the child's dominion over 'the Kingdom', over 'Being within the Whole'. To this liberating conception Nietzsche returns in the first of Zarathustra's parables[1] and in a note (as fragmentary as any of Heraclitus) in *The Will to Power*, dated 1885/6 (§ 797). Reflecting on a childlike divinity of supreme innocence, whose 'play' comprises – perhaps *is* – 'the Kingdom', Nietzsche is offering the image of the Child as an 'aesthetic justification', not only beyond good and evil, but beyond all conflict, all antagonisms. We can make little of the few words on the page.[2] The intimation is too brief, the air too thin to carry the argument. Among Nietzsche's many inconclusive conclusions, this vision of the world, justified in its totality as a child's play, characterizes his deepest yearning: yet it is the least conclusive and the least convincing. Conflict and lethal strife are inseparable from his view of the world, even from those euphoric reflections with which he leaves it and enters the night of madness. 'Dionysus' is the name he signs on his last notes; *and* 'The Crucified'. 'Here you have the antithesis.'

---

[1] See Erich Heller, *The Poet's Self and the Poem* (London 1976), chapter 2, 'Nietzsche in the Waste Land'. It does not seem likely that the image of 'the child' in this passage (Z I § 2: 'The three metamorphoses') can be connected with Matthew 18 and 19 ('except ye be converted and become like little children...'), which is ridiculed in Z IV § 18, i and ii, and accused of 'psychological naïveté' in *WzM* § 197. Whether the Greeks had any notion of identifying 'the child' with Wordsworthian innocence, as both Nietzsche and many of his critics do (rather than with caprice and mischievousness), is another question.

[2] Not so Heidegger (see *Nietzsche*, I, pp. 333ff) and Fink (*Nietzsches Philosophie*, pp. 187 to the end). Thomas Mann symbolizes Nietzsche's yearning for a final affirmation in his account of Adrian Leverkühn's last composition, where he represents 'the high G of a 'cello [as] the last word, the last fainting sound, slowly dying in a pianissimo fermata, a hope beyond hope' (see *Doktor Faustus*, chapter xlvi).

The dichotomy between the moral and the aesthetic, between strenuousness and the grace of play, remains unreconciled. And since this conflict to the last is a sign of his truthfulness, victory is not with 'the aesthetic'.

3

And many such like 'as'es' of their charge...

(*Hamlet* v: 2)

One more task remains: to consider how to read Nietzsche's work, how to understand the mode in which it is cast. The task is made easy because we can approach it through his own observations about language. The point at issue is not how accurate these observations are as fundamental (true or false) statements about the nature of language, but what they reveal of Nietzsche's own literary practice.

In 1873 (a year after *The Birth of Tragedy*) Nietzsche dictated to his old schoolfriend, Carl von Gersdorff, an essay entitled 'On Truth and Falsehood in an Extra-Moral Sense'.[1] Although this is only a short essay of fifteen pages, hardly corrected by Nietzsche and not published until 1903, it is probably the longest single essay on a traditional philosophical subject he ever wrote. It is an imperfect piece, and we shall have to supplement its argument from Nietzsche's contemporary note-books and later reflections, but it contains his only considered statement on the nature, which turns out to be the metaphysics, of language.

Its purpose is to elucidate and evaluate a linguistic variant of Kantian criticism (by which I do not mean that Nietzsche's argument owes anything to Kant, whose linguistic views were naïve and uncritical). Kant had maintained that we are incapable of unmediated knowledge of whatever is outside ourselves – of 'things in themselves' – since we know these things only in the forms imposed on them by our perception; subsequently Kant's position had been exaggerated, indeed falsified, to the point where it amounted to a denial of the possibility of any reliable knowledge and to the assertion of a radical subjectivism. Similarly Nietzsche claims that language, far from giving us a true account of things as they are in the world, and far from having its grounds in 'true reality', is a referentially unreliable set of

[1] *WKG* III/2 pp. 369–84. An excerpt from the essay is contained in *The Portable Nietzsche* (pp. 42–7); a complete translation appeared in the Oberlin *Undergraduate Journal of Philosophy*, May 1976.

almost entirely arbitrary signs, made up by us for various
concrete and practical ends, mainly to do with the safeguarding
of life and preservation of the species. And whereas we like to
think that the value of language is commensurate with the
amount of truth about the world it secures for us, its real value
to us is merely a pragmatic one, to do with whether or not it works.
Its principal function is to hide from us the hostile nature of the
universe in order to preserve us from destruction – at least for
a little while; therefore the lie about what the universe is really
like is not a contingent aspect of language, but its very essence.
The lie of language in an 'extra-moral sense' (as the title of the
essay puts it) consists in the vital pretence that language is able
to relate the world of men to some wider, benevolent cosmic
scheme by offering them reliable knowledge of that scheme,
whereas the universe can get on perfectly well without the world
of men and is merely waiting for an opportunity to continue on
its desolate journey through man-less aeons. The 'moral' sense
of lying, on the other hand, is confined to violating the linguistic,
lexical or semantic conventions men have set up in order to get
on with each other as best they may. No knowledge of a world
beyond our world is available to us. All statements pretending
to such knowledge are false, whereas all statements claiming to
be true accounts of our world are mere tautology:

If someone hides a thing behind a bush, looks for it there and indeed
finds it, then such searching and finding is nothing very praiseworthy:
but that precisely is what the searching and finding of 'truth' within the
realm of reason amounts to.

(Incidentally, we may wonder how men, said to be incapable of
knowing anything about the universe in which their world is
travelling, nevertheless 'know' that it is malevolent, destructive
and desolate. The answer to that question is given in *The Birth
of Tragedy*, where a pre-rational, instinctive intuition of primal
suffering and fear is postulated as the ground and origin of
humanity.)

How then (Nietzsche asks),[1] if we cannot have any positive
contact with the real world, can we sustain life? How is it that
the world works? It works with the help of an illusion, on an 'as
if...' principle. We act in the world as if we were in touch with
a benevolent reality, as if we were capable of comprehending its

[1] In a series of notes written at this time; see *Mus* VI pp. 18–19.

cosmic purpose, as if there were a divinity whose decrees we fulfil and who gives meaning to our individual lives.

While we establish and try to stabilize this 'as if . . .' relationship through language, the function of language nevertheless remains *ad hoc* and its uses largely arbitrary. Between words and things there is no direct relationship (things are not simply the causes of words), and yet the two are not completely unrelated: words are said to be the distant and distorted 'echoes of nervous impulses'. These 'echoes' or rudimentary elements are poeticized and given coherence according to rules which are entirely invented by man. Thus the relationship that obtains between words and 'the real world' is a metaphorical or aesthetic one. Man as the idealist philosophers saw him – that is, man as the unstable and contingent perceiving subject of an objective world – is re-interpreted in Nietzsche's scheme as man the creator of language. The relationship which obtains between subject and object – between human language and the real things in the world from which language is excluded – is not a causal relationship, for between two such heterogeneous things as subject and object no direct relationship can exist. Nor is it mimetic or expressive, but what Nietzsche calls 'at most an aesthetic attitude',

. . .by which I mean an intimatory transference, a sort of halting, stammering translation into an entirely foreign language: for which purpose we need a freely poeticizing, a freely inventive middle sphere and middle faculty.

(We shall see these words – 'a middle sphere and middle faculty' – are more revealing than Nietzsche is likely to have intended.) This 'poeticizing translation into an entirely foreign language' Nietzsche now likens to the production of Chladny's figures,[1] which are obtained by drawing the bow of a violin across a board of very thin plywood covered with fine sand; the regular geometrical patterns into which the grains of sand arrange themselves thus reproduce or 'reflect' the vibrations of the music. These figures are as it were metaphorical representations of the music – metaphors of a metaphor. Though it might not be absurd to claim that you can tell from these patterns what it is that men mean by the word 'tone', the patterns will certainly not tell you anything about the nature and meaning of music.

[1] For Schopenhauer's use of these 'figures' see *Die Welt als Wille und Vorstellung* vol. I iii § 52, and vol. II § 39.

This picturesque yet accurate image aptly illustrates Nietzsche's historical situation. We note his predilection for an analogy drawn from the realm of natural sciences – it is, as always, a not very sophisticated bit of science – such as was fashionable in the heyday of the scientific ideology; and we are left with the impression that in order to explain the mental operation involved in the creation of language, all we need to do is translate the mechanical causality of Chladny's figures into the sphere of mind. A good many of the psychological insights and reflections in the books of Nietzsche's most mature period – especially in *Beyond Good and Evil* and its sequel, *The Genealogy of Morals* – are supported by analogies which involve just such a psycho-physical causality, so that it looks as though Nietzsche were on the point of accepting one of the mechanistic and materialistic psychologies current at the time. *Almost* the opposite is the case. By pointing to Chladny's sound patterns, and to the fact that, whatever else they do, they do not explain the meaning of music, Nietzsche is in fact showing how inadequate the analogy – the argument from the Chladny figures – really is, and thus pointing to the break between the psychic and the physical, between mechanical purpose and human meaning. ('We feel,' writes Wittgenstein in the *Tractatus*, 6.52, 'that even when all *possible* scientific questions have been answered, our problems of life have still not been touched at all.')

The system of language sketched out in this early essay is a system not without meaning, but it is meaningful only in itself. The way Nietzsche chooses to describe it (and we recall that he started life as a classical philologist) is by saying that words do not designate things and are not little labels stuck on to things, but are *metaphors* for real things in the world:

What then is truth? A mobile army of metaphors, metonymics, anthropomorphisms – in short, a sum of human relations which, poetically and rhetorically intensified, became transposed and adorned, and which after long usage by a people seem fixed, canonical and binding on them. Truths are illusions which one has forgotten *are* illusions

– and if, so far, the passage was cast in the form of a fairly neutral philosophical hypothesis, now the point has been reached where Nietzsche can no longer let go without using the entire energy of his style to thrust a value-judgement over the whole argument –

Truths are illusions which one has forgotten *are* illusions, worn-out metaphors which have become powerless to affect the senses, coins which have their obverse effaced and are now no longer of account as coins, but merely as metal.

There is no need to emphasize the powerful imagination at work in this metaphorical account of the nature of metaphors, an imagination that points to and intimates rather than sets out to prove its insights. (In this respect, as in so many others, Nietzsche agrees with Schopenhauer, who had claimed that 'erweisen' rather than 'beweisen' was philosophy's proper task.)[1] What the statement reveals is fundamental to Nietzsche's literary practice and therefore to the way in which we must read his writings. If 'truths...are metaphors', then truth (such as we are capable of conceiving) is in metaphor only: this 'linguistic' insight goes hand in hand with – is the stylistic correlative of – Nietzsche's 'experimental' thinking. It enters Nietzsche's style, or rather the many styles he acknowledged as his own, at the most intimate and instinctive level of his writing, sometimes to its detriment. All he wrote is distinguished by a richness and appropriateness of metaphor, by a splendid liveliness and adaptability to the purpose in hand. Seen as a whole, his work is the most powerful invitation to think that we have, yet occasionally it is marred by a curious mannerism which escapes his conscious control: it is his redundant use of the particle 'als', meaning 'as', 'in the role or function of...'. Even without having to undergo the deadly tedium of 'stylo-statistical' word counts, we note whole paragraphs, by no means only in the early writings, where his use of this particle cannot be justified on grammatical or stylistic grounds. The linguistic tic signifies an instinctive, sometimes monotonous re-enacting of a fundamental movement of Nietzsche's thought: a movement in which a never-ending interchange in the function of words – metaphorical intimations of divers spheres of experience – is allowed to become the dominant feature of language, where language is taken to be the metaphorical, and therefore inexact, approximate intimation of our being in the world.

[1] *Ibid.* vol. 1/i § 14.

4

Words, words, words...

(Hamlet II: 2)

Neither in this essay of 1873 nor anywhere else does Nietzsche offer a radical criticism of the language of universal and metaphysical concepts (in the way that Wittgenstein does). He sanctions generalizations and conceptual statements of every kind – metaphysical or empirical – as a part of that complex system of linguistic conventions by means of which men are enabled to live in the world. Concepts (Nietzsche writes in the concluding section) are not fundamentally different from other aspects of our language. He likens them to dice – 'they are made of hard bone...octagonal and negotiable, like dice...; but even in this form they show that they are the residue of metaphors', that is, of 'nervous impulses' translated into particular names.[1] When Nietzsche likens concepts to coin (money), he illuminates their nature in much the same way as the young Marx had illuminated the nature of money (coin) by likening it to concepts and thus identifying the function of coin as that of a mediator between men and the goods they would have, their *'demande'*:[2] but whereas Marx's ultimate aim is to subject the metaphorical shift to a radical criticism, Nietzsche accepts it as part of 'the lie' and thus as the *donnée* of our situation in the world. (We note however that, although Nietzsche shows how 'the language of science', too, springs from the common ground of metaphor, none of the important passages in the essay itself is cast in the conceptual language of 'Wissenschaft'.) And again he does not criticize the Kantian and Schopenhauerian notion of 'the things in themselves' beyond asserting that *'for us'* they are convenient because life-sustaining fictions. This is the first move in an argument which ten years later produces the definition of 'the supreme will to power' as a man's determination 'to impose on "becoming" the character of "Being"' (*WzM* §617), and by the

---

[1]   Nietzsche's argument here resembles Hegel's, who also derives 'Begriff' from 'begreifen', but tries to preserve the dynamic character inherent in the verb; see his *Ästhetik*, ed. F. Bassenge (Berlin 1955), pp. 136–7.

[2]   See Marx's section on money in the *Paris MSS (Ökonomisch-philosophische Manuskripte)* of 1844 (ed. G. Hillmann, München 1966), pp. 103–7; also Jacques Derrida, 'White Mythology: Metaphor in the Text of Philosophy' in *New Literary Review* VI/1, Autumn 1974, pp. 12ff.

end of 1888 makes of all 'Being an empty fiction. The "apparent" world is the only one there is; the "true" world has merely been mendaciously added [hinzugelogen]' (*GD* III § 2). And the lie is ineradicable: language (we recall the passage from *The Anti-Christ*) is 'fixed, all that is fixed kills'. It cannot adequately express 'becoming', which is the very nature of our existence (*WzM* § 715, also of 1888).

What are we to make of this strange, idiosyncratic insistence on the 'lying' nature of language? Why does Nietzsche refuse to distinguish between 'fictions' and 'lies'? Plato (in the tenth book of the *Republic*) ignores the distinction because by branding fiction as a lie he hopes to safeguard the *polis* from the effects of poetic irresponsibility. (The myths of poets, he suggests, are hardly better than the evil lies of demagogues.) Nietzsche on the other hand cares little for the *polis*. 'Life', not the *polis* nor even 'the world', is the real object of his concern. (And 'life', we recall, being the source and origin of rational distinctions and of language, can never be defined and designated by them – a sophistry that does not worry him enough.) Thus life, for Nietzsche, is never a concept but a vision, a metaphor which embraces all kinds of being but is devalued when it is seen unheroically, under the aspect of association. Yet to us who live in the world it is obvious to the point of banality that there *is* a difference between myth or fiction or poetry on the one hand and the lie on the other, and this difference derives its entire meaning from an organized legal or moral and therefore social context. However, only to one who is prepared to take institutionalized life in the world seriously is this difference of any consequence. *Sub specie aeterni*, in terms of an aesthetic justification, the difference disappears. And here Nietzsche leaves the argument.

We can never speak of 'fiction', 'myth' or 'lies' without implying some kind of truth. And if Nietzsche claims that 'truth, for us, is no more' than the agreement to count the dots and play a game of dice always in the same way, his formulation, '*for us*', implies that there must be something other, something more...: but again the space occupied by that other thing is empty.

The aesthetic (we saw in the first part of this chapter) is at odds with the truth about the world. Language (we may now add), being merely 'a mobile army of metaphors', is seen predominantly as an aesthetic phenomenon; and from this two important conclusions follow.

First, the activity of artists – traditionally seen as the makers of metaphors – and the aesthetic activity in general assume an entirely central position in the world. Art is in no sense esoteric or marginal, but becomes the human activity par excellence: it is creative existence. The 'justification' of the world through 'the aesthetic activity' is identical with the 'justification' or meaning imprinted on the world through man the maker of linguistic conventions, that is, of a system of 'metaphors'. This in turn implies that gnosis on which Nietzsche's theory of tragedy was founded and with which the essay of 1873 begins: it implies the existence of a hostile universe of silence before and beyond language, within which our little human world of language is an oasis of life, comfort and sustenance, but not of *truth*.

Secondly, to see language as an army of metaphors is to see it as a system of signs which, unlike other such systems, is tied to an historical dimension. Its changing nature – that is, its historicity – is built into this scheme by means of its very formulations:[1] Nietzsche speaks of the 'long usage' in the course of which words become 'fixed, canonical and binding on' a people; metaphors become 'hard' and 'rigid', or again they wear out and 'lose their sensuous power', images are effaced and cease to be valid...In all this there is change, movement, a course of history. But this history turns out to be no more than a process of cliché-formations – a process which runs all one way, from pristine freshness to ossification, decadence, and an apocalyptic ending; and this, we know, is the way Nietzsche saw European history from the golden age of pre-Socratic Greece to his own day and to the early twentieth century as he anticipated it. This is the pattern of Pietist historiography. But the German literary tradition, too, from Hölderlin through Heine to Stefan George, Karl Kraus and beyond, is full of such apocalyptic visions, in which moral prophecy combines in strange ways with a destructive, Samsonian intent.[2] Nietzsche's catastrophe-mindedness, too, entails a powerfully negative evaluation of each subsequent historical stage, but – and this is inherent in his value judgements – it also entails an unequivocal condemnation of everything that

[1] See also Heinrich von Staden, 'Nietzsche and Marx on Greek Art and Literature: Case Studies', *Daedalus*, 1976, p. 89.

[2] See J. P. Stern, *Re-Interpretations: Seven Studies in Nineteenth-Century German Literature*, pp. 221 ff.

is 'fixed, canonical, and binding', because it is supposed to be hostile to 'life'. 'Being', we recall, is the lie imposed on 'Becoming'. Words make no sense unless they are arranged in a way that makes them 'fixed, canonical and binding', yet once they are so arranged, they cease to communicate with 'life'. Any extended regularization of the elements of language is condemned because it too (Nietzsche believes) proceeds from, and magnifies 'the lie' at the heart of the language–'reality' relationship. Our criticism of Nietzsche's linguistic views merges with our criticism of his moral and religious reflections: language too belongs to that sphere of association which for him is the sphere of the derivative and inauthentic, because he shares that strange (German and Lutheran?) superstition which values origins and singularities more highly than continuities and collectives, and sees every structure as a betrayal of the elements that compose it. The language of poets, on the other hand, more than any other, escapes the 'petrifaction' of clichés. The main reason why, in accordance with his view of language, Nietzsche places the aesthetic activity at the heart of human existence is because, more than any other human product, the work of art escapes the sphere of association and lives by the appearance of uniqueness.

The reflection and the aphorism as units of literary expression, the bright idea as the unit of philosophical thinking, the anecdote[1] as the unit of biography and history, the moment and the single mood – these are the lodestars that guide Nietzsche's venture. With the poet Rainer Maria Rilke he shares 'that dark premonition that this would be life: full of single, particular things, which are made for each man only, and which cannot be *said*'. But it is not only a dark premonition. Those 'moments of assent to all Being', too, are part of Nietzsche's venture, and to them he owes that 'light- and colour-scale of Dionysian happiness' which Rilke celebrates in the Ninth Duino Elegy:[2]

Ein Mal
jedes, nur *ein* Mal. *Ein* Mal und nicht mehr. Und wir auch
ein Mal. Nie wieder.

---

[1] See Bertram, *Nietzsche*, pp. 249–59, chapter 'Anekdote'.

[2] '...dark premonition': R. M. Rilke, *Die Aufzeichnungen des Malte Laurids Brigge* I (Leipzig 1919), p. 139; 'moments of assent': *WzM* § 1032; 'light- and colour-scale': *WzM* § 1051; for both, see above p. 180; for the relationship between Rilke's '*ein* Mal' and Nietzsche's 'eternal recurrence' see Erich Heller, *The Disinherited Mind*, pp. 128–30.

Once
Each thing but *once*. *Once* and no more. And we also
are *once*. Never again.

How are we to explain this strange contempt for language in a
writer whom we acknowledge among the finest stylists in
German? It has little to do with nominalism. Its source takes
us back, beyond Nietzsche, to the centre of Schopenhauer's
aesthetics. We must see it as a radicalization of all those passages
in *The World as Will and Idea* where, following on his *aperçu* that
'the world is the product of the Will', Schopenhauer claims that
music, not language, is the medium in which the true essence of
the world is represented. Music, he argues (book III § 52), is not
like the other arts. What it represents are not the Platonic Ideas
in which the partial, individuated aspects of the world are
subsumed. Whereas language gives us merely an indirect,
mediate account of those Ideas – the world at a double remove
– music re-enacts the all-encompassing, cosmic Will itself, it is its
'objectivization and image'. Thus music alone brings man into
unreflective, intuitive contact with the essence of the world, its
dark chthonic forces, with what ultimately matters. And here
Schopenhauer's aesthetics turns into ethics: music alone enables
us to contemplate the world *sub specie voluntatis* and at the same
time to withdraw from it.

Nietzsche, as we have seen, takes over the idea of 'the Will'
as creator of the world, reverses Schopenhauer's ascetic rejection
of it, and replaces it by a fragmentary but emphatic doctrine of
assent. Yet all those note-books full of dithyrambs to the 'will to
power' do not contain a re-valuation of language. The system
sketched out in the essay of 1873 remains essentially unchanged,
some of its main points are merely given a more abstract
formulation in the notes intended for *The Will to Power*: the bond
between men corresponds to no 'reality' and is merely a useful
verbal fiction (*WzM* § 676); language is less precise and less
truthful than, and derivative from, other ways of experiencing
the world; an indeterminate causal connection obtains between
words and things (§ 506); the use of metaphysical concepts, which
in the 1873 essay had been ridiculed as mere tautology, is now
(§ 409, written 1885) described as part of our misguided philosophical tradition... In short, Nietzsche's conception and assessment of language remain as negative as ever. Language is still
placed at the opposite pole to 'reality', outside the world which

Zarathustra blesses with his 'yea-saying', or indeed outside any world; and there, by and large, it remains. There are occasions when Nietzsche shows how acts are determined by valuations and valuations by the verbal forms in which they occur (e.g. *GM* I); when he tells us that grammar (*GD* III § 5, *WzM* § 484) or syntax (§ 549) colour and shape our thinking, create fictitious opposites and contrasts (§§ 124, 699) and linguistic chimeras – when language holds us captive in a picture. All such observations, we can see, imply a recognition of what we have come to call the 'performative' or 'perlocutionary' function of language – a recognition which, if he were to make it explicit, would make nonsense of the idea that language is located somewhere outside, or opposite, the world, or 'reality', or 'life'. As it is, the criticism remains casual, mere piecemeal exhortations.

It is Ludwig Wittgenstein's early work which helps us to place Nietzsche's language-conscious observations in their proper perspective, if only because that work too has its roots in Schopenhauer. The *Tractatus Logico-Philosophicus* of 1922 is designed to secure for language that stability of reference which Nietzsche failed to find there. The main proposition on which the *Tractatus* rests is that language and the world display 'the same logical form' (2.2). (Whether Wittgenstein succeeds in this claim I cannot tell.) The hypothesis of such a total accord – a sort of pre-established harmony – does not, however, lead to a rehabilitation of language but, on the contrary, to its radical devaluation: the harmony is complete, Wittgenstein is in effect saying, but empty ('If someone hides a thing behind a bush', &c.). In more detail: language represents (or forms a picture of) things in the world, but it cannot represent their totality or the rules governing that representation (4.2). (A picture of that totality, or of those rules, would have to be taken from outside that totality; there is no outside.) And this apparently innocuous statement, which has its parallel in Nietzsche's claim (in the essay of 1873) that the relationship between words, propositions and things is indeterminable, leads Wittgenstein to a number of conclusions which Nietzsche (and not only he) would regard as wholly nihilistic. To represent these rules of representation, a 'higher order' of language would be required,[1] yet in the scheme of the *Tractatus* only one order is possible, for 'all propositions are of

---

[1] See *Philosophical Investigations* (Oxford 1953), I, § 197, and Max Black, *A Companion to Wittgenstein's 'Tractatus'* (Cambridge 1964), chapter 8.

equal value' (6.41). Hence all propositions of a 'higher order' – not only those containing the rules of representation but also those of ethics and aesthetics (6.41), and indeed all propositions of traditional philosophy – are ruled out of court. (Ethics = aesthetics = 0) And here all three – Schopenhauer, Nietzsche and the young Wittgenstein – agree: whatever are the deepest, most fundamental concerns of man, language cannot express them, nor can they be contained in the world that is co-extensive with language. Hence the world is without value or meaning: 'If there is value that does have value, it must lie outside the whole sphere of what happens and is the case...It must lie outside the world' (6.41). This is Wittgenstein's conclusion, as it was Schopenhauer's before him. And Nietzsche's too? 'Life', 'the will to power', Zarathustra's paeans to the earth – all these are arrayed to stave off just this conclusion; but: 'I do not wish for life again...I have tried to affirm it myself – ah!'

There are two ways out of this impasse. The first is taken in the *Tractatus* itself, where Wittgenstein appeals to our innermost experience of a 'feeling' for the totality of things in the world (6.45). (Nietzsche too, we recall, is apt to argue for the primacy of 'instinctive feeling' over rational discourse.) And this feeling Wittgenstein calls 'the mystical'. It cannot be 'said', put into propositional language, but it 'shows itself' (6.522). To recast this in its original Schopenhauerian terms: what 'the mystical' expresses are not the individuated aspects of the world, not the individual 'wills' that compose it, but 'the Will's' essential totality. For Schopenhauer the expression of that totality (as we saw at the beginning of this argument) is not in language but in music; or, to put *that* in Nietzsche's terms, 'the mystical' – music – is the primal ground of suffering, unworded, unindividuated; it is the Kingdom of Dionysus.

The other way out is to abandon the metaphysical concern of the *Tractatus* – the harmony between world and language established through the idea of a common 'logical form' – and to set out on a series of 'philosophical investigations' into the ways we actually use language. What Wittgenstein does in the work to which he gave that name is to examine the diversity of the functions of language in a series of exploratory journeys through areas where language does quite other things than label, designate, name or describe. One of the results of this procedure is to show that, by virtue of these other activities, language turns out to be, not the isolated, unique thing that stands outside the world or 'reality' and all other experience but, on the contrary, a ubiquitous, protean, all-permeating 'form of life' or mode of being in the world. Unlike Wittgenstein's, Nietzsche's visits in this region of linguistic analysis are unplanned, fortuitous. He offers no consistent recognition that language is not merely represent-ational or 'referential', that one can 'do things with words'. And if he sees language as merely 'referential', so, on the whole, he does literature. From his anti-Aristotelian and anti-mimetic first book onwàrds Nietzsche will argue, or insinuate, that only in its pristine, anti-literary, near-musical form does tragedy offer a positive contribution to 'life'. True, in *The Genealogy of Morals* there are frequent hints that moralities and religious command-ments alike depend for their content and efficacy on the verbal forms in which they are cast – but this again reduces language to a weapon in the fight against untrammelled 'life', and here too an independent, value-free enquiry fails to get under way.[1]

Nietzsche's idea of philosophical criticism is bound to remain unspecialized and unrestricted, he will never confide it to a single kind of enquiry. He is too eager to find out what makes people do whatever it is they do to be able to devote himself wholly to doing it. Jakob Burckhardt, we recall, decided to see the world *sub specie* of the Courtauld Institute. Nietzsche will never have a 'Hauptfach'.

6

...caviare to the general...

(*Hamlet* II: 2)

In speaking of language as a dynamic system of signs with an inherent organization of meanings, Nietzsche goes a little way beyond the traditional linguistic theory of his period – the theory which looks on all words as static names of things. Yet he does not contribute significantly to twentieth-century linguistic think-ing because he does not anticipate the discoveries on which

---

[1] At the end of *GM* I Nietzsche suggests that an academic prize should be offered for an answer to the question, 'What light does the science of linguistics, and especially the study of etymology, throw on the evolution [Entwicklungs-geschichte] of moral concepts?' A notorious cul-de-sac lies at the end of the Hegelian (or Heideggerian) etymologizing that is here being proposed. Again one is bound to ask why it should be assumed that the (true or assumed) origins of a word have necessarily anything to do with its later uses.

it is founded. Among these is Saussure's[1] demonstration that the elements of language cannot be physically described (the metaphor from Chladny's figures does illustrate a causal relationship of sorts), and his view of language as a self-contained system or structure. Nietzsche thinks that he has disposed of the truth-value of language by calling its arrangements a mere convention (a structure or system), without apparently realizing that a convention which works is more than a free-floating, arbitrary imposition. He argues throughout on the tacit assumption that the elements of language receive their particular meanings from the contexts in which they occur. Yet he ignores the fact that any system or structure is more than its parts; that by virtue of being what it is, a structure imposes stability upon its constitutive elements; and that these elements are defined by their relations within the structure. (In just this way he was uninterested in the rule of custom and law, and in every moral or religious institution which related single insights and truths to each other, and thus stabilized them.) Perhaps he takes some parts of this argument for granted. He is not interested in language for its own sake, but in its relationship with all that seems to lie beyond it. Is he then saying that a non-linguistic, non-metaphorical numinous world does exist after all? Sometimes it seems to enter Nietzsche's argument inadvertently (as when he complains that language is 'not an *adequate* expression' for...what realities?), at other times the existence of such an ineffable world is irresistibly implied (in words like '*meta*phor' and '*trans*lation', or again in his insistence that something – 'mere metal' – is left over once the inscription on the coin has been rubbed off by wear). He uses every occasion to attack the idea of such a world as a Platonist–Christian–Idealist swindle, yet he never finally relinquishes it either. His linguistic observations must be seen as a foreground argument. Behind them he postulates a non-metaphorical, 'true' order of things to which language does not belong, but to which it is somehow related – 'aesthetically', by way of a 'halting, stammering' reproduction of...we cannot say what. This, precisely, is the linguistic analogy to the idea of a social system that works by virtue of its relationship to something outside itself.[2]

---

[1] Ferdinand de Saussure, *Course in General Linguistics* [1915] (New York 1959), especially chapter iii; cf. also J. Culler, *Saussure* (Fontana Modern Masters, London 1976).

[2] See above, p. 132.

That there is a numinous order of things to which language does not belong was the central metaphysical claim on which *The Birth of Tragedy* was founded. The anti-Socratic attitude, central to that book, culminated in an attack on all language-dominated cultures. There is hardly a book of Nietzsche's in which the value and 'authenticity' of language are not slighted. In that tone of bravado characteristic of his last reflections he writes, under the heading 'From a Moral Theory for the Deaf and Dumb, and Other Philosophers':

We do not set a high enough value on ourselves when we communicate what is in our minds. Our real experiences are not at all garrulous. They couldn't communicate themselves, even if they wished to. That is because they lack the right word. Whatever we have words for, we have already outgrown. In all talk there is a grain of contempt. Language, it seems, has been invented only for the average, for the middling and communicable. Language vulgarizes the speaker. (*GD* IX § 26)

How then should he convey his vision of the metaphysics of language, Zarathustra's conviction that 'man is a rope, tied between animal and Superman', and that 'what may be loved in man is that he is a transition'? There is no direct way of doing it, yet Nietzsche's passion for *writing* – the obverse of the enticement of insanity and of the fear of silence – remains with him to the end: it is to resolve this dilemma that his character-istic style of indirection and metaphors, and the argument by 'intimation and transference', come into their own. Yet, as he never ceases to remind himself and warn his reader, these devices can do no more than demonstrate the inadequacies of utterance:

All names for Good and Evil are parables. They do not express, they merely beckon. A fool is he who desires knowledge from them. (*Z* I § 23)[1]

Where does this style find its vocabulary, how is it assembled? The essay of 1873 ends with a description of the creative intellect that has freed itself from all practical considerations and tasks and sets out, disinterestedly, to re-enact the world in images and concepts. So far the young Nietzsche's argument is pure Schopenhauer. But when Nietzsche goes on to show how this creative mind in its freedom takes up the vocabulary of common discourse and the scaffolding of concepts 'in order to dismantle

---

[1] 'Gleichnisse sind alle Namen von Gut und Böse: sie sprechen nicht aus, sie winken nur. Ein Tor, welcher von ihnen Wissen will.'

them, break up their order and reconstitute them ironically, bringing together things farthest apart and separating those closest together', for no other purpose than to play with them; and when he concludes that

...no regular way leads from such intuitions to the land of ghostly abstractions, it is not for them that the word was created; seeing them, man falls silent or speaks in forbidden metaphors and extravagant combinations of concepts, so that by demolishing and mocking the old conceptual boundaries (if in no other way) he may show himself equal to the impression with which the mighty intuition seized him

– Nietzsche is giving the most accurate description we have of his own future philosophical and literary procedure. (Did he, one wonders, know Baudelaire's description of the artistic imagination: 'It created, at the world's beginning, analogy and metaphor. It de-constructs the whole of creation and, using the materials it has collected and arranged in accordance with the rules which originate in the soul's innermost depths, it creates a new world, the sensation of newness'?)[1]

There is a sense in which every forceful, original metaphor is a 'forbidden metaphor'. Metaphoricity itself is a challenge – in some languages perhaps the most radical challenge there is – to the conventionality or, as Nietzsche would say, the disheartening commonness of language. More than once he tells us that communication is not what he is concerned with, that he wishes to be misunderstood, that thought debases itself and the thinker when it strives to be made commonly accessible. Is this merely a grotesque paradox? Is it not belied by the brilliant clarity of his writings? The clarity of his metaphors can deceive. And, after all, he had his wish: *Zarathustra*, his only experiment in a predominantly metaphorical style, *was* misunderstood. He calls it 'a book for all and no-one', that is, for 'all' who would be prepared to read it on his, Nietzsche's own, metaphorically encoded terms, which, in the event, turned out to be 'no-one'. At least, most of the people he could have had in mind read it on *their* terms, as a rallying call to militarism, pan-Germanism, imperialism and racism, yet *that* was a misunderstanding we may be sure he did not wish for.

The forbidden metaphors work only when they are used sparingly, tactically, when they are allowed to form patterns of

[1] Charles Baudelaire, *Curiosités esthétiques*, ed. Henri Lemaître (Paris 1962), 'Salon de 1859' § III p. 321.

contrast with usages which do not challenge the convention, and this of course is how Nietzsche writes at his best. This is not a very surprising conclusion, yet it does not mean that he writes like everybody else. What that image of the artist at work among forbidden metaphors and untoward combinations of concepts suggests is the act of writing as demolition and de-construction: the breaking up of accepted order is manifest in the pointed brevity of each utterance. And with this goes Nietzsche's discovery that his discrete reflections have value and make sense (*Mus* XXI p. 80); that discontinuity can be significant; that '*notes for*' *a philosophy are a philosophy.* (Anton von Webern, Bertolt Brecht, Jorge Luis Borges, Picasso and Braque in *their* media made similar discoveries.) In just this way Nietzsche will 'bring together and separate' the elements of those cardinal metaphors for which his writings are famous: 'amor fati', invoking choice motivated by love where blind fate is sovereign; 'the aesthetic justification' where there is to be no justifying or judging; 'the lie in a supra-moral sense'; 'the eternal recurrence' where 'eternity' is to be merely hideous endlessness; 'the death of God' which does not tell us whether he was ever alive; and 'the will to power' which is forever destroying its products and itself – all examples of a metaphysics of which the least confusing thing to say is that it consistently avoids the dangers of dogma and petrifaction at the price of being consistently paradoxical.

7

There are critics of Nietzsche who have read his work as that of a traditional nineteenth-century German conceptual philosopher or ideologist who, from irresponsibility, demagogy, or sheer ineptitude, made things unnecessarily difficult for himself and his readers by indulging in metaphor-mindedness; critics of this sort see it as their task to demythologize Nietzsche's writings and, having freed them from their metaphors, to consider how much – or rather how little – remains valid in terms of a conceptually legitimized scheme or system. Others have taken the opposite view: they have seen him as a poet – either as a heroic poet of the German soul (in a tradition that goes from Hölderlin to Rilke, Stefan George and Paul Celan) or as a pre-fascist poet manqué with a penchant for *art nouveau* heraldic beasts and a permanent place in Pseud's Corner. By now it should be clear that the present study is written in the belief that the alternative, poet *versus* philosopher, is misleading.

Assuming that the way a writer theorizes about language and describes it contains at least some hints of the way he uses it, we can see that what Nietzsche has evolved in those sixteen years he was granted for his philosophical venture is a variety of styles which are metaphorical in the sense outlined in the essay of 1873 and the later observations that spring from it. It is a mode of writing somewhere between individuation and concern with particulars which is the language area of creative literature, and conceptual generalities and abstractions which make up the language area of traditional Kantian and post-Kantian philosophy. When Nietzsche refers to the image of the silver coin with its effaced inscription, its value reduced to that of the metal alone, he has in mind neither the coin itself (he is not telling a story), nor a generality which would make the actual image of the coin merely an illustration and therefore dispensable. The metaphor of the coin is intended as an intermediary between two modes of thinking and writing, as a pattern which determines neither a narrative line nor a piece of philosophical poetry or 'Begriffs-dichtung', but a philosophical argument.

This middle mode of discourse can certainly be *shown* (and to show it has been the purpose of this chapter), but I am not clear how it can be defined more precisely. It is not poetry: Nietzsche's poetry is less distinguished and less important than his prose. Nor is it poetic prose – the poetic prose he wrote is only rarely successful, in parts of *Zarathustra* it is (in itself and in its influence) a disaster. Nor is it aphorism – Nietzsche's strictly aphoristic utterances are less interesting than those of La Rochefoucauld and Lichtenberg, the two practitioners of the genre whom he most admired. And it is certainly not the unalloyed language of concepts: on the occasions when, in his treatment of traditional philosophical problems (e.g. in his polemics against Kant), he uses such a language, his style becomes impatient, repetitious and often perfunctory. The true distinction of his work, and the true ground of his immensely wide and often overpowering influence, lies in this middle mode of language, which I suppose we may call 'literary–philosophical'; to have devised this mode and applied it to an almost infinite variety of contemporary issues is his greatest achievement. Yet from this mode too springs that entirely modern (and depressingly familiar) habit of talking metaphorically about 'God', 'saintliness', 'divine creation', 'sin' and the like without ever quite deciding what non-metaphorical meanings, and what beliefs (if any) go with the talking.

Content and form of what he wrote do not always coincide. First, and most fortunately, this is so in his observations on 'the morality of strenuousness' and on the 'God-less theology', which are as unlaboured, unstrenuous and brightly clear (each within its narrow compass) as almost everything else: writing about 'the spirit of gravity', he is informed by the spirit of lightness and (literary) grace. And there is a second area where content and form do not coincide. Was Heidegger right when he declared that Nietzsche's work was *finis metaphysicae*? In Nietzsche's philosophizing, and through its very form, a series of traditional metaphysical topics is challenged and rendered problematic. Yet in spite of the form in which they appear, these topics are never wholly refuted; they remain implied in the terminology of the refutations. Moreover, Nietzsche's ultimate intention was not to destroy metaphysics but to create a new, more timely system. In that, as in all his extended projects, he failed – again I think we may say, fortunately. There is no Nietzschean revolution, but there is a new way of looking at the world – his world and ours – and a new style of describing it. And yet he has wrought change: no description undertaken with any intensity leaves things as they are, least of all Nietzsche's.

The disdain with which he treated the sphere of association and the consequent limitations of his view of life in the world have been mentioned, but there is another, positive side to this story. The guiding intention of his philosophical prose is to convey not the general or the average but the unique, to preserve the dynamic, unsteady, the irregular and above all the individualized nature of life. Schopenhauer once described his own philosophical style as the outcome of 'my trick...of suddenly and instantly freezing the most living sense–experience or the deepest feeling the hour has brought with the coldest abstract reflection, in order to preserve it in a transfixed state'.[1] Nietzsche intends the opposite. He fears being 'formulated, sprawling on a pin'. His aim is to let the process of 'becoming' speak, to remove the descriptions of 'life' as little as possible from its uncertain, unstable, catastrophic origins and destination, even

---

[1] Quoted from O. Jenson, *Die Ursache der Widersprüche im Schopenhauerschen System* (Rostock 1906), p. 64.

at the price of intellectual coherence itself. Language, metaphor and thought are related to 'the real world' as patterns and paradigms of our being in *its* relationship to 'the real world': there is no such thing as 'Being at rest with itself, identical with itself, unaltering: the only "Being" vouchsafed to us is changing, not identical with itself, it is involved in relationships...' (*WKG* v/2 p. 468).

Being involved in relationships: the ever-renewed attempts to preserve these 'relationships' from petrifaction fill Nietzsche's books and notebooks, this is what he sees as the task of his philosophical *and* literary undertaking. It is not surprising that Nietzsche's hybrid mode of writing is forever in danger of being impatiently dismissed as 'neither one thing nor t'other', for it constitutes a provocation of the genre theories and tacit assumptions on which French and English kinds of discourse are founded. But it has its antecedents (great writers are hardly ever formal innovators), in the Book of Proverbs and in what remains of the writings of the pre-Socratics, in Pascal and a host of German writers as well as a few English ones (chief among them William Blake); and among its many successors is the (equally irreducible) language of 'family likenesses', 'indistinct photographs', and metaphors of games of Wittgenstein's *Philosophical Investigations*. What Nietzsche teaches us is not to read philosophy as literature, let alone literature as philosophy, but to read both as closely related forms of life. In challenging, through this mode of writing, the dichotomy of 'scientific' *versus* 'imaginative', or again the antitheses between 'concept' and 'metaphor', 'abstract' and 'concrete', Nietzsche is at the same time intent on challenging those divisions in our areas of knowledge-and-experience and that fragmentation of knowledge which he (together with other nineteenth-century thinkers, men like Marx, Carlyle and Matthew Arnold) saw as one of the chief blights of modern Western civilization.

More than the work of any other philosopher, Nietzsche's work is experiment and hypothesis, not precept. This means that any valid criticism of it must concern itself with the question of how to read him. Best, perhaps, as we read the turbulent late autumn sky with its dramatic greens and melancholy blue-greys and lurid streaks of vermilion; its broken towers and crenellations, its wild riders and other shapes, too, 'like a camel...very like a whale': to read him for the signs of today and tomorrow. But signs of such intensity must always be more than signs.

A speculative conclusion

Aspects of the contemporary philosophy of language enable us to place Nietzsche's unsystematic philosophizing in a perspective and so to view it comprehensively. A scheme emerges which enables us to survey language, experience in the world and human character from three different points of view.

The first shows a picture, somewhat rounded out, of the world made up of Nietzsche's own moral–existential reflections as they were presented in the first nine chapters of this study.

In the tenth chapter I was concerned with Nietzsche's attempt to re-interpret and 'justify existence aesthetically'. The first condition of such a re-interpretation, it seems to me, would have to be a radically different understanding of the function of language in the world. Therefore, in constructing *the second* perspective as an antithesis of the first, I have inverted Nietzsche's view of language and have tried to show what such an inversion implies for experience at large.

In *the third* section Nietzsche's aesthetic experiment is seen as his attempt to impose certain aspects of the second 'linguistic' view (2 . . .) upon the moral–existential (1 . . .). *The fourth* and final section contains a brief assessment of Nietzsche's philosophical undertaking as a whole.

The aim of this Summary is neither to paper over nor to exaggerate the contradictions of Nietzsche's thinking but to give them their due weight and then to show how far, in spite of them, a coherent and illuminating reading of Nietzsche is possible. Each of the three perspectives is presented first as a view of language and then as a view of 'experience' or 'reality' (or whatever is not language). Each perspective has also certain implications for a view of human character, but there seemed no need to make them explicit at this stage.

1. According to the first view, human language is seen as a *special* phenomenon, set against 'experience' or 'reality' or 'being'.
1.1. It is *superior* to certain other modes of experience – hence the isolation of poets and their pride in their elect status.

The rest of experience is silent, 'irrational', instinctive...

1.2. But language is also *inferior*, incapable of expressing certain special or privileged segments of experience – hence Nietzsche's lament, 'Only a poet! only a fool!'

Thought is distinct from, is more than, words.

There is the inexpressible, the flame fed by knowledge which (as Plato says in the Seventh Epistle) burns wordless in the soul and is the unutterable sum of all wisdom. It 'shows' itself (as Wittgenstein says at the end of the *Tractatus*), it is 'the mystical', 'beyond' all language. It is 'the meaning of all things' to which countless poets have referred throughout the ages; more 'real' and (or: and therefore) more valuable than language; having a higher 'ontic' status.

For Nietzsche the inexpressible is 'life'. All descriptions of it are axiomatically inadequate.

1.3. This is the 'mimetic' or '*referential*' view, where language is seen as a means of pointing to, re-presenting or labelling, that which it is not and that which it does not contain. (This view underlies most of the literary and philosophical productions of the nineteenth and early twentieth centuries.)

It is the *dynamic* view of language. Here language is predatory: it strives to encompass more than it possesses.

'The will to power' is the non-linguistic equivalent of this predatory aspect of language.

1.4. There is genealogy and history; this is the *historical*, 'vertical' view.

History is the product of the will to power of the gifted, modified by the resentments of the weak.

Similarly, the aesthetic is the product of historical situations thus determined.

The present does not count, except as a transition between past and future.

What counts is progress: it is the effort of language to usurp more than it encompasses.

In non-linguistic terms: though the improvement of man is concentrated in certain privileged moments in the past, it is also a *future* goal.

The improvement of man in the direction of the Superman, and of a strengthened and purified will to power, is Nietzsche's critique (and equivalent) of the nineteenth-century conception of progress.

But since language is always getting the better of what it has conquered – since conquest always renders worthless that which it conquers – 'progress' always brings with it disenchantment.

Nihilism is the paralysing yet necessary consciousness of this state of things.

'The eternal recurrence of the same' is Nietzsche's way of representing the disenchantment in its most radical, nihilistic form.

1.5. This is the *moral* view of things. (Morality, like aesthetics, is the product of every superior power, appropriated, modified and thus corrupted by the weak.)

The aesthetic is in the service of 'life'.

Relating language to 'experience' is being involved in *judgements*: in judging, for instance, how far language succeeds in conquering that which it does not encompass.

Similarly, men are judged according to the efforts with which they overcome their own inadequacies and weak desires.

The only source of each man's efforts, as well as the only source of his limitation, is 'his' will to power. The only source of moral problems is the self, not society.

There is truth and falsehood. They are judgements relating to the correspondence between language and 'reality', i.e. that which language is not.

The judgements inherent in this view are absolute, black-and-white, Manichean; whether they are 'supra-moral' or 'beyond good and evil', they are *moral* judgements.

The values which inform the world seen as the antagonist of language are the values of unique and strenuous effort, exacted under existential duress, and assessed in terms of sacrifice. These are the only values Nietzsche consistently acknowledges.

Though these values (like the aesthetic ones) are historicized – as the determined products of situations in time – they are not dissolved by historical analysis, not explained away.

All that belongs to the sphere of association is antagonistic to these values. What counts are originality, creativity, the *unique* effort.

All extension and continuity is boring and without value.

Since the difference between fiction and falsehood is rooted in social and legal arrangements (which do not belong to 'the ground of reality'), there is no difference between them.

There are two tests to which these values must be subjected: the death of God (which is a part of our past), and the eternal recurrence of all things (which is 'in time without a goal', the equivalent of the Christian idea of hell). These are essentially moral tests.

The creator and bearer of these values is the Superman; he belongs to, and is an ideal of, moral philosophy.

The conception of the eternal recurrence, as a radical test entailing the destruction of all 'meaning' and purpose in history and in individual life, is a moral conception.

1.6. This is the *causal* view.

Causality is the name we give to the function of the will to power, it is that will at work in nature and in history.

1.7. It is the *hierarchic* view.

It is what it is by virtue of being permeated with judging, with choices and the drama of choice; tragedy here is the irredeemable, irremediable heartbreak.

This finality is not assuaged, not made less poignant, by the eternal recurrence of all things.

1.8. Nietzsche brings this view and its implications to a head. (In this sense Heidegger is right when he calls Nietzsche's philosophy the culmination and destruction of recent Western metaphysics.) Here lies Nietzsche's importance and a substantial source of his influence.

1.9. To this view belongs the characterology of *the tragic*. It is the *Dionysian* view.

2. According to the second, opposite view, language is seen as 'a form of life', a mode of 'experience' or 'reality'.

2.1. It is *equal* – in value, 'reality' or whatever – to other 'forms' or modes. There is no competition.

Language fulfils a variety of functions. Among them are communicating, labelling things, but also a number of 'performative' uses ('words are deeds').

2.2 It is a *self-contained* system of signs which requires no referents outside itself for its validation. The '*signifiant*' has no need of a '*signifié*', except for a special purpose. But since it is a *system*, its internal organization is not arbitrary.

At the same time language is entirely *open toward*, it dovetails with, other 'forms' or modes of experience.

It is neither special nor privileged, neither superior nor inferior to other modes, but different from them and at one with the whole of experience, 'the world *sub specie linguae*'.

Words are no less than thoughts – we know thoughts *as* words.

There is no reason why 'the mystical' should not 'show' itself in language, any less than other concepts do. 'The inexpressible' is a word in the system like other words; the proposition, 'language is inadequate', contributes to the adequacy of language like any other proposition.

No one kind of language (e.g. 'scientific' or 'conceptual') has a special claim to exactness, but each kind is (or is not) appropriate to a given purpose.

The meanings of words are in their uses, and all are (potentially) present.

2.3. This is the *static*, 'horizontal' view.

It is a way – one of the ways – of exploring the world, of doing things in the world.

It is not concerned with conquest, it is not trying to be, or to encompass, that which it is not.

2.4. Hence there is no progress, and no history as the enactment of progress.

There is (in non-linguistic terms) no future improvement of man. His fulfilment is ever possible, ever present.

Progress, disenchantment with progress, and nihilism are like scenes from a picture book.

Past and future are what they are by virtue of being enacted in the *present*. Things and relationships are assembled, not in a one-way sequence of before and after, but in a panoramic view.

Time itself is one of the dimensions of that panorama, one of the *rules* according to which 'experience' is enacted and the world has its being. And so is causality.

2.5. This is the *aesthetic* rather than the moral view of things. The good and the true are subsumed in the beautiful; 'reality' is at one with appearance.

It is a view which allows for judgements. But these relate to the elegance and economy – the *consistency* – of the internal arrangements of this mode, not to its referential efficiency, its capacity for conquest.

It abhors black-and-white contrasts. Instead, it is concerned with transitions and rainbows of meaning.

2.6. This is the view of the world seen as a dream – a dream which includes the consciousness of dreaming.

The metaphor of *play*, or of *the game* (Heraclitus speaks of the world as 'a child playing draughts', Wittgenstein and Saussure liken language to a game of chess) with its rules is not an arbitrary metaphor.

2.7. It is a *hieratic* view. Only the great aesthetic achievements - the finest spectacles – count; the Superman is one of them, 'the eternal recurrence of the same' is another.

2.8. This is the view of language underlying the writings of a few modern poets, among them Hölderlin, Mallarmé and Rilke, and the later writings of Wittgenstein, though not all its implications are always present.

2.9. To this view belongs the aesthetic characterology. It is the *Apolline* view of tragedy and of the world.

3. Nietzsche undertakes to aestheticize the world and the being of man; he does this by imposing certain aspects of the second view upon the first.

3.1. Language is seen as inferior to 'reality' (cf. 1.2), as *relatively* incapable of conveying what matters most.

Although Nietzsche often writes on the assumption that 'words are deeds', he offers no consistent recognition that language is 'a form of life'.

3.2. Language here is *largely* but not entirely self-contained. (If it is open toward other 'forms' of life, it is so inadvertently, not – as in 2.2 – by its very nature.)

Words demand to be validated by reference to 'their' *signifiés* (i.e. things in the world), but strictly speaking no such validation is possible. (The idea that language is validated because it is a *system* or structure is not considered.)

Words are less than thoughts and less than the *pathos* of feelings, yet under special conditions – in certain arrangements – they can validate (i.e. 'justify') 'reality'.

3.3. Their relation to 'reality' is approximate, metaphorical. Here lies the formal (cf. 1.8) source of Nietzsche's influence.

There is thus one kind of language – the middle mode between metaphors and concepts (i.e. petrified metaphors) – which has a special claim to being exact and faithful.

3.4. Faithful to what? This is a dynamic and, in a limited sense, a referential view of language.

Its aim is to reproduce 'being in relationships', the movement of things in the world. It too (cf. 2.5) is concerned with transitions, shades of meaning, with turning blocks of facts into scales and spectrums.

3.5. This is not simply *the* aesthetic view of things (i.e. 2...), but an undertaking to encompass and then to justify the world aesthetically.

The aesthetic is the product but also the validation of history.

It is the meaning, or at least one important meaning, of Nietzsche's 'revaluation of all values'.

3.6. The values by which the world subsists, as well as those which result from Nietzsche's own 're-valuation', are to be like the colour-values of painters.

The value-scheme of strenuous effort, especially, is to be replaced by the value (of the appearance) of effortless grace.

After 'the death of God' there is to be 'Amor fati' – the serene acceptance of Come-what-may.

Anti-Christ is the attempt to de-moralize and then to aestheticize the religious. (If Nietzsche's claim that 'in my heart I was never base toward Christianity' is not simply a self-delusion, we must see his attacks on Christian morality as undertaken for the sake of an aesthetic re-interpretation of the spirituality that is left over once the Christian moral values have been destroyed.)

Appearance and reality are one. The spiritual and the worldly are one. Both are blameless, guiltless.

There is 'the innocence of Becoming' – everything that is alive and moving toward its own self-fulfilment is innocent. (Yet there is no – Hegelian – progress, no perfectibility of man and thus no – enlightened – optimism.)

There is guilt. It is the state of mind and heart informed by 'the spirit of gravity', by everything that is static and claims to be absolute. Hence to assert unchanging universal 'Being' is the paradigm of falsehood.

How to change and yet remain the same? The contradiction is to be resolved, and the self-consistency – 'authenticity' – of man is to be salvaged, through the Pindaric 'be thou that which thou art'.

The Superman – embodiment of that authenticity – is an aesthetic ideal.

The will to power by which he subsists does not cease to be a dynamic principle (1.3) as soon as it becomes an aesthetic spectacle, for there is a language (3.4) which can represent 'being in relationships'. (Nietzsche's projected book, *The Will to Power*, is to be seen 'only as a book, made for thinking'.)

3.7. Time and causality are to be preserved in the image of 'the Great Noon'; genealogy and history, too, are series of images of moments out of time.

If genealogy and history were seen (1.5) as the content of the eternal recurrence of all things, and thus the material of the most vigorous moral test that can be devised, *now* the eternal recurrence, too, along with all other moral considerations, becomes an aesthetic spectacle.

3.8. Significance, value and truth lie, not in duration (cf. 1.5), but in *the moment*, the anecdote, the bright philosophical idea.

The sphere of association is validated, not in the act of the aesthetic justification, but as its object; it becomes the material of beautiful recurrent patterns.

3.9. If, finally, any meaning is to be attached to Nietzsche's occasional praise of the scientific attitude and of the pursuit of truth for its own sake (as opposed to his more common view that science and truth are to be placed at the service of 'life'), these 'positivist' commendations of the pursuit of truth, too, must be seen as part of the aesthetic theodicy. (Modern scientists are unlikely to baulk at this part of Nietzsche's project.)

4. An assessment.

4.1. Why does Nietzsche attempt this aesthetic justification?

His profound dissatisfaction with all the moral schemes he knows is manifest throughout. And so is his dissatisfaction with the Hegelian ideas of history and progress, with Darwinian genealogy, and with the moral–spiritual content of Christianity.

The otherworldly, metaphysical elements of Christianity, too, he regards as worthless, but not the 'yearning for infinity' from which he sees them arise, and not the *pathos* they represent.

Both the ethics and the aesthetics of Schopenhauer's philosophy he comes to reject as decadent (and thus a transient phenomenon); as mere passive reactions to, and means of escaping from, the world of the will.

His own 'revaluation of all [moral] values' remains fragmentary: Nietzsche can hardly have failed to see that it too, when completed, would turn out to be merely *yet another* '*morality*'. (Whether he was ever struck by its inadequacy as a morality which by definition cannot be institutionalized – a scheme that is not a scheme – is less certain.)

Above all – and some of his last observations are written by an anguished, haunted man – he wishes to put an end to *judging*. He wishes to destroy the crudities of the black-and-white view of everything; to get beyond the conception of strenuousness and seriousness as moral and existential values, beyond the 'sweaty',

'German' view of morality to which idealism, but his own philosophy no less, are committed.

The aesthetic vindication of the world is not to be a Schopenhauerian escape from the excellence created by the great men of will, nor is Nietzsche able to acquiesce in the Wagnerian paradox (the origin of great art in a morally indifferent or inferior, 'theatrical' personality). These problems are to be resolved by deciding – it is impossible to see this as anything more than a forcible and thus arbitrary *decision* – to define 'the aesthetic' as the product of an élite of 'the finest hearts and minds'. This is to be the new '*joyous* science', informed by a 'mediterranean serenity', a combination of seriousness and playfulness. It is to represent what Nietzsche does not wish to give up: the search for the unity of knowledge and life, a total *account* that would also be a valid and comprehensive *precept* and a search for excellence, however defined.

Yet it is impossible to overlook the movement from criticism and self-criticism to self-destruction which accompanies this search. The rejections in which this 'aesthetic justification' is grounded include most of the nineteenth-century elements in Nietzsche's mind and character, most of what makes him the man he is. Seen in biographical terms, the aesthetic accompanies Nietzsche's thinking from beginning to end, and it is part of the euphoria he experienced on the threshold of his final madness.

4.2. Why does Nietzsche fail?

If I speak of a failure in his attempts at an aesthetic justification of the world, what I have in mind is not only his inability to offer an aesthetic 'system' as an alternative to a moral one – his distrust of system, one of his virtues as a thinker, is too deep for that. There is also the practice of judging – a part of his Protestant morality. It is too deeply ingrained to allow for more than glimpses of an alternative way of responding to the world; hence his inability to show with any richness of detail comparable with the richness of the scenes he presents from the moral world, what this other, aesthetic 'world and being of man' might be like.

No man's freedom from the restraints of his time and place is absolute; the project of a total self-creation of values is chimerical. Nietzsche's attacks on, and rejections of, every aspect of Christian dogma and faith still leave him an apostate Christian. His understanding of the spirit of classical Greece does not make him into a Greek thinker. And his criticisms of the traditional 'referential' view of language are too scattered and too few to allow him to develop a consistent alternative.

4.3. Where then does he succeed?

Nietzsche's failure is also his success. He understands, and 'unmasks', the ethic of blame and praise, punishment and reward, and of the agony of conscience, better than any other thinker. Respecting the variety of life more than he respects the variety of men, he shows what it means to approach each moral–existential issue with a fresh mind; what it means to philosophize against the greatest intellectual and personal odds a man can devise; and what it means to philosophize in an age without a living faith, 'at the torpid turn of the world'. For these purposes he fashions, not a whole new language (which would be as absurd as the project for totally new values), but a new style of understanding, and therefore also participating in, his world and ours. That 'God is dead', that the world is the product of the will to power, and that true value lies only in a morality of strenuousness, are Nietzsche's formulations for convictions on which much of our lives is based. He is often more perceptive and persuasive than those who tell us (rightly, I believe) that these convictions are not true. But no man has been more imaginative in trying to see what the world would be like if they were.

Bibliography

NIETZSCHE'S WORKS

Die Geburt der Tragödie (The Birth of Tragedy)   1872
Unzeitgemässe Betrachtungen (Thoughts Out of Season)   1873–6
Menschliches, Allzumenschliches (Human, All-too-Human)   1878–80
Morgenröte (Aurora)   1881
Die Fröhliche Wissenschaft (The Joyous Science)   1882
  Book v (§§ 343–83) added in 1887.
Also sprach Zarathustra (Thus Spoke Zarathustra)   1883–5
Jenseits von Gut und Böse (Beyond Good and Evil)   1886
Zur Genealogie der Moral (The Genealogy of Morals)   1887
Der Fall Wagner (The Wagner Case)   1888
Die Götzen-Dämmerung (The Twilight of the Idols)   1889
Der Antichrist   1895
Ecce Homo   1908
Der Wille zur Macht
  Numbering and dating of the 1,067 reflections of this posthumous
  compilation are taken from *The Will to Power* (ed. W. Kaufmann,
  New York 1968), which follows the 1911 German edition.
Gesammelte Werke, Musarionausgabe.
  23 vols. Munich 1920–9.
Werke in drei Bänden
  ed. K. Schlechta, Munich 1954–6.
Werke: Kritische Gesamtausgabe
  ed. G. Colli and M. Montinari, Berlin 1967ff, unfinished.
Nietzsche Studien
  Berlin 1972ff.

TRANSLATIONS

Beyond Good and Evil: Prelude to a Philosophy of the Future
  (W. Kaufmann) New York, Vintage Books (paperback) 1973.
  (R. J. Hollingdale) Harmondsworth, Penguin Books (paperback)
  1973.
The Birth of Tragedy and *The Case of Wagner*
  (W. Kaufmann) New York, Vintage Books (paperback) 1967.
The Gay Science [The Joyous Science]
  (W. Kaufmann) New York, Vintage Books (paperback) 1974.
On the Genealogy of Morals and *Ecce Homo*
  (W. Kaufmann and R. J. Hollingdale) New York, Vintage Books
  (paperback) 1973.

Human All-too-Human
(Helen Zimmern) 2 vols. New York, Gordon Press 1974.
The Antichrist and *Twilight of the Idols*
(R. J. Hollingdale) Harmondsworth, Penguin Books (paperback)
1969.
Thus Spoke Zarathustra
(W. Kaufmann) New York, Viking Books (paperback) 1966.
(R. J. Hollingdale) Harmondsworth, Penguin Books (paperback)
1969.
The Will to Power
(W. Kaufmann and R. J. Hollingdale) New York, Viking Books
(paperback) 1968.
Thoughts Out of Season
(J. M. Kennedy) 2 vols. New York, Gordon Press 1974.
The Dawn of Day [Aurora]
(Anthony M. Ludovic) New York, Gordon Press 1974.
The Portable Nietzsche
(W. Kaufmann) New York, Viking Books (paperback) 1954.
Contains translations of: *Thus Spoke Zarathustra, Twilight of the
Idols, The Antichrist* and *Nietzsche contra Wagner*
A Nietzsche Reader
(R. J. Hollingdale) Harmondsworth, Penguin Books (paperback)
1977.

CRITICAL LITERATURE

C. Andler, *Nietzsche: Sa vie et sa pensée.* 6 vols.: Paris 1920–31.
C. A. Bernoulli, *Franz Overbeck und Friedrich Nietzsche: eine
Freundschaft.* 2 vols. Jena 1908.
E. Bertram, *Nietzsche: Versuch einer Mythologie.* Berlin 1918, Bonn
[8]1965.
P. Bridgewater, *Nietzsche in Anglosaxony.* Leicester 1972. (With full
bibliography.)
F. Copleston, *Friedrich Nietzsche: Philosopher of Culture.* London and
New York [2]1975.
A. C. Danto, *Nietzsche as Philosopher.* New York 1965, [2]1971.
P. Deussen, *Erinnerungen an Friedrich Nietzsche.* Leipzig 1901.
E. Fink, *Nietzsches Philosophie.* Stuttgart 1960, [3]1973.
I. Frenzel, *Friedrich Nietzsche: An Illustrated Biography.* Indianapolis
1967.
I. Frenzel, *Friedrich Nietzsche in Selbstzeugnissen und Bilddokumenten.*
(rowohlts monographien, 115) Reinbek 1966.
G. Grant, *Time as History.* Toronto 1969.
M. Heidegger, *Nietzsche.* 2 vols., Pfullingen 1961.
M. Heidegger, 'Nietzsches Wort "Gott ist tot"...' in *Holzwege,*
Frankfurt/Main 1950, [4]1963.

Bibliography

E. Heller, *The Artist's Journey Into the Interior and Other Essays*. New York, Vintage Books (paperback) 1968

E. Heller, *The Disinherited Mind*. Cambridge 1952. (chapters 'Burckhardt and Nietzsche', 'Nietzsche and Goethe', 'Rilke and Nietzsche').

E. Heller, 'The Modern German Mind: the Legacy of Nietzsche', in *Literary Lectures presented at the Library of Congress*, Washington 1973.

E. Heller, *The Poet's Self and the Poem*. London 1976. 'Nietzsche in the Waste Land' (pp. 28–50).

P. Heller, *Dialectics and Nihilism: Essays on Lessing, Nietzsche, Mann and Kafka*. Amherst, Mass. 1966.

P. Heller, '*Von den ersten und letzten Dingen*': *Studien und Kommentar zu einer Aphorismenreihe von Friedrich Nietzsche*. Berlin and New York 1972.

R. J. Hollingdale, *Nietzsche: The Man and His Philosophy*. Baton Rouge 1965.

R. L. Howey, *Heidegger and Jaspers on Nietzsche: A Critical Examination of Heidegger's and Jaspers's Interpretations of Nietzsche*. The Hague 1973.

K. Jaspers, *Nietzsche: Einführung in das Verständnis seines Philosophierens*. Berlin 1947. (English translation by C. F. Wallraff and F. J. Schmitz, *Nietzsche: An Introduction to the Understanding of His Philosophical Activity*. Tucson 1965.)

W. Kaufmann, *Nietzsche: Philosopher, Psychologist, Antichrist*. Princeton [4]1974.

J. Lavrin, *Nietzsche: A Biographical Introduction*. London 1971.

F. A. Lea, *The Tragic Philosopher: A Study of Friedrich Nietzsche*. London 1973.

K. Löwith, 'Nietzsche nach sechzig Jahren' in *Gesammelte Abhandlungen*. Stuttgart 1960.

K. Löwith, *Von Hegel zu Nietzsche. Der revolutionäre Bruch im Denken des neunzehnten Jahrhunderts*. Stuttgart 1964 (English translation by D. E. Green, *From Hegel to Nietzsche*. New York 1967, paperback).

F. R. Love, *Young Nietzsche and the Wagnerian Experience*. Chapel Hill 1963.

Thomas Mann, *Nietzsche's Philosophie im Lichte unserer Erfahrung*. Berlin 1948.

J. Nolte, *Wahrheit und Freiheit: Meditationen über Texte aus Friedrich Nietzsche*. Düsseldorf 1973.

Nietzsche: Imagery and Thought. A collection of essays edited by J. M. S. Pasley. London 1978.

E. F. Podach, *Nietzsches Zusammenbruch*. Heidelberg 1930.

T. B. Strong, *Friedrich Nietzsche and the Politics of Transfiguration*. Berkeley 1975.

G. Wilson Knight, *Christ and Nietzsche*. London and New York 1948.

H. M. Wolff, *Friedrich Nietzsche: der Weg zum Nichts*. Bern 1956.

Index